Broken Promises

Jesus & The Second Coming

-------Mark Smith 2020-------

****

*****

ISBN 9798695036824
Independently Published via Amazon's Kindle Direct Press

Email: Mark@JCnot4me.com   **Web Page**: www.JCnot4me.com

*****

Table of Contents

Introduction

I started my study of The Second Coming as a dedicated & serious Christian. Had someone pointed the proverbial gun at my head and said denounce Jesus or die, I would have gladly responded "here I come Lord!". As I said, I started my study as a Christian. I ended my study the opposite.

My curiosity for the topic of The Second Coming had been sparked decades earlier. I remember a particular Sunday School class I was in as a young teenager. In the Church of Christ (non-instrumental), they would pick out an entire book of the New Testament and proceed one chapter a week for a very detailed verse-by-verse analysis. Well, when we got to the 24th chapter of Matthew, something seemed fishy to me. I asked the instructor about Matthew 24:34, which seemed to indicate that the Second Coming was due within the lifetime of Jesus' Apostles- and how could that be, because obviously it never happened. His response was the classic "get out of jail free card" of any public speaker: "That's an interesting question- thank you. I'll get back to you later on that". And, of course, he never did. But I did- it took me decades, but I got back to it, and this book you're reading right now is the result.

Thus sparked by that teenage Sunday School class, throughout my adult Christian life I had always wanted to get to the bottom of the issue and solve the confusion over The Second Coming. I was, and am, a student of the Bible such that once I have a particular topic in my sights, I latch onto it like a pitbull and won't let go until I know almost everything there is about it. I have never walked away from a deeply studied Biblical topic confused over what the conclusion should be. So I dived into The Second Coming, determined to solve this mystery. However, when I started my intense study, I had no idea that six months later it would lead me to the rock-solid conclusions that ended up ending my Christianity.

For six months I ate, breathed, and lived The Second Coming. First thing I did was to gather every single verse in the New Testament that I could find that had anything whatsoever to do with the topic, and each verse got it's own place in a three-ring binder. For these kinds of studies, I want ALL the data. I started studying these verses- organizing them, categorizing them, checking out various translations, looking up the key words in the original Greek and checking commentaries as needed. But I started to notice something, and it was disturbing. It looked like a lot of the verses were predicting this Second Coming should have taken place way back in the First Century. This was an unexpected problem for me.

In doing research for this book, I flew to Chicago to spend time in the well-stocked library of The Moody Bible Institute, which had many out of print books and Bible translations that were no longer available otherwise. On this same trip I also visited the library at Notre Dame, in Indiana. Back in California, I spent time in the beautiful library of The Fuller Theological Seminary, in Pasadena. Much time was also spent in the libraries of BIOLA, as well as Vanguard University, a Christian school in Costa Mesa California, where I had attended the public lectures of the original "Bible Answer Man" Dr. Walter Martin. I also spent time in the library of Lutheran Concordia University, in Irvine California. In all these journeys, whenever I found relevant data, I was sure to make a trip to the Xerox machine in the library so that all this data would be available to me later.

And these Xeroxed sheets, after I got home, would be three-hole-punched and put into large binders- all organized, tabbed & indexed.

As research for this book continued, I also attended every public lecture that afforded me the opportunity to pick the brains of some popular theologians. I attended lectures by Dr. William Lane Craig (and managed to stay awake!), Greg Koukl of "Stand To Reason", Dr. Dominic Crossan speaking on Eschatology at Chapman University, and Dr. H. Wayne House. I really did give it my best shot.

All the data ended up focusing to one logical conclusion} Jesus's second coming was due to happen in the First Century. The fact that it had not happened led me to reject Christianity- and write this book you are now reading. I had spent 30 years in the religion, and if I can help others to not do likewise, all this effort was worth it.

A scene in the classic movie "Patton" has George C. Scott, as General Patton, on a hilltop overlooking the desert battlefield of North Africa below, as his tanks and artillery wreck havoc among Rommel's vaunted Afika Corp. As he's watching the battle through his binoculars, a smile comes across his face and he exclaims outloud, "Rommel, you magnificent bastard, *__I read your book!!!__*"

The same thought goes thru my mind whenever I think about my discovery that Jesus had been a false prophet. I find myself, time and again, paraphrasing the words of Patton: *Jesus, you magnificent bastard, I read your book!!!* And that's really all it took to win this battle. Even just a simple reading of the New Testament enables one to see through the smoke-screens and defensive maneuvers and theological gerrymandering thrown up by a desperate (but doomed) clergy, fighting to "save their savior" and thus protect their careers and paychecks. And yes, I use the word "smoke screen" intentionally, for most of what theologians write on this topic is meant not to excavate but obfuscate the truth of the matter. And if you give up and walk away from the topic totally confused after reading thru their verbose and confusing meanderings as to why Jesus didn't really *__mean__* what he plainly *__said__*, they feel they have succeeded. If you are a Christian, they want you to give up on the topic, be happy with their several contradictory "explanations", and just go back to being a good sheep that does not ask questions.

It took me a full 30 years, as a "Bible Believing *__REAL__* Christian", to finally get to the point where I could see what Jesus & Company had been saying all along in the New Testament concerning the Second Coming. And what they had been saying all along was that Jesus would return within the *__First Century__*, set up his kingdom, commence Judgment Day- and then, in the First Century, all the Christians would live happily ever after. That's what was promised 2,000 years ago- with no if's, and's, or but's, and that's what the Christians of that era expected, based upon what they were promised. And this book of mine has not put any words into Jesus' mouth- there's no need to; rather, it's about revealing what he and his Apostles had actually been saying all along.

Do you remember how the Apostle Peter, to save his own skin, lied his butt off after Jesus had been arrested? Well, he wasn't the only one back then comfortable & skilled with lying, because the promises by Jesus and his Apostles on this topic all turned out to be lies. These lies make Jesus & Company false prophets, liars, and therefore people unworthy of the trust and faith of Christians. As for Jesus, having shown himself a false prophet, he became unworthy of my worship.

As a Christian I had overlooked a lot of difficult things to understand, but this massive lying could not be overlooked. This was a make-or-break issue. Worshipping a false prophet is where I, as a Christian, and I hope you as well, draw the line. Regardless of the cost, I refused to worship a false prophet, and thus began my journey out of Christianity.

I hope you will take The New Testament at face value and uncover what has been covered. Stop putting off that in-depth study of Eschatology you've always wanted to do. This jigsaw puzzle called Eschatology originally formed a clear and unbroken picture- it can once again. Re-assemble the pieces and the portrait shines forth, a portrait kept scrambled by self-serving theologians and Christian spin doctors, a picture that portrays a Jesus who with all his heart prophesied that his "Second Coming" would occur within the First Century era. But the fact is it did not (regardless of what Preterists may claim), and no other conclusion can possibly be reached from this, other than Jesus turns out to be just another false prophet from long ago. Like General Patton reading Rommel's book, it's always been there for you to see- all you've ever really had to do was to wake up and read the book.

---Mark Smith---

Awake, sleeper,
And arise from the dead

Ephesians 5:14 NASB

DEDICATION

I dedicate this book to Henry Clay Grayson, a fine southern gentleman and businessman from Tennessee who, as an Elder in Florida, at the Sarasota Church of Christ, when sixteen year old me told him they were doing it all wrong at his church by not having a paid preacher, instead of arguing with me, he casually challenged me to prove them wrong from the Bible. I ended up proving myself wrong, and set a life course of always digging out & confirming the truth for myself. Thank you, Mr. Grayson.

Word Definitions

Knowing the definitions of key words used by the authors of the New Testament is essential to understanding what they meant. Without this information gained from good dictionaries and Greek lexicons, it is impossible to make an informed decision. As Christian scholar Gleason Archer says:

> *No interpretation of Scripture is valid that is not based on careful exegesis, that is, on wholehearted commitment to determining what the ancient author **meant** by the words he used. This is accomplished by a painstaking study of the **key words** as defined in the **dictionaries** (Hebrew and Greek) and as used in parallel passages... A good 90% of the problems will be dealt with in **good commentaries**. Good **Bible Dictionaries** and **encyclopedias** may clear up many perplexities.*
>
> **Encyclopedia of Bible Difficulties,** Gleason Archer, pp.15-16 [#125]

Prophecy, from a Christian perspective, is about speaking God's truth into the lives of people. The purpose of prophecy is to instruct, encourage or warn. This may or may not include predictions of future events, either conditional (if you do that - this will happen) or unconditional. **Prophet**

Prophet

	ASSERTION
	When the word "prophet" <u>helps</u> their Jesus, Christians define **prophet** as one who <u>***does***</u> *"predict the future." *When the word "prophet" <u>hurts</u> their Jesus,* Christians **then** define prophet as one who <u>***does not***</u> **"predict the future." ********************** ** Christians demand that the definition of prophet include "predicting the future" when wanting to "prove" from the prophets of the Jewish Bible that Jesus was the prophesied messiah.* ** Christians demand that the definition of prophet NOT include "predicting the future" when wanting to defend their own prophet Jesus from the consequences of his own false prophecies.

certainly true of individuals but is it fair to generalise?

I will define the word as including within it <u>the ability to predict the future.</u> — *not always* I base my definition on the following evidence.

Bible in Basic English [#20]	But the prophet who **takes it on himself** to say words in my name which I have <u>**not**</u> given him orders to say… will come to his death. And if you say in your hearts, how are we to be <u>***certain***</u> that the word does <u>**not**</u> come from the Lord? When a prophet makes a statement in the name of the Lord, if what he says does <u>**not**</u> take place and **his words do <u>not</u> come true**, then his word is **not** the word of the Lord: the words of the prophet were said in the pride of his heart, and you are to have no fear of him. (Deuteronomy 18:20-22)
The American Heritage Dictionary [#8]	1. A person who speaks by divine inspiration or as the interpreter through whom the will of a god is expressed. 2. A person gifted with profound moral insight and exceptional powers of expression. 3. A predictor; a soothsayer. 4. The chief spokesperson of a movement or cause.
Harper's Bible Dictionary p.585 [#39]	Prophesying, in the N.T., included… (3) an <u>occasional ***prediction***</u>.
The Westminster Dictionary of The Bible p.492 [#40]	They were accredited by signs, **by the <u>fulfillment</u> of their <u>predictions</u>**, and by the conformity of their teaching to the Law.
Vine's Expository Dictionary of New Testament Words Vol. III p.222 [#43]	The prophesying of the N.T. prophets was <u>both a</u> preaching of the Divine counsels of grace already accomplished <u>and the</u> ***fore-telling*** of the purposes of God **in the future**.
Reasonable Faith Dr. William L. Craig pp.47&159 [#130]	<u>***Jesus***</u> appealed to miracles and to <u>***fulfilled prophecy***</u> to **prove** that his claims were true. What about the apostles? In dealing with Jews, **they appealed to <u>fulfilled prophecy</u>**… According to this approach, one supported the authority of Scripture by the empirical signs of credibility, mainly miracle and **prophecy**.
Lost Christianities Dr. Burton Mack p.150 [#209]	How can we imagine that God has spoken to his prophets, even his theologically correct prophets, **if their predictions do not come true**? — *fair*

Soon

Greek: mello μέλλω

This is never ~~translated 'soon'~~ in NIV (word 3516)

most common translation is 'about to'
e.g.
Mk 13:4
Lk 7:2
Lk 9:31
Lk 10:1
Lk 21:7
Lk 21:36
Ac 16:27
Ac 18:14
Ac 20:3
Ac 21:37

Vine's Expository Dictionary of New Testament Words p.15 [#43]	Mello} signifies (a) of intention, to be **ABOUT TO DO SOMETHING**
A Comprehensive Lexicon of the Greek Language [#148]	**ON THE POINT TO DO OR SUFFER SOMETHING**
Keyword Concordance p.7 [#149]	To be **ON THE VERGE** of an action… impending
The NIV Interlinear Greek – English New Testament p.547 [#6]	In Acts 17:31, a verse dealing with the "when" of Judgment Day, it translates "mello" as **ABOUT TO BE** meaning that Judgment Day is **IMPENDING**
A Manual Greek Lexicon of the New Testament p.282 [#150]	**ABOUT TO BE OR DO**
A Greek And English Lexicon of the New Testament Edward Robinson p.449 [#75]	To be **about to do** or suffer any thing, to be **ON THE POINT OF**
Thayer's Greek-English Lexicon of the New Testament p.396 [#65]	To be **about to do** anything. To be **ON THE POINT OF DOING** or suffering something
Mounce Concise Greek-English Dictionary of The New Testament [#211]	**TO BE ABOUT TO, BE ON THE POINT OF**

*NIV translates mello as 'will' [God] has set a day when he **will** judge the world*   *no it doesn't!*

also 'going to'
e.g.
Mt 2:13
Mt 16:27

also 'future'
Rom 8:38
1 Cor 3:22

also 'to come'
e.g. Gal 3:23
Eph 1:21
Col 2:17

Mounce's Complete Expository Dictionary: 'mello communicates true intention or inevitability rather than wishful thinking'

Quickly

Greek: takos ταχύς NIV 5443, 5444

Vine's Expository Dictionary of New Testament Words p.60 [#43]	Tachu: swift **QUICK,** signifies quickly} Rev. 2:16; 3:11; 11:14; 22:7,12,20
A Manual Greek Lexicon of the New Testament p.441 [#150]	Quickly, speedily, forthwith **AS QUICKLY AS POSSIBLE** soon, speedy
A Greek And English Lexicon of the New Testament p.710 [#75]	Quickness, swiftness, speed, quickly, **speedily**, shortly, **haste**, nimble
Thayer's Greek-English Lexicon of the New Testament p.616 [#65]	Quickly, speedily **WITHOUT DELAY** fleet, speedy
A Greek-English Lexicon of the New Testament p.814 [#66]	Speed, quickness, swiftness, haste, quickly **AT ONCE** **WITHOUT DELAY** soon, in a short time.
A Greek-English Lexicon p.1,762 [#151]	**SWIFTNESS** speed, hastiness
Mounce Concise Greek-English Dictionary of The New Testament [#211]	Swift, quick, ready **PROMPT**
Commentaries & Quotes	
Four Views on the Book of Revelation Ken Gentry's Chapter p.40-41 [#247]	The events of Revelation "must soon [Gk. *tachos*] take place" (v.1) because "the time is near [Gk. *Engys*]." Greek lexicons and modern translations indicate TEMPORAL PROXIMITY. Throughout the New Testament *tachos* means "QUICKLY, AT ONCE, **WITHOUT DELAY**, SHORTLY". The term *engys* ("near") also speaks of temporal nearness: of the future (Matt. 26:18), of SUMMER (24:32), and of a FESTIVAL (John 2:13) The inspired apostle John clearly informs his original audience nearly two thousand years ago that THEY should expect the prophecies to "take place" (Rev 1:1) in their LIFETIME. As Milton Terry notes, the events of Revelation are "BUT A FEW YEARS IN THE FUTURE WHEN JOHN WROTE.".

"At Hand"

Greek: engizo / engus ἐγγίζω / ἐγγύς

Vine's Expository Dictionary of New Testament Words Vol. 2, p.90 [#43]	<u>Near</u>, <u>nigh</u>, at hand. Engus} (b) of time, e.g., Matt. 26:18; Luke 21:30,31; "nigh," "nigh at hand;" ...the phrase is a translation of the Aramaic **Maranatha**, a Christian watchword.
Keyword Concordance p.204 [#149]	<u>Relatively close</u>, approach, be at hand, be nigh, come near, draw near.
A Manual Greek Lexicon of the New Testament p.127 [#150]	To **bring near**, to come near.
A Greek And English Lexicon of the New Testament Edward Robinson p.200 [#75]	To bring near, to cause to approach, **to draw near**, to approach, to have drawn near, to be near, to be at hand.
Thayer's Greek-English Lexicon of the New Testament p.164 [#65]	To bring near, to **draw or come near**, has come nigh, is at hand.
A Greek-English Lexicon of the New Testament Arndt & Gingrich p.212 [#66]	Approach, come near, of **approaching in time**.
A Greek-English Lexicon Liddell & Scott p.467 [#151]	Bring near, bring up to, *to be* **ON THE POINT OF DOING**.
Luke and the Last Things A.J. Matill pp.71-72 [#35]	It denotes that an event **WILL HAPPEN SOON** by which is meant or presumed that there will **NOT BE A LONG TIME TO WAIT** before it happens. ...Luke uses *engus* and *engidzo* interchangeably.
Theological Dictionary of the New Testament Dr. Gerhard Kittel pp.330-332 [#67]	To bring near... Thus in the early days of Christianity (these words)... expressed hope of **THE IMMINENCE OF THE COMING WORLD**.
Mounce Concise Greek-English Dictionary of The New Testament [#211]	To approach, draw near, to be at hand **TO BE AT THE POINT OF DEATH** Close at hand, near as to time

Imminent

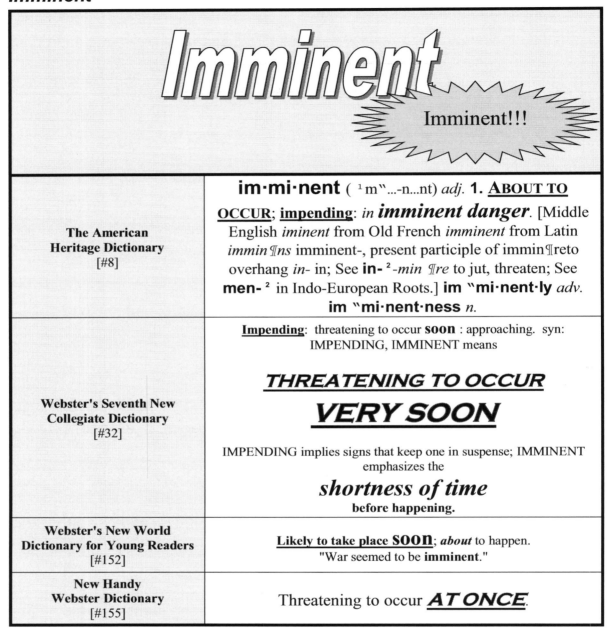

Time

As Defined by The Bible

"Long Time" **3,000 Years or More**	### From The Bible: For <u>certain men</u> whose condemnation was **written about <u>*LONG AGO*</u>** (by Enoch) have secretly slipped in among you. (Jude 4 NIVUS [#16]) <u>Enoch</u>, the seventh from Adam, <u>prophesied</u> about <u>these</u> men: 'See, the Lord is coming with thousands upon thousands of his holy ones…' (Jude 14 NIVUS [#16]) <u>Note</u>: According to the author of <u>Jude</u>, "long ago" certain men were written about by Enoch, of Old Testament fame. Taking Bishop James Ussher's date of the creation being Saturday, October 22, 4,004 BC, then calculating forward per Genesis 5: 1-24, Enoch would have been alive to prophesy from 3,382 BC → 3,017 BC. This puts Enoch about 3,000 years distant from the author of Jude. Therefore, according to the author of Jude, **3,000 years** is officially a *long time*.
"Short Time" **1,000 Years Max, Possibly Even Less Than 7 Years**	### From The Bible: And he laid hold of… the devil…, and bound him for *A THOUSAND YEARS*, and threw him into the abyss… so that he should not deceive the nations any longer, until the thousand years were completed; after these things he must be released for *A SHORT TIME*. (Rev. 20:2,3 NAS [#1]) <u>Note</u>: The "Devil" will be locked up for a thousand years, then in contrast to this one thousand years, he'll be released for "**a short time**", thus showing that a short time is *less than* 1,000 years. How much less than a thousand years? According to many Christian theorists, the "Devil" will be running around loose for **WELL LESS THAN 7 YEARS**, showing even more how short a "short time" is.

Time (con't)

Short Time -vs- **Long Time**	**ACTS 26:28-29 NIV** *Then Agrippa said to Paul, "Do you think that in such a **SHORT TIME** you can persuade me to be a Christian?" Paul replied, "**SHORT TIME** or **LONG**- I pray God that not only you but all who are listening to me today may become what I am, except for these chains."* ------------------------ Around 59 CE, Paul had the opportunity to present his message to King Agrippa and Agrippa's wife Berenice, along with others, in the city of Caesarea Maritima. A "**short time**" would be the amount of time that Paul has been speaking to this crowd- maybe a **few hours** at most, and a "long time" would have been well **within the lifetime of the crown listening**. Paul desires, in short or long time, that the crowd be persuaded to become Christian. If, however, the "long time" were over a hundred years, there is no way Paul could have expected them to convert, as they'd all be dead by then. If one is selling Amway, you don't tell your customer that you hope they'll buy your product 300 years from now- that would make no sense. Furthermore, Paul's phrase "all who are listening to me today" rules out anyone in the distant future. Paul clearly expects the end of the world to occur well within the lifetime of the audience he spoke to that day.

2nd Coming Due
Within Their Lifetime- Within the Preaching Ministry of The 1st Century Apostles

Matthew 10:22-23

NASB [#1]	And you will be hated by all on account of My name, but it is the one who has *endured* **TO** the end who will be saved. But whenever they persecute you in this city, flee to the next; for truly I say to you, you shall *not* finish going through the cities of Israel, until **the Son of Man comes**.
The Scholars Version [#11]	When they persecute you in this city, flee to another. I *swear* to you, you certainly *won't* have exhausted the cities of Israel *before* the son of Adam comes.
NIV [#16]	All men will hate you because of me, but he who *stands firm* **TO** the end will be saved…

My Comments

A = B = C = D

For those who would argue otherwise, a quick comparison of Matthew 10 to passages found within the gospel, show that all are indeed speaking of the same subject:
The Second Coming of Christ.

Matthew 10:22-23		Matthew 16:27-28		Matthew 24		Matthew 26:57-64	
Hated by all	22			Hated by all	9		
Endure to end = will be saved	22			Endure to end = will be saved	13		
On account of my name	22			On account of my name	9		
Persecution	23			Persecution	9		
Preaching city to city.	23			Preaching nation to nation	14		
Truly I say to you	23	Truly I say to you	28	Truly I say to you	34		
Son of Man	23	Son of Man		Son of Man	27-30	Son of Man	
		Angels	27	Angels	31		
				Coming on clouds	30	Coming on clouds	64
		Comes in glory	27	Comes in glory	30		
Promised within their lifetime	23	Promised within their lifetime	28	Promised within their lifetime	34	Promised within their lifetime	64

2nd Coming Due

Within Their Lifetime- Within the Preaching Ministry of The First Century Apostles

Matthew 10:22-23

My Comments (con't)

Another indication that Jesus expected to return within the lifetime of his Apostles is that Jesus told his Apostles that, before these 12 men finished preaching the Gospel to Israel, which the inhabited part is 1/3 the size of Florida, the Second Coming would have taken place. While they were still in the process of traveling around this small small mostly desert country Israel and preaching to their fellow countrymen, their mission would be cut short by the Second Coming.

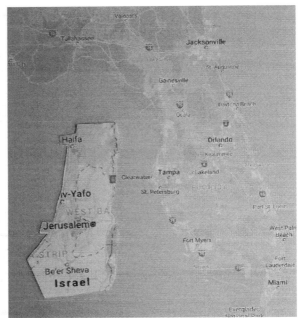

How Long for Twelve Men, Preaching Full Time, to Cover the Inhabited Portion of Israel? Maybe 5 Years if They Crawled Instead of Walked.

"Stand Firm To The *End" = Expected Within Their Lifetime

You cannot be expected to "**stand firm to the end**" if said end is *thousands* of years past your own death. Imagine telling someone in the here and now to "stand firm" until the sun explodes from old age five billion years from now. It would be complete nonsense. You can *only* tell someone to "stand firm to the end" if you yourself expect "the end" to be within their lifetime. Even the context of Matthew 10 implies an era within their lifetime: verse 17 predicting Christians being scourged in synagogues. Has *that* been a viable threat to Christians anytime lately? Of course not. Therefore, unless Jesus taught complete nonsense, Jesus ***himself*** expected his return to Earth to be within the lifetime of his Apostles.

*The End refers to the end of human governments on Earth, and the beginning of BibleGod's promised wonderland. (Mt 13:39-40; 24:3,6,13-14; 28:20 // 1C 1:8; 15:24 // Heb. 3:6; 6:11 // 1Pt. 4:7 // Rev. 2:26)

2nd Coming Due Within Their Lifetimes

Commentaries & Quotes
Matthew 10:22-23

The Historical Jesus & The Kingdom of God Dr. Richard Hiers p. 66-67 [#119]	What He taught them about the Kingdom of God we do not know, but not long before, he had sent out the Twelve to proclaim its **nearness**. _He_ had _expected_ it to come _before_ **they returned from completing their mission (Matt 10:23)... before his apostles could complete their work.**
Apocalypse of The Gospel Rev. Milton Terry p.9 [#120]	The coming of the Son of man is to be understood here as in all other passages.
The Parousia J. Stuart Russell p.28 [#33]	Look at his words. Can anything be more specific and definite as to persons, place, time, and circumstance, than this prediction of our Lord? It is to the twelve that He speaks; it is the cities of Israel which they are to evangelize; the subject is His own **speedy coming**; and the time **so near**, that _before_ their work is complete His coming _will_ take place... the words simply mean what they say—that _before_ the apostles completed their life-work of evangelising the land of Israel, the coming of the Lord _should_ take place.
The Quest of the Historical Jesus Dr. Albert Schweitzer pp.358-360 [#36]	He tells them in plain words that **he does not expect to see them back in the present age**. The Parousia of the Son of Man, which is logically and temporally identical with the dawn of the Kingdom, **will take place _before_ they shall have completed a hasty journey through the cities of Israel to announce it**. _That the words mean this and nothing else, that they ought not to be in any way weakened down, should be sufficiently evident..._ It is equally clear.. that **this prediction** # WAS _NOT_ FULFILLED. The disciples returned to Him; and the appearing of the Son of Man had **not** taken place... The whole history of 'Christianity' down to the present day... is based on the **delay** of the Parousia, the **non-occurrence** of the Parousia... the _non_-**fulfillment of Matt. 10:23** is the first postponement of the Parousia.
Is Christianity Good for The World? C. Hitchens p.23 [#228]	The late C.S. Lewis helps make this point for me by emphasizing that the teachings of Jesus _ONLY_ make sense if the speaker is the herald of an _IMMINENT_ kingdom of heaven. Otherwise, would it _NOT_ be morally _UNSAFE_ to denounce thrift, family, and the "taking of thought for the morrow"?
Forgery in Christianity J. Wheless p.93 [#246]	So **quickly** would this "second coming" be, that when the Twelve were sent out on their **first preaching tour** in **little** Palestine, their Master assured them: "Ye shall **not** have gone over the cities of Israel till the Son of man come" (Mt x,23)

2nd Coming Due Within Their Lifetimes

Commentaries & Quotes (con't)
Matthew 10:22-23

Treastise on The Gods H.L. Mencken [#239]	He (Jesus) believed **THE END OF THE WORLD WAS AT HAND** and sought to induce His fellow Jews to prepare for it. (p.191) The chief professional difficulty that confronted the early Christian theologians was explaining away the **FAILURE** of the **SECOND COMING**. ...Jesus had given them plenty of reason for that expectation... **BUT AS DAY FOLLOWED DAY WITHOUT THE AWAITED SIGNS AND PORTENTS**, and many believers, in the face of His clear promise, began to "**TASTE OF DEATH**" without seeing "the kingdom of God come with power," it became necessary to revise the orthodox doctrine. So the Second Coming was quietly **POSTPONED**: it would come, not tomorrow, or next day, but in a few months or years—at worst, within a **GENERATION**. ...But as the years lengthened and the troubles of the time piled up, there was a revival of impatience, and many converts, including some of influence, **LEFT THE YOUNG CHURCH.** (pp. 227-228)

Matthew 16:27-28

2nd Coming Due Within Their Lifetime
---along with---
Judgment Day

Matthew 16:27-28

New American Standard Bible [#1]	"For the ***Son of Man*** is going to come in the **glory** of His Father **with His angels**; and WILL **THEN** RECOMPENSE EVERY MAN ACCORDING TO HIS DEEDS. **"Truly I say to you, there are some of those who are standing here who shall not taste death until they see the *Son of Man* coming in His kingdom."**	
The Scholars Version [#11]	Remember, the son of Adam is going to come in the glory of his Father with his messengers, and **then** he will reward everyone according to their deeds. I swear to you: Some of those standing here **won't ever taste death before** they see the son of Adam's imperial rule arriving.	
Today's English Version [#14]	For the Son of Man is ***about to come*** in the glory of his Father with his angels, and then he will reward each one according to his deeds. I assure you that there are **some here who will *not* die until they have seen the Son of Man come as King**.	(ENB)
Concordant Literal New Testament [#4]	For the Son of Mankind is ***about to be coming*** in the glory of His Father, with His messengers, and then He will be paying each in accord with his practice. Verily I am saying to you that there are some of those standing here **who under no circumstances should be tasting death** till they should be perceiving the Son of Mankind coming in His kingdom.	Hyper-literal
A Literal Translation of The Bible [#23]	For the Son of man is ****about to come*** in the glory of His Father, with His angels…	Single author: Jay P. Green.
Centenary Translation of the New Testament [#102]	For the Son of man is ****about to come*** in the glory of his Father, and his angels with him…	Single translator Helen Barrett Montgomery
The Riverside New Testament [#108]	For the Son of Man ***will *soon come*** in the glory of his Father…	Single translator Wm. Ballantine
The Authentic New Testament [#112]	****Very soon*** the Son of Man will come in his Father's state…	Single translator Hugh J. Schonfield
Weymouth [#2]	For the Son of Man is ****soon to come*** in the glory of the Father with His angels, and then will He requite every man according to his actions. I ***solemnly*** tell you that some of those who are standing here will certainly ***not*** taste death till they have seen the Son of Man coming in His Kingdom."	Single translator Richard Weymouth
Westcott & Hort [#7]	27 **mellei** gar o uioj tou anqrwpou ercesqai en th doxh tou patroj autou meta twn aggelwn autou kai tote apodwsei ekastw kata thn praxin autou	

*Greek: mello: On the point of happening, about to occur, impending, ***ON THE VERGE OF TAKING PLACE.***

2nd Coming Due Within Their Lifetime

Matthew 16:27-28

My Comments

A = B = C = D

As previously shown in the Matthew 10 section, the four major promises of Jesus within the Gospel of Matthew (to return within their lifetime) are all basically the same. And, as *will* be shown in the Matthew 24 section, they are also, therefore, equal to the Second Coming passages found in 1st & 2nd Thessalonians. Therefore, it is reasonable to conclude these kind of passages are all pointing toward the *same* event- The Second Coming, and *not* transfigurations, "holy spirit" baptisms, the founding of the church or any other excuses theologians manage to pull out of thin air.

TRIPLE REINFORCEMENT OF PROMISE

Jesus, in an attempt to ensure that he would *not* be misunderstood about the nearness of his Second Coming, uses three lines of reasoning to anchor down his promise that it would occur before the end of the First Century:

1. I am coming back *soon*.
2. I *promise you* that I am coming back soon.
3. I am coming back *sooooo* soon, that I am coming *within your lifetime*.

How he could have made it any clearer is beyond me. But in spite of his plain talk, many theologians still pretend to misunderstand the clear intent of his words in *their* attempt to "save the savior's butt" from being a false prophet. Such transparent intellectual dishonesty is disgusting.

(1: mello = soon, on the verge of happening // 2: "verily" "I swear" " I *solemnly* tell you" // 3: "shall not taste death")

"COMING OF THE SON OF MAN" = SECOND COMING / JUDGMENT DAY

To reinforce the fact that Jesus is NOT talking here about anything other than the Second Coming / Judgment Day promise, I present the following verse.

> But when the **Son of Man** comes in His g l o r y and *all the angels with Him*, then He will sit on His g l o r i o u s throne. And all the nations will be gathered before Him; and He will separate them from one another, as the shepherd separates the sheep from the goats;   and He will put the sheep on His right, and the goats on the left.
>
> (Matthew 25:31-33 NASB [#1])

Notice below the parallels that jump out immediately:

Matthew 16:27-28	Matthew 25:31-33
Son of Man comes	Son of Man comes
Comes in glory	Comes in glory
Comes with angels	Comes with angels
"then he will reward each one according to his deeds"	"then He will sit on His g l o r i o u s throne. And all the nations will be gathered before Him; and He will separate them from one another, as the shepherd separates the sheep from the goats

2nd Coming Due Within Their Lifetime

Matthew 16:27-28

My Comments (con't)

≠ TRANSFIGURATION

Some Christians, noticing that these words of Jesus wrap up the end of Matthew, chapter 16, assume the fulfillment of Jesus' promise is found in the beginning of the very next chapter, 17, where Jesus gets a radioactive-like glow on the "Mount of Transfiguration."

But chapter 17 does not fulfill what Jesus promised in the previous chapter, for Jesus promised that *this* coming would bring along with it hordes of angels, as well as the final day of Judgment. Neither of these is recorded in chapter 17, especially "Judgment Day" which would bring along with it the end of the world. The world, as you notice, still exists. Therefore, these words of Jesus remain unfulfilled.

2nd Coming Due Within Their Lifetime

Matthew 16:27-28

Commentaries & Quotes

A Critical & Exegetical Commentary [#121]	…mellein, which here emphasizes the ***nearness*** of the coming (of the Son of Man)…
Last Days Madness Gary DeMar pp.34-35 [#34]	Some claim that the 'coming' Jesus had in mind was the **TRANSFIGURATION**. But the transfiguration ***cannot*** be its fulfillment since Jesus indicated that ***some*** who were standing with Him would still be alive when He came but ***most*** would be dead. If we adopt the view that the Transfiguration is the fulfillment of Matthew 16:27-28, we must conclude that **MOST** of the people with whom Jesus spoke were **DEAD** within seven to ten days (Mt 17:1)!!! Hardly possible. Others see the Feast of Pentecost, with the coming of the Holy Spirit, as the fulfillment. But the same problem arises— nearly ***all*** the disciples would have had to die within a period of a few months after the events described by Jesus… Such a scenario does not fit with the language of the text or the history of the time. (pp.34-35) Jesus clearly stated that He would come ***BEFORE*** THE LAST APOSTLE DIED. (p.59)
The Parousia Stuart Russell pp.29-33 [#33]	To suppose that it refers merely to the glorious manifestation of Jesus on the mount of **TRANSFIGURATION**, though an hypothesis which has great names to support it, **is so palpably *inadequate* as an interpretation that it *scarcely requires refutation*…** The very form of the expression shows that the event spoken of could ***not*** lie within the space of a few months, or even a few ***years***: it is a mode of speech which suggests that not all present will live to see the event spoken of; that not many will do so; but that some will. **It is exactly such a way of speaking as would suit an interval of THIRTY OR FORTY YEARS**, when the majority of the persons **then** present would have passed away, but **some** would survive and witness the events referred to… THE PAROUSIA, OR GLORIOUS COMING OF CHRIST, WAS DECLARED BY HIMSELF TO FALL WITHIN THE LIMITS OF THE ***THEN EXISTING GENERATION***.

Apocalypse of the Gospels Milton Terry p.10 [#120]	Some have understood that the reference is to the **TRANSFIGURATION**, which all three synoptists record immediately afterward. But two decisive objections stand in the way of such a reference:
	  1. That event occurred ***only*** six or eight days afterward.
	  2. It could ***not*** with any propriety be called a **coming of the Son of man** in the glory of his Father **with the *angels***, or **coming in his *kingdom***…
	The plain teaching of the passage is that ***before*** some of those who heard him speak should die the Son of man ***would*** come in glory, and his kingdom would be established in power.

The Holy Bible with an Explanatory & Critical Commentary F.C. Cook p.87 [#122]	Many expositors (e.g. some mentioned by Origen on this place, Hilary, and Jerome) refer this verse to the **TRANSFIGURATION**, in which case the promise relates only to the three Apostles: Peter, James, and John. This interpretation, however, seems open to objection:
	  1. Because it does ***not*** satisfy the **usual** meaning of the kingdom in the Gospels.
	  2. Because our Lord's words seem naturally to point to a more ***remote*** event.

2nd Coming Due Within Their Lifetime	
Matthew 16:27-28	
Commentaries & Quotes (con't)	
Bertrand Russell on God and Religion p.66 [#123]	For one thing, he (Christ) certainly thought that his second coming would occur in clouds of glory *before* **the death of all the people who were then living at the time**. There are a **great many texts** that prove that. …there are a lot of places where it is quite clear that he believed that his second coming would happen **during** the lifetime of many then living.
The Quest of the Historical Jesus Dr. Albert Schweitzer p.20 [#36]	There is no justification for twisting this about or explaining it away. It simply means that Jesus promises the fulfillment of all Messianic hopes **before** the end of the *existing* generation.
The Five Gospels p.80 [#11]	*…this apocalyptic event will take place **within the *lifetime*** of some of Mark's congregation… within the lifetime of some of the members of their respective congregations. *(NOTE: Comment is on the parallel passage of Mark 8:9)
Why I Believed Kenneth Daniels p.220 [#204]	There is **no ambiguity** here concerning the meaning of "<u>GENERATION</u>"; the terms are explicitly laid out. There is **NO CLEARER WAY** to say "this <u>GENERATION</u> will not pass away" than to say "**There are some of those who are standing *here* who shall not taste death until**…" Since denying the meaning of this timeframe is not an option, the only recourse… is to interpret the phrase "see the Son of Man" coming in his kingdom" as something OTHER than Jesus' literal return. Accordingly, many apologists suggest that the story of the **TRANSFIGURATION**, which immediately follows Jesus' speech in the narrative, represents the fulfillment. …This may seem plausible at first, until all the details are taken into account.

First, if the Transfiguration followed on the heels of Jesus' prediction, what could have been the purpose of including the clause, "there are some of those who are standing here who shall not taste **death** until…"? Though there is wiggle room for interpreting Jesus' meaning, this is not language ordinarily used to describe an event that is to take place in **SHORT ORDER**. …it seems strange for him (Jesus) to have placed the event within his disciples' LIFETIME, rather than "**soon**," "**within a week**," or "**within a year**". |
| **St. Peter verses St. Paul** Michael Goulder p.41 [#124] | Mark [i.e. Mark 9:1, a parallel passage] like all early Christians, was expecting the end of the age <u>SOON</u>; and in this case he is specific. *Some standing here*, (say AD 30), *will not have tasted death*, will not be dead, *before they see the kingdom come in power*… In other words, *Jesus' return was expected **IN THE LIFETIME**** of some of his hearers, or in rough terms, **before 90AD**: that would be when the kingdom of God would begin. Notice Mark's phrase *in power*, echoing Paul's in 1st Cor. 4:20. What we have *now* is talk; what we are *looking for* is power, when we will look out of the door and *not* see beggars starving and Roman soldiers driving Jews off in slavery. |
| **The Greek Testament: Vol 1** Henry Alford p.177 [#219] | This declaration refers, in its full meaning, **CERTAINLY <u>NOT</u> TO THE TRANSFIGURATION** which follows… (it) indicates a **DISTANT EVENT**. |

	2nd Coming Due Within Their Lifetime
	Matthew 16:27-28
	Commentaries & Quotes (con't)
Critical & Exegetical Hand-Book to the Gospel of Matthew Heinrich Meyer p.304 [#220]	Having affirmed the certainty of the **second coming** and divine retribution, He now proceeds to do the same with regard to their <u>NEARNESS</u>… they will **STILL BE LIVING** when it takes place. …Others… have so strangely <u>**PERVERTED CHRIST'S PREDICTION**</u> as even to make it refer to the incident of the <u>**TRANSFIGURATION**</u> immediately following.
Matthew Douglas Hare p.197 [#140]	…His glorious coming will occur **WITHIN THE NATURAL <u>LIFETIME</u> OF SOME OF JESUS' CONTEMPORARIES**. This idea is repeated at **24:24** Early Christians, including Paul and the seer of Revelation, **EXPECTED JESUS TO RETURN SOON**. For later generations the promise of Matt. 16:28 and its parallels has **POSED A PROBLEM**, because **IT IS APPARENTLY AN** ***<u>UNFULFILLED PROPHECY</u>***. Consequently, some have proposed that the prediction of verse 28 is… the story of the **TRANSFIGURATION**… These proposals are **NOT CONVINCING**. The promise of Jesus glorious arrival with his angels remains **UNFILLED**.
The Prophecy of Matthew 24 Thomas Newton 1754 AD p.66 [#251]	In another place he says, Matt xvi.28- "There are some standing here…" intimating that is would not succeed **IMMEDIATELY**, and yet **NOT AT SUCH A DISTANCE OF TIME, BUT THAT SOME THEN LIVING SHOULD BE SPECTATORS OF THE CALAMITIES** coming upon the nation. …It is true our Saviour declares, "All these things shall be fulfilled in **THIS** generation."
The Prophecy of the Destruction of Jerusalem Nisbett (1787 AD) pp.13-14 [#157]	Besides, to foretell that the disciples would not die till an event took place which was to happen but **SIX DAYS** after this, as Bishop Newcome observes, would be a prophecy unworthy of Christ.

	2nd Coming Within Their Lifetime		
	Matthew 21:36-45		
NRSV [#17]	**Parable of the Evil Tenants** 36 Again he sent other slaves, more than the first; and they treated them in the same way. 37 Finally **he sent his son** to them, saying, 'They will respect my son.' 38 But when the tenants saw the son, they said to themselves, 'This is the heir; **come, let us <u>kill</u> him** and get his inheritance." 39 So they seized him, threw him out of the vineyard, **and killed him.** 40 Now when the owner of the vineyard **<u>comes</u>**, what will he do to those tenants?" 41 They said to him, "**He will put those wretches to <small>A MISERABLE DEATH</small>**, and lease the vineyard to other tenants who will give him the produce at the harvest time." 42 Jesus said to them, "Have you never read in the scriptures: 'The stone that the builders rejected has become the cornerstone; this was the Lord's doing, and it is amazing in our eyes'? 43 Therefore I tell you, the kingdom of God will be **taken away from *you*** and given to a people that produces the fruits of the kingdom. 44 The one who falls on this stone will be broken to pieces; and it will crush anyone on whom it falls." 45 When the **chief priests and the Pharisees** heard his parables, **they realized** [in 33 CE] **that he was speaking about *them*.**		

My Comments

2nd Coming Within Lifetime of Those Who Murdered Jesus

This "Parable of the Evil Tenants" is obviously alluding to the Second Coming of Jesus. When Jesus *comes*, he will return to *extract revenge upon <u>the same people</u> who earlier had cut short his career*. These people are First Century "chief priests" and "Pharisees" and they understood quite well that this parable was *targeted directly at them*. They could look forward to "a miserable death" when "the owner of the vineyard comes". But **THE ONLY WAY THEY COULD BE "PUT TO A MISERABLE DEATH" IS IF**

THEY WERE STILL ALIVE

to BE "PUT TO DEATH" when Jesus came!!! Thus, one more indication Jesus was promising to return within the lifetime of the First Century people.

All Hell To Break Loose Upon

THIS

1st Century Generation

Matthew 23:33-36

NASB [#1]	**You** serpents, **you** brood of vipers, how shall **you** escape **the sentence of hell**? Therefore, behold, I am sending **you** prophets and wise men and scribes; some of them you will <u>kill</u> and <u>crucify</u>, and some of them you will <u>scourge in your synagogues</u>, and persecute from city to city, that <u>upon **you**</u> may fall the guilt of all the righteous blood shed on earth, from the blood of righteous Abel to the blood of Zechariah, the son of Berechiah [Zech. 1:7], whom you murdered between the temple and the altar. Truly I say to you, **all these things shall come upon** `this` generation.

The Scholars Version [#11]	I swear to you, **<u>ALL THESE THINGS</u> are going to rain down on THIS** GENERATION.

Commentary

Jesus and 'This Generation' Evald Lovestam p.670 [#147]	The presentation varies in the two Gospels, but in both of them 'this genea' is in focus. It is to be struck by the ***impending*** punishment.

My Comments

2nd Coming Due Within Their 1st Century Lifetime

The resemblance of this to Matthew 24 and the "Parable of the Evil Tenants" of Matthew 21 is so obvious I refuse to belabor the point. These same men that did the killing of Jesus and others, these men would themselves be cut down upon the Second Coming of Jesus. And again, the only way they could **be** killed by the Second Coming is if they were **STILL ALIVE** to *be* killed. Jesus was *not* threatening some future generation of Jews thousands of years away. Why on earth should they be punished for something their ancient ancestors had done? He was rather threatening *those* Jews that plotted *his* death- the same Jews who would later "kill and **crucify**" and "**scourge in their synagogues**" the Christians that lived in the decades after his death. I think most would agree that the racist accusation of Jews **scourging Christians in synagogues and doing crucifixions of Christians** indicates more of a FIRST CENTURY ERA racism than anything modern.

Matthew 23:33-36

Generation = Race?

For those using the "generation = race" theory as an emergency escape route from the truth, this verse presents a problem. Contrary to anti-Semitic Christian racists throughout the centuries, Jesus does ***not*** here condemn the ***entire*** Jewish race- hundreds of generations past, present, and future. He rather rails against one *specific* generation- the generation which, having had front row seats to all that Jesus had **REALLY** done (as opposed to what others 40+ years later **CLAIMED** he had done), and having thus examined the *real* evidence, as opposed to the CLAIMED evidence, they determined NOT that he was a god, but that he was delusional, and rather than worship him, strung him up.

"This Generation"

The phrase "this generation" is the ***exact*** same phrase found in ***all*** the so-called controversial passages where some theologians can't bring themselves to tell the truth as to what "this generation" really means. As the real definition, if used in this verse, doesn't endanger their employment, they are happy to let it alone and not torture / contort / distort it into meaning something else. This same phrase is also found in Luke 17:25, where Jesus says that he must be "rejected by THIS GENERATION." Again, for some strange economic reason, the theologians also leave *that* "this generation" alone. It's funny how they pick and choose their hatchet jobs.

This Generation

2nd Coming Due Within Their
1st Century Lifetimes

Matthew 24:1-51
Weymouth's Version [#2]

1   Jesus had left the Temple and was going on His way, when **His disciples** came and called His attention to the Temple buildings.

> His disciples bring to his attention the beautiful buildings of the Jewish temple, one of the wonders of the world at that time.

2 "**You** see all these?" He replied; "in solemn truth I tell **you** that there will not be left here one stone upon another that will not be pulled down."

3 Afterwards He was on the Mount of Olives and was seated there when **the disciples** came to Him, **apart from the others**, and said, "Tell **us** when this will be; and what will be the sign of your Coming **and** of the Close of the Age?"

> **The Address on the Envelope**
> Jesus is being questioned, and responds to, his Apostles, and no one else. The text goes out of its way to communicate this. This is not an envelope addressed "Occupant" but rather addressed specifically "To The Apostles". The entire discourse shows the message was for the First Century Apostles, and not concerned with people living thousands of years in the future. Please follow the "us's" and "you's" etc. that I have put in bold formatting, to see exactly whom Jesus was speaking to.

4 "Take care that no one misleads **YOU**," answered Jesus;

> **"You" = First Century Apostles**
> The warnings are to those he was speaking to, face to face in 33AD, the First Century Apostles, and NOT to people millions of years distant

5 "for many will come assuming my name and saying `I am the Christ;' and they will mislead many.

6 And **before long you** will hear of wars and rumours of wars. Do not be alarmed, for such things must be; but the End is not yet.

> **"Before Long" = Soon**
> The "before long" is reinforced in the Greek by the word "mello" meaning, "to be **on the point of** doing or suffering something".

7 For nation will rise in arms against nation, kingdom against kingdom, and there will be famines and earthquakes in various places;

8 but all these miseries are but like the early pains of childbirth.

> **"Pains of Childbirth" = Soon**
> Again, no room for thousands of years. This was all due- and soon.

9 "At that time they will deliver **you** up to punishment and will put **you** to **death**; and **you** will be objects of hatred to all the nations because you are called by my name.

Persecution Fulfilled in First Century

This is another indication this is a First Century event. In fact, an entire book (William McBirnie, "The Search for the Twelve Apostles" [#37]) claims to document **how**, within the First Century, all these Apostles to whom Jesus spoke ended up being persecuted, some even to death.

10 Then will many stumble and fall, and they will betray one another and hate one another.

11 Many false prophets will rise up and lead multitudes astray;

12 and because of the prevalent disregard of God's law the love of the great majority will grow cold;

Apostasy: Fulfilled in First Century

"The Apostasy" was a daily fact of First Century church life. Judas Iscariot, and Ananias & Sapphira were apostates near the beginning of the Christian era, and toward the end of the First Century, 1st John 2:18 records the then current existence of not one, but many, "anti-Christs". Paul even names some apostates

> "For Demas, having loved this present world, has deserted me... Alexander the coppersmith did me much harm; the Lord will repay him according to his deeds... he has vigorously opposed our teaching." (2nd Timothy 4:10-15)

13 but those who *stand firm to the End* shall be saved.

"Stand Firm To End" = Within Lifetime

This is just one of several places within the New Testament where it is indicated that the Second Coming is something these Apostles (and others of that century) could, if they "stood firm", hope to see *within their lifetime*. Other references are: Heb. 3:6,4; Rev. 2:25-26 etc. The "shall be saved" is *not* the "instant-karma" salvation Televangelists hawk on their gaudy TV shows, but rather being saved from the destruction that was due to take place upon the Earth when the excrement hit the fan during BibleGod's "days of vengeance" (Lk 21:22) at the Second Coming.

14 And this Good News of the Kingdom shall be proclaimed **throughout the whole world** to set the evidence before all the Gentiles; and *then* the End will come.

Gospel → Whole Earth: First Century Also

The New Testament claims that well before the First Century ended the entire world had been evangelized with the gospel:

> So faith comes from what is heard, and what is heard comes by the preaching of Christ. But I ask, have they not heard? Indeed they have; for "Their voice has gone out to **all the earth**, and their words to the **ends of the world**." (Rm 10:17-18 RSV [#18])

> The gospel... has been proclaimed to **every creature** under heaven, and of which I, Paul, have become a servant. (Col. 1:23 NIV [#16])

15 "When **you** have seen (to use the language of the Prophet Daniel) the `Abomination of Desolation', standing in the Holy Place" --let the reader observe those words—

"Holy Place" = First Century Temple
In case no one noticed, there hasn't been a temple of Jehovah to "stand in" since the Jewish temple was razed (i.e. torn down) in 70 AD. Once again, this points to a First Century era.

As for Christians who teach that *another* temple may some day be constructed, does that mean that your BibleGod is *behind* said construction, thus making it a "Holy Place"? Can just anybody, at any time, with or without prior authorization from your BibleGod, go around building temples that somehow then automatically become "holy"? If so, then what of the Mormon temples? What if all the Atheists got together, and built a temple there in Jerusalem? Constructing an object that *looks like* a living human body (i.e. a statue) or a "holy" temple does not **make** said object a living human body or a "holy" temple.

16 "then let those who are in Judaea escape to the hills;

17 let him who is on the roof not go down to fetch what is in his house;

18 nor let him who is outside the city stay to pick up his outer garment.

19 And alas for the women who at that time are with child or have infants!

20 "But pray that your flight may not be in winter, nor on the Sabbath;

21 for it will be a time of great suffering, such as never has been from the beginning of the world till now, and assuredly never will be again.

First Century Israel
These phrases "those who are in Judaea" and "on a Sabbath" are a big *hint* that in location, this scenario is placed in the Israel of yesteryear. Another clue is the mentioning of people being up on roofs, indicates the flat roofs that were common back then during the First Century.

22 And if those days had not been cut **short**, no one would escape; but for the sake of God's own People those days will be cut short.

How Short is Short
I hope that modern theologians are not the ones allowed to define the word "short" in this verse, seeing how when "short" refers to the wait for the Second Coming, they have stretched THAT "short" out to about 2,000 years now. In this verse, a "short" like that would be anything BUT short, to describe the length of how long these people would suffer.

23 "If at that time any one should say to **you**, `See, here is the Christ!' or `There!' give no credence to it.

24 For there will rise up false Christs and false prophets, displaying wonderful signs and prodigies, so as to deceive, were it possible, even God's own People.

25 Remember, I have *forewarned YOU*.

"Remember" = Must Be Alive = Must Be First Century
Jesus couldn't ask these people to **stop** in the **middle** of all these future disasters to **remember** what he had told them years in their past, unless they would yet be alive **in the midst of** all these future disasters. No future generations are in view here.

26 If therefore they should say to **you**, `See, He is in the Desert!' do not go out there: or `See, He is indoors in the room!' do not believe it.

27 For just as the lightning flashes in the east and is **SEEN** to the very west, so will be the Coming of the Son of Man.

Visibility = Problem for Preterist View
As with all things Christian, this doctrine of the Second Coming is fractured amongst various splinter groups. One such group, called the "Preterist", (and even *this* small splinter group is *further* splintered into even smaller groups) more or less believe that Jesus *did* return, however he returned in an "invisible" returning in 70 AD, and *that's* why everybody missed it.

The wording of Matthew, however, seems to contradict this belief. Matthew implies that if you were facing west- maybe toward where the sun just "set" an hour ago, and lightning strikes in the east, even miles behind your back, you can not *help* but see the entire sky light up. Likewise, Jesus is saying that his return will be **so obvious and visible**, that even if you **weren't** looking for it, you couldn't **help** but see it. Thus groups that have advocated an invisible "Second Coming" of Jesus do so in **contradiction** to what Jesus **himself** taught. The reason Jesus' return was **not** noticed in the First Century (or in 1914 if you're a Jehovah's Witness) is *not* because it was *invisible*, but rather because it *never happened*.

28 Wherever the dead body is, there will the vultures flock together.

29 "But **immediately** after those times of distress the sun will be darkened, the moon will not shed her light, the stars will fall from the firmament, and the forces which control the heavens will be disordered and disturbed.

Immediately = First Century
Having already established that previous events were predicted to take place within the First Century, these **remaining** events, which were to **immediately** follow, would also have to be within the First Century. As for stars falling off the firmament, please check my website JCnot4me.com for my "The Universe According To The Bible".

30 **Then** will appear the Sign of the Son of Man in the sky; and then will all the nations of the earth lament, when they see the Son of Man coming on the clouds of the sky with great power and glory.

"Immediately...Then" = First Century
Next, a "sign" is said to appear in the sky, following all the other sky disturbances mentioned above. The use of the "then's" implies a fast-paced sequence which does not allow for any theorized thousand-year "gaps": "*Then* will appear the Sign...*then* will all nations lament". Thus, once again, the era is locked into the First Century.

Also, the "Son of Man" theme is the same as in all the *other* 2nd Coming texts, texts whose fulfillment were likewise promised within the lifetime of the First Century hearers.

31 And He will send out His **angels** with a **loud trumpet-blast**, and they will bring together His own People to Him from north, south, east and west--**from one extremity of the world to the other**.

Yet Another Problem for the Preterist View

As the Preterists *try* to explain how Jesus returned invisibly in the First Century, they also need to explain how this verse was fulfilled without anyone noticing. How do you hide a worldwide infestation of billions of angels fluttering about in the sky while blowing horns at maximum volume? The preterists "answer" this via a common Christian dodge- they hide behind figurative language.

32 "Now learn from the fig-tree the lesson it teaches. As soon as its branches have now become soft and it is bursting into leaf, you all know that summer is near.

33 So **you** also, when *you* see all these signs, may be sure that He is near--*at your very door*.

"When YOU See" = First Century Apostles

Jesus tells his Apostles "when **YOU** see all these signs". *Not* "if" or "maybe" but **when**. Jesus was thus guaranteeing them that **all** these signs would take place *within* their lifetime, *including* the Second Coming.

"At Your Very Door" = First Century

The phrase "He is near--at your very door" implies a few things. First, it implies the **very next step** will bring Jesus **THROUGH** the door. Second, whose "door" was he near? The Apostle's "door".

34 I tell **you** in *solemn* truth that **the present generation** will certainly **not** pass away without **all these things** having first taken place.

"Present Generation" = First Century

There is much more said elsewhere about this verse and its key word "generation." For now, let me point out that this 34th verse does not exist in a vacuum; it is the **culmination** of the last several verses, all *time references*, and all of which lead up to make a specific point: Jesus' Second Coming was due **within their lifetime**. The context allows no other interpretation.

"Trust Me, I'm Not Lying"

Jesus *precedes* the prophecy with "I tell you in solemn truth" and *follows* it in verse #35 with a claim that his words would outlast even the *Universe*. These facts should be a major hint this prophecy was an extremely important issue for him, and he wanted to be dead sure that nobody misunderstood him. In his own mind, even though he *sincerely* believed that he'd be back within that century, he was **SINCERELY WRONG**. He did *not*, within the lifetime of *that* generation, return in the clouds, in the glory of BibleGod, with hordes of angels, with trumpets blowing. His prophecy turned out to be false, and that makes him a *false prophet*.

"All These Things" = Complete Package

Jesus says emphatically that "*all these things*" would happen *before* his then *current* generation had passed away. Jesus presents the entire package as a "take it or leave it" situation, picking and choosing not allowed. Some Christian "explanations" of this verse have attempted to **slice & dice** the 24th chapter into "some for back then, some for now, and maybe... some for the future". This fragmenting of the chapter is not allowed by Jesus' clear statement "**all these things**". ANY Christian theory that tries to explain away this "problem chapter" has to treat the chapter as a *whole*, and explain how all of it happened or *didn't* happen. Of course, since the date for the destruction (v. 2) of the Jewish temple is firmly established in history at 70 AD, and everything in this chapter is promised within a short time frame, this entire chapter is thus locked into the First Century, from which it can not escape.

35 Earth and sky will pass away, but it is certain that my words will not pass away.

36 "But as to that day and the exact time no one knows--not even the angels of heaven, nor the Son, but the Father alone.

Within Certain Limits ≠ Exact "Day & Time"
Some have quibbled in the best Clintonian tradition that Jesus' no-show can't be objected to because Jesus said no one knows the *exact* day & time. The exact day & time Jesus never gave, but I bet if he had, the Christians would invent an excuse for *that* blooper, too.

Jesus didn't give the exact year, or month, or day, or hour, or minute- but so what? He gave limits-time *limits*, an "expiration date" if you will. He himself said he'd be back *before* that generation died off, therefore *within* the lifetime of his Apostles. As to the exact *millisecond* within that generational limit that he was due back, it doesn't matter. What matters is that his "**expiration date**" long since **expired**. Christians should deal with *that* LOG in their theological eye, and ignore the *splinter* presented by this verse.

37 For as it was in the time of Noah, so it will be at the Coming of the Son of Man.

38 At that time, before the Deluge, men were busy eating and drinking, taking wives or giving them, up to the very day when Noah entered the Ark,

39 nor did they realise any danger till the Deluge came and swept them all away; so will it be at the Coming of the Son of Man.

Noah's Flood Was Within Noah's Generation
The flood that "Noah" warned everyone about was due within "Noah's" generation, not 10,000 years later. It would have been completely ludicrous for Noah to have been warning his neighbors to escape! Run! Flee! some flood that was yet thousands of years past their lifetimes. In light of this, when Jesus promised his Apostles that, as it was with "Noah", so also with the Second Coming, this nails down the due-date of the Second Coming to within their lifetime.

40 Then will two men be in the open country: one will be taken away, and one left behind.

41 Two women will be grinding at the mill: one will be taken away, and one left behind.

42 Be on the alert therefore, for **you** do not know the day on which your Lord is coming.

43 But of this be assured, that if the master of the house had known the hour at which the robber was coming, he would have kept awake, and not have allowed his house to be broken into.

Keep Awake = Within Their Lifetime
If the burglar who was going to rob the house wasn't even *due* until centuries *after* both house and owner had dissolved into dust, Jesus' advice to the home owner (i.e. his Apostles) to "keep

awake" is total and complete *nonsense*. Therefore, Jesus *must* have believed his Second Coming would occur within their lifetime.

44 Therefore **you** also **must be** _ready_; for it is at a time when **you** do not expect Him that the Son of Man will come.

"Be Ready" = Within Their Lifetime

It has been around 2,000 years since Jesus sounded the alarm warning his Apostles about his Second Coming. Looking back with hindsight, him getting his Apostles all worked up about this event makes no sense at all, unless he himself expected to be back within their lifetime. One does not pull a fire alarm _thousands_ of years in advance of the fire.

45 "**Who** therefore is the loyal and intelligent **servant** to whom his master has entrusted the control of his household to give them their rations at the appointed time?

Within Peter's Lifetime

"*Who is the loyal and intelligent servant*"??? Peter, that's who, as recorded earlier in this same book of Matthew, 16:18,19

> ... you are Peter, and on this rock I will build My church... And I will give to you the keys of the kingdom of Heaven.

If the fulfillment of the Second Coming prophecy was _**not**_ due until centuries _**after**_ Peter's death, pray tell who is _**NOW**_ the one the "master has entrusted the control of his household" of faith to???? Who is the one living _**today**_ who's been appointed to "give them their rations at the appointed time"??? Who is _**NOW**_, Mr. & Mrs. Protestant, holding the keys???

46 Blessed is that servant whom his master when he comes shall find so doing!

Within Peter's Lifetime

Jesus, in this story, tells of a departing master (i.e. Jesus) who puts a slave (i.e. Peter) in charge of the household until his return. In the story, the master returns _**within**_ the lifetime of the slave.

Jesus (as seen previously) put Peter in charge of the household of faith _**until**_ Jesus should have returned. Therefore Jesus, like the master in the story, expected to be back _**within**_ Peter's lifetime. If Jesus was _**NOT**_ going to have returned within Peter's lifetime, Jesus would have made arrangements for NEW "slaves" to watch over his household until if and when he _**DID**_ come back. To imply otherwise is to say that Jesus was a deadbeat dad, who just walked out on his family, abandoned them, without a second thought as to their welfare.

The fact that Christianity, after the death of the Apostles, _**has been**_ torn asunder time & again over the issue of "who's in charge here" is proof that Jesus really _**was**_ a deadbeat dad who orphaned his kids. Jesus neither _**returned**_ when he promised he would, nor did he clearly _**provide**_ someone to watch over his kids in the meantime until he _**did**_ return. (As for the knee-jerk response of "That's what the Holy Ghost is for", this "ghost" must have been asleep all this time, as it allowed thousands of Christian splinter groups to develop, all over this very issue of "who's in charge here."

47 In solemn truth I tell **you** that he will give him the management of all his wealth.

48 But if the man, being a ***bad*** servant, should say in his heart, `My master is a ***LONG TIME*** in coming,'

But It **HAS** Been A Long Time!!!

Jesus here ***condemns*** as a "bad servant" he who says Jesus' return is "a ***long time*** in coming". Yet to say anything ***else*** in our era, is evidence of total and complete ***blindness*** to the passage of about **2,000** years. The simple, undeniable ***fact*** is that his return ***HAS*** been "a ***long*** time in coming" and no amount of theological BS by Jesus or anyone else can change that fact into a fiction. And every century, Christians have to answer anew why their master ***has been*** such a long time in coming. How many more centuries have to go by, before Christianity will admit the obvious? When the sun goes super nova in several billion years and he ***STILL*** hasn't shown up, will they finally admit what to everyone else has been obvious???

Even a New Testament writer- disguising himself as the Apostle Peter, felt obligated to throw in his two cents on ***why*** their heavenly father seems to have orphaned them. He wrote that a short time is really a long time as long as you're not the one telling time (2nd Peter 3:8). I think he also sold used chariots on the side. For more on this, see the chapter *"Christian Math: 1 = 1,000 (2ⁿᵈ Peter 3:8"*.

Jesus Missing!! Kids Orphaned!!

Modern Christians, via 2,000 years of disappointments, have been ***forced*** into becoming "bad servants;" for the return of Jesus has ***indeed*** been "a long time in coming". They themselves stand condemned by their own god when they point out his "delay" in returning. But it's not their fault- it's his- ***he never came back!!!*** He ***abandoned*** his kids. He ***walked out on them*** and left them orphans, and now they delude themselves into thinking daddy's really coming home someday. Umpteen years ago, their daddy walked out to the corner liquor store to pick up some whiskey & cigarettes, and he just never came back, never wrote, never called. Thousands of years later his great-great-great etc grandkids wait for him by the front door like dogs, barking in excitement at every passing "sign" they think indicates the Second Coming. But it never comes. And their Jesus remains... M.I.A. Missing in Action.

49 and should begin to beat his fellow servants, while he eats and drinks with drunkards;

50 the master of that servant will arrive on a day when he is not expecting him and at an hour of which he has not been informed;

51 he will treat him with the utmost severity and assign him a place among the hypocrites: there will be the weeping and the gnashing of teeth.

My Final Comments
The 24th Chapter of Matthew

Multiple Questions ≠ Different Eras

Some, in yet another attempt to "save the savior" have suggested that there are two or three separate questions in verse #3 concerning future events, and therefore the timing of these events may be thousands of years apart.

Regardless of how many questions may have been originally asked by the Apostles, the man answering the questions was very explicit that everything in this narrative would be fulfilled within a short time span, certainly not to extend past the First Century.

- "Before long" the Apostles would hear of war rumors. (v.6) (The "before long" is Greek word "mello" means "to be **on the point of** doing or suffering something".)
- " The early pains of childbirth " (v.8) is another is another phrase that indicates there is not much time left till all these things are supposed to take place.
- "Those who stand firm to the End" (v.13) indicates that "The End" will be something these Apostles can reasonably hope to "stand firm to" long enough to see, i.e., within their lifetime. One can't "stand firm" to an end millions of years distant.
- "But *immediately* after those times of distress…" (v.29) certainly doesn't grant much time between events.
- "*Then* will appear the Sign of the Son of Man…" (v.30) is the very next step past the "immediately" of the preceding verse. Again, no room for thousands of years of delays.
- "So you also, *when YOU see all these signs*, may be sure that **He is near--at your very door**.." (v.33) Now Jesus is telling his First Century Apostles that when they've seen all the signs described, the Second Coming will be just around the corner- "at your very door," which implies the very next step will bring him *through* the doorway. Again, another lock-in for the First Century era.
- " I tell **you** (his 1ˢᵗ century Apostles) in solemn truth that the **present** generation will certainly not pass away without

ALL THESE THINGS

having *first* taken place." (v.34) As if I needed any more evidence to show that this entire scenario is locked up into a First Century time frame, along comes Jesus to drive the killing nail into the theory that any other era besides the First Century would suffice. Regardless of how many questions were asked by the Apostles, "**ALL** these **things**" are predicted to take place before *that* present generation of then-living First Century men died off.

- "But if the man, being a **bad servant**, should say in his heart, `My master is a **LONG TIME** in coming…'" (v.48) cinches the argument that whatever questions may have been asked regarding their future, their answers were all due within the First Century. The fulfillment of the predictions, according to Jesus, would *not* be "a long time in coming."

"This Generation" = Due in 1st Century

Matthew 24:34
90+ Translations

New American Standard Bible [#1]	Truly I say to you, this generation will not pass away until **all** these things take place.
The Holy Bible R. Knox [#95]	Believe me, this generation will not have passed, before all this is accomplished.
Concordant Literal New Testament A.E. Knoch [#4]	Verily, I am saying to you, that **by no means** may this generation be passing by till all these things should be occurring.
The Modern Reader's Bible R. Moulton [#96]	Verily I say unto you, this generation shall not pass away, till all these things be accomplished.
The Complete Bible: An American Translation Smith & Goodspeed [#12]	I tell you, **before** the present generation passes away, these things will all happen.
The New Testament Cunnington [#101]	Verily I say to you, this generation will not pass away, till all these things have come to pass.
The Emphasized New Testament Rotherham [#5]	Verily I say unto you—In nowise shall this generation pass away until **all** these things shall happen.
The New King James Bible [#104]	Assuredly, I say to you, this generation will by no means pass away till all these things are fulfilled.
The New Testament in Modern English J.B. Phillips [#15]	Believe me, this generation will **not** disappear till all this has taken place.
The New International Version [#16]	I tell you the truth, this generation will _**certainly**_ **not** pass away until all these things have happened.
New Revised Standard Version [#17]	Truly I tell you, this generation will **not** pass away until all these things have taken place.
Revised Standard Version [#18]	Truly, I say to you, this generation will **not** pass away till all these things take place.
The New Testament Anderson [#106]	Verily I say to you, this generation shall not pass away till all these things take place.
Young's Literal Translation [#3]	Verily I say to you, this generation may **not** pass away till all these may come to pass.
American Standard Version [#10]	Verily I say unto you, this generation shall **not** pass away, till all these things be accomplished.
King James Version [#19]	Verily I say unto you, this generation shall **not** pass, till all these things be fulfilled.
Bible in Basic English [#20]	Truly I say to you, **This generation will <u>not</u> come to an end** till all these things are complete.
Darby Bible [#21]	Verily I say to you, **This generation will not have passed away** until all these things shall have taken place.

Matthew 24:34 Via 90+ Versions
(con't)

21st Century King James Version [#22]	Verily I say unto you, **this generation shall not pass** until all these things be fulfilled.
A Literal Translation of The Bible [#23]	Truly I say to you, **In no way will this generation pass away** until all these things have occurred.
Green's Modern King James Version [#24]	Truly I say to you, This generation shall **not** pass until all these things are fulfilled.
The Bible in Living English Byington [#99]	I tell you verily that this generation shall not pass away till all this has taken place.
The New Jerusalem Bible [#26]	In truth I tell you, **before** this generation has passed away, **all** these things will have taken place.
The New Testament [#107]	Amen I say to you, this generation will not pass away till all these things have been accomplished.
The New World Translation [#98]	Truly I say to you that this generation will by no means pass away until all these things occur.
The New American Bible [#29]	I assure you, **the present generation will not pass away** until all this takes place.
An American Translation [#30]	I tell you the truth, these people will **not** pass away till all this happens.
The Riverside New Testament Ballantine [#108]	Truly I tell you, this generation will not pass away before all these things happen.
The New Testament John Wesley [#109]	Verily I say to you, this generation shall not pass away till all things be done.
The Good News According to Matthew Einspruch [#110]	I assure you, this generation will not pass away before all these things will have taken place.
The New Testament in Basic English Hooke [#111]	Truly I say to you, this generation will not come to an end till all these things are complete.
The Authentic New Testament Schonfield [#112]	I tell you truly, this generation will by no means pass away before all these things take place.
The Corrected English New Testament Lloyd [#113]	Verily, I say unto you, this generation will not pass away, till all these things have come to pass.
The Four Gospels: A New Translation Torrey [#114]	Verily I say to you, **before** this generation passes away, all these things will happen.
Douay-Rheims 1899 American Edition [#185]	Amen I say to you, that this generation shall not pass, till all these things be done.
Evangelical Heritage Version [#186]	Amen I tell you: This generation will certainly not pass away until all these things take place.
English Standard Version Anglicised [#187]	Truly, I say to you, this generation will not pass away until all these things take place.

Matthew 24:34 Via 90+ Versions
(con't)

The New Testament- According To The Eastern Text (Aramaic) Lamsa [#115]	Truly I say to you, that this generation will not pass away, until all these things happen.
(Pre-published translation from the Aramaic) Alexander [#156]	Amen, I am telling you, that this generation will not pass away, until all these things have been fulfilled.
God's New Covenant- A New Testament Translation Cassirer [#116]	Indeed, I can give you **_solemn_** assurance that this generation will not have passed away before all this has taken place.
Tyndale's New Testament Wm. Tyndale [#117]	Verily I say unto you, that this generation shall not pass till all these be fulfilled.
The Twentieth Century New Testament [#103]	I tell you, **even the _present_ generation** will **_not_** pass away, till all these things have taken place.
The New Life Testament Ledyard [#105]	For I tell you, the people of **THIS DAY** will not pass away before all these things have happened.
Centenary Translation of the New Testament Montgomery [#102]	I tell you in solemn truth, that the present generation shall not pass away till all these things happen.
The Holy Bible in Modern English F. Fenton [#28]	I tell you indeed, that **this present generation** shall not pass away until all these things arrive.
The Bible: A New Translation J. Moffatt [#27]	I tell you truly, the **present** generation will **not** pass away, till all this happens.
The New English Bible [#25]	I tell you this: **the _present_ generation will live to see it all**.
The New Testament in Modern Speech Weymouth [#2]	I tell you in solemn truth that **the _present_ generation** will certainly not pass away without all these things having first taken place.
The Berkeley Version G. Verkuyl [#13]	I assure you, **all these things** will take place **before this _present_ generation** passes on.
The Scholars Version Robert Funk [#11]	I **swear to God**, this generation certainly **won't** pass into oblivion before all these things take place!"
Holy Bible- Contemporary English [#100]	I can promise you that **_some_** of the people of **_this_** generation will **_still be alive_** when all this happens.
The Amplified New Testament [#9]	Truly, I tell you, **this generation—that is, the whole multitude of people living at the same time, in a definite, given period**—will not pass away till all these things **_taken together_** take place.
The Everyday Bible, New Century Version Word Pub. [#97]	I tell you the truth. **_All these things_** will happen **while the people of this time _are still living!_**

Matthew 24:34 Via 90+ Versions (con't)	
Today's English Version [#14]	Remember that **all these things will happen _before_ the people _now_ living have all died.**
Mounce Reverse Interlinear N.T. [#161]	I tell you the truth, this generation will not pass away until all these things take place.
Disciples' Literal N.T. [#162]	Truly I say to you that this generation will by no means pass away until all these things take place.
Easy to Read Version [#163]	I assure you that **all these things** will happen while **some of the people of _this_ time are still living.**
English Standard Version [#164]	Truly, I say to you, this generation will not pass away until all these things take place.
1599 Geneva Bible [#165]	Verily I say to you, this generation shall not pass, till all these things be done.
God's Word Translation [#166]	I can **GUARANTEE** this truth: **This generation will _not_ disappear** until all these things take place.
International Children's Bible [#167]	I tell you the truth. All these things will happen while the people of this time are still living!
Jubilee Bible 2000 [#168]	Verily I say unto you, This generation shall not pass until all these things are fulfilled.
Lexham Bible [#169]	Truly I say to you that this generation will **never** pass away until all these things take place!
Names of God Bible [#170]	I can guarantee this truth: This generation will not disappear until all these things take place.
New American Bible Revised Edition [#171]	Amen, and I say to you, this generation will not pass away until all these things have taken place.
New English Translation [#172]	I tell you the truth, this generation will not pass away until all these things take place.
New International Readers Version [#173]	What I'm about to tell you is **true**. The people living **now** will certainly not pass away until all these things happen.
New Life Version [#174]	For sure, I tell you, **the people of _this day_** will not pass away before all these things have happened.
New Living Translation [#175]	I tell you the truth, **this generation will not pass from the scene** until all these things take place.
Orthodox Jewish Bible [#176]	Omein, I say to you, that this dor (generation) will by no means pass away until all these things come about.
Tree of Life Version [#177]	Amen, I tell you, this generation will not pass away until all these things happen.
World English Bible [#179]	Most certainly I tell you, this generation will not pass away, until all these things are accomplished.
Wycliffe Bible [#180]	Truly I say to you, for this generation shall not pass, till all things be done.
BRG Bible [#182]	Verily I say unto you, This generation shall not pass, till all these things be fulfilled.
Christian Standard Bible [#183]	Truly I tell you, this generation will certainly not pass away until all these things take place.
Common English Bible [#184]	I assure you that this generation won't pass away until all these things happen.
Complete Jewish Bible [#184]	Yes! I tell you that this people will certainly not pass away before all these things happen.

Matthew 24:34 Via 90+ Versions
(con't)

Good News Translation [#188]	Remember that all these things will happen **BEFORE** the people **NOW LIVING** have all **died**.
Holman Christian Standard Bible [#189]	I assure you: This generation will certainly **not** pass away until all these things take place.
Modern English Version [#190]	Truly I say to you, this generation will not pass away until **all** these things take place.
New International Version UK [#191]	Truly I tell you, this generation will certainly not pass away until all these things have happened.
New King James Version [#192]	Assuredly, I say to you, this generation will by no means pass away till all these things take place.
New Matthew Bible [#193]	Truly I say to you that this generation shall not pass till all these thing be fulfilled.
New Revised Standard Version, Anglicised [#194]	Truly I tell you, this generation will not pass away until all these things have taken place.
New Revised Standard Version, Anglicised Catholic Edition [#195]	Truly I tell you, this generation will not pass away until all these things have taken place.
New Revised Standard Version Catholic Edition [#196]	Truly I tell you, this generation will not pass away until all these things have taken place.
New Testament for Everyone [#197]	I'm telling you **THE TRUTH**: this generation won't be gone **BEFORE** all these things happen.
The Passion Translation [#198]	I assure you, the end of this age will not come until all I have spoken comes to pass.
Revised Geneva Translation [#199]	Truly I say to you that *this* generation shall not pass until all these things are done.
The Original New Testament Schonfield [#181]	So you, when you see all this, will know that **it is at hand**, **at the very doors**. I tell you truly, **this** generation will by no means pass away before all these things take place.
The Voice [#178]	I tell you this: *THIS* generation will see **ALL** these things take place **BEFORE** it passes away.

40

Matthew 24:34   The Greek Word Genea

Lexicons, Dictionaries, Commentaries, Quotes	
Matthew 24:34 **Generation "γενεα"**	
Greek Lexicons	
Greek & English Lexicon of the New Testament Edward Robinson p.140 [#62]	1. a generation, pr. <u>the interval of</u> **time between father and son**, a <u>SINGLE STEP</u> or succession in natural descent… from **thirty to forty years** as a generation. 3. a generation of men, the men of any age, *those living in any **one** period*; this *PRESENT* generation.
The New Analytical Greek Lexicon W. Perschbacher p.77 [#63]	a generation of mankind, a *step* in a genealogy.
The Analytical Lexicon To The Greek New Testament William Mounce p.123 [#64]	a **generation**, an **interval of time**.
Thayer's Greek-English Lexicon of the New Testament p.112 [#65]	3. the whole multitude of men living *at the same time*: **Mt xxiv.34**… used esp. of the Jewish race living at <u>one and the *same*</u> period.
A Greek English Lexicon of the New Testament, Vol. 1 Arndt & Gingrich [#66]	2. basically, the sum total of **those born at the <u>same time</u>**, expanded to include all those living at a given time, generation, **contemporaries**… Jesus looks upon the whole contemp. **generation** of Jews as a uniform mass confronting him, **Mt 24:34**; Mk 13:30; Lk 21:32

Lexicons, Dictionaries, Commentaries, Quotes
Matthew 24:34
Generation "γενεα"

Biblical Dictionaries

The New International Dictionary of New Testament Theology pp.35-36 [#59]	**Genea:** Those born at the **same time** constitute a generation… the body of one's **contemporaries**…In the LXX *genea* is almost always the translation of *dor*, and means generation, in which case the whole history of Israel is often regarded as a work of God extending through many generations ("**from generation to generation**" , "**from all generations**")… In Jesus' discourse about the future… Mk 13:30; **Matt. 24:34**; Lk. 21:32… the discourse refers to this *genea* "passing away"… By using this phrase, **Jesus appears to set a TIME LIMIT** for certain events… **Genos:** The noun genos, formed from the same stem and related to the verb ginomai, is frequently translated by race… Both in the LXX and in the NT its prime meaning is nation, people, or tribe.
The Imperial Bible Dictionary Rev. Patrick Fairbairn pp.351-352 [#61]	…Thus Herodotus says, 'three generations of men make an hundred years.' 3. Finally, the word is sometimes taken more concretely to denote the persons actually constituting a *specific* generation, as exponents of its state or character
New Bible Dictionary Douglas, Hillyer, and Wood p.412 [#68]	**Genea**: Used chiefly in the LXX to translate *dor*, and like it including among its meanings much the same range as Eng. "generation". It is used of the people living at a given time… and by extension, of the time itself… **40 years**… is to be taken as a round number indicating a generation. **Genos**: "Race". AV translates the phrase genos eklekton in 1 Pet. 2:9 "chosen generation", but RV "elect race" or RSV "chosen race" is to be preferred.
Exegetical Dictionary of the New Testament Balz & Schneider p.24 [#60]	1. Of the 43 references to genea in the NT, 33 are in the Synoptics, where the word refers in 25 of its occurrences to **the Jewish people in the time of Jesus**, 17 times in the expression "this generation."… For Mark 8:12 only the **final judgment** awaits the condemned Israel *of the time of Jesus*… Consequently in an apocalyptic threatening word **13:30** affirms, along with **Matt 24:34** and **Luke 21:32**, that *this* generation must experience the horrors of the **end time**.
Vine's Expository Dictionary of New Testament Words "age" p.42 [#43]	Genea: The whole multitude of men living *at the same time*, **Matt 23:34**; Mark 13:30; Luke 21:32… a period ordinarily occupied by *each successive generation*, say, of **thirty or forty years**.
Theological Dictionary of the New Testament Gerhard Kittel p.663 [#67]	In the NT, γενεα is common in the Synoptics, rare in Paul, absent from Jn, including Rev. …It mostly denotes "generation" in the sense of **contemporaries**. We often have the formula… Mk 13:30; **Mt 24:34**; Lk 21:32… This generation is to be understood *temporally*.

Matthew 24:34
Generation "γενεα"

	Mostly Biblical Dictionaries (con't)
The Westminster Dictionary of The Bible John Davis p.198 [#40-A]	The age or period of a body of *contemporaries… as determined by the normal span of life. The generation lasts as long as any of the members **survive**. *con·tem·po·rar·y *adj. Abbr.* **contemp. 1.** Belonging to the same period of time: *a fact documented by two contemporary sources.* *(The American Heritage Dictionary,* [#8])
Smith's Bible Dictionary William Smith p.209 [#41]	In the long-lived Patriarchal age a generation seems to have been computed at 100 years… but subsequently the reckoning was the same which has been adopted by other civilized nations, viz., **from thirty to forty years**… Generation is also used to signify the men of an age, or time, as **cotemporaries**…
Harper's Bible Dictionary p.218 [#39]	Used in the singular, generation usually signified the sum total of **individuals forming a <u>contemporary</u> group.**
The Harper Collins Bible Dictionary P. Achtemeier p.366 [#45]	(Heb. *dor*) The period of time between the birth of parents and the birth of their children; all of the people alive during that time. …most biblical writers seem to consider **thirty to forty years** to be a normal generation.
The Interpreter's Dictionary of the Bible p.366 [#47]	…**the period from a *man's* birth to that of his *son***—and collectively the people who live in that period. In the NT, *genea* generally corresponds to this meaning.
Mercer Dictionary of the Bible Watson Mills p.321 [#48]	In its strictest temporal sense, a generation is the period of time *between* the birth of parents **and** the birth of their *children*… the term simply refers to **all people living at a particular time.**
Nelson's Illustrated Bible Dictionary Herbert Lockyer p.411 [#49]	A body of people who live **at the same time** in a given period of history.
The Oxford English Dictionary Vol. VI of XX p.436 [#50]	**The whole body of individuals born about the same period**; also, the time covered by the lives of these. In reckoning historically by 'generations', the word is taken to mean the interval of time between the birth of the **PARENTS** and that of their **CHILDREN**, usually computed at **thirty years**, or three generations to a century. †6. [*obsolete* usage indicated by †] family, breed, **race.**
Peloubet's Bible Dictionary F.N. Peloubet p.215 [#52]	…the reckoning was the same which has been adopted by modern civilized nations, viz. from **thirty to forty years**. Generation is also used to signify the men of an age or time, as **contemporaries**.
Concise Dictionary of The Bible Neill, Goodwin, & Dowle p.120 [#54]	Frequently used in the general sense of a period of time, **the span of one human life**, or of those who live at a particular period of time.

Matthew 24:34
Generation "γενεα"

Biblical Dictionaries (con't)

The Eerdmans Bible Dictionary p.408 [#57]	The 'circle' of life, spanning from a man's birth to that of his son; this period was reckoned to be **FORTY YEARS**. The term was also used to refer collectively to all people living in such a period.
Easton's Bible Dictionary M.G. Easton [#69]	Matt 24:34, "This generation" = the persons **then living contemporary with Christ**.
Davis Dictionary of the Bible John D. Davis p.265 [#131]	3.) The age or period of a body of **contemporaries**… The generation lasts as long as _**any**_ of the members survive.
Today's Dictionary of the Bible T.A. Bryant p.254 [#132]	**24:34**, "This generation" = the persons then living **contemporary with Christ**.
A Dictionary of the Bible and Christian Doctrine in Everyday English A. Trusdale pp.113-114 [#135]	A generation is the time period between the age of parents and their children. A generation is **about 25 years**. A generation is all the people living at about the same period of time (Matthew 11:16-19; **24:34**…)
Dictionary of The Bible John McKenzie p.301 [#136]	In general the word generation in the Bible refers to any **contemporary** group.
A Biblical and Theological Dictionary p.401 [#139]	It was fixed by some at a hundred years, by others at a hundred and ten, by others at thirty-three, thirty, twenty-five, and even at twenty years.
A Dictionary of the Bible James Hastings p.142 [#145]	1b) of all men living at any given time… as 1.(b), **Mt 24:34**… a period of **about 30 to 33 years.**
Cruden's Dictionary of Bible Terms Alexander Cruden p.127 [#133]	**Matt. xxiv. 34**, "This generation shall not pass…" _**All**_ who are at _**present living**_ shall _**not**_ be dead _**when**_ this shall come to pass. There are _**some at this day living**_, who _**shall**_ be witnesses of the evils which I have foretold shall befall the Jews.
The New Unger's Bible Dictionary Merrill Unger p.464 [#143]	(3) The word is also taken to denote the persons actually constituting a specific generation… We must adhere to the ordinary usage, according to which _dor_ signifies an age, or **the men living in a particular age**.

Matthew 24:34
Generation "γενεα"

Christian Encyclopedias	
The International Standard Bible Encyclopedia G. Bromiley p.431 [#46]	Hebrew *dôr*, Aram. *dar*, and Gk *geneá*; refer to a period of time loosely defined as **the TIME BETWEEN A PARENTS' PRIME AND THAT OF HIS CHILD**… Those living at a given time in history are referred to as a generation.
The Popular and Critical Bible Encyclopaedia Samuel Fallows p.697 [#51]	**Matt 24:34**, η γενεα αντη, means the generation or persons ***THEN*** *living* **contemporary** with Christ.
Wycliffe Bible Encyclopedia p.664 [#53]	**Genea**: It has the concept of the sum total of those born at the same time-**contemporaries**. **Genos**: The term connotes the meaning of *'race.'*
Cyclopaedia of Biblical, Theological, and Ecclesiastical Literature McClintock & Strong p.776 [#58]	**Genea** means the generation of persons then living ***contemporary*** with Christ.
The Cyclopaedia of Biblical Literature p.748 [#134]	**Matt. xxix.34**, η γενεα αντη means the generation or persons ***then*** **living contemporary** *with* **Christ.** …The Greeks reckoned three generations for every hundred years, i.e. 33 1/3 years to each.
The Comprehensive Critical & Explanatory Bible Encyclopaedia Edward Robinson pp.452-453 [#137]	"The present generation" comprises **all those who are *now* alive.** **Matt. xxiv.34.** "This generation shall not pass away, till all be fulfilled;" **some now living shall witness the event foretold.** …Our Lord uses the term generation to express a period of about ## 36 OR 37 YEARS when he says, "This generation shall not pass away, till all be fulfilled;" say **A.D. 70.**

Matthew 24:34
Generation "γενεα"

Christian Commentaries

Matthew Douglas Hare pp.281-282 [#140]	…verse 34 solemnly **promises** that Jesus will return **while some of his contemporaries are STILL ALIVE** (a reprise of 16:28). …**THIS PREDICTION WAS NOT FULFILLED.** ..The gospel testimony provides strong support for *this* view: **Jesus did *not* know all things**.
The Expositor's Bible Commentary D.A. Carson p.507 [#55]	(This generation) can only with the *greatest difficulty* be made to mean **anything *other*** than **the** generation living when Jesus spoke.
Commentary on the Gospel of Mark William Lane p.480 [#56]	…in Mark, 'this generation' clearly designates the **contemporaries** of Jesus.
The Wesleyan Bible Commentary Ralph Earle p.104 [#142]	So, when you see <u>all these things</u>—presumably what had been described so far in this chapter—then know that he…is **right at the doors** (v. 33). The statement in **verse 34** is another ***difficult*** one. On the surface it seems to say that **Christ would return DURING that very generation**… The word for **generation** is *genea*. Its first meaning is "family, descent," and so "**race**." It may mean "nation," or even "age" (period of time). But **its *primary* meaning**, especially in the Gospels, is this: Basically, the sum total of those **BORN** at the same time, expanded to include all those living at a given time, generation, **contemporaries**. If generation is to be taken in this strict sense, then <u>all these things</u> ***must be*** limited to the events **culminating** in A.D. 70 …The **MAJORITY OF THE *BEST* SCHOLARS TODAY** insist that generation be taken in its **strictest** sense.
The Expositor's Greek Testament Bruce & Dods p.296 [#84]	Jesus was quite certain that they would happen *within the **then** living generation*.
The Interpreter's Bible p.551 [#42]	He [Matthew] probably believed, however, that the end would come ***before*** all of Jesus' hearers had died.
The Gospel of Matthew T. Robinson p.200 [#88]	Further, he [Jesus] insists that his words are **infallible**, and that they are **more certain than the material universe itself**…it is interesting to note that this evangelist [Matthew] has allowed the words "the **present generation** will **not** pass away till all this happens" to stand.
New Century Bible: The Gospel of Matthew p.323 [#146]	This verse recalls 16.28, and affirms that **some of the disciples would live to see the Parousia**. This would presuppose a **relatively early date** for the event…*Was Jesus in ERROR* in his prediction of the nearness of the End…?

Christian Commentaries (con't)

Word Pictures in the New Testament A. Robinson pp.193-194 [#90]	In the Old Testament a generation was reckoned as **forty years**. This is the **natural** way to take verse 34… He had <u>**plainly stated**</u> in verse 34 that those events (destruction of Jerusalem) would take place **in that generation**. …One may, of course, accuse Jesus of <u>**hopeless confusion**</u>…It is <u>**impossible**</u> to escape the conclusion that Jesus as Man, expected the End, <u>**within the lifetime of his contemporaries.**</u>
Primative Christian Eschatology E.C. Dewick pp.175-177 [#91]	And further, a straightforward interpretation of the Synoptic narratives… implies that the "coming of the Son of Man" was to take place at the time of the Fall of Jerusalem. …while our Lord foretold that "all things" would certainly be accomplished <u>within a generation</u>, He did **not** know the exact date of the final crisis. …there were limits to our Lord's human knowledge…if our Lord did actually use the words "This generation shall not pass, until all these things be accomplished,"… **He believed Himself to know something which He did <u>not</u> really know.** …But the hard **fact** still remains, that if Jesus spoke the sayings of St. Mark xiii. and St. Matthew xxiv. in the exact order and under the exact circumstances which the Evangelists relate, He MISJUDGED the extent of His <u>own</u> knowledge, and uttered a <u>definite</u> **prediction** which *was **not** fulfilled.*
The Eschatology of Jesus Luis Muirhead p.50 [#92]	The Synoptists fell into the contradiction…of making Jesus declare at one moment that He did *not* know the time of the glorious Advent, and at another that **it would** *INFALLIBLY* **happen within that generation.**
The Jerome Biblical Commentary p.106 [#94]	The affirmation that "<u>all these things</u>" will happen <u>in this generation</u> is ***clear***, and there is ***<u>no</u>*** reason to alter the meaning of the word "generation" from its ***usual*** sense except a **fear** that the Scriptures **<u>may be in error</u>** if it is ***<u>not</u>*** so altered.
The Interpreter's Bible Vol. 7 p.864 [#42]	Indeed, the fulfillment *will take place* **<u>before</u>** this *present* generation has passed away. And the certainty rests upon what Jesus *himself* has said.

Matthew 24:34

Generation "γενεα"

	Christian Commentaries (con't)
The Interpreter's Bible Vol. 8 p.370 [#42]	A **solemn** assurance that the apocalyptic events will take place in the ***near*** future. …When the *later* church **adjusted its thinking** [i.e. did some **spin control**. – M.S.] to an indefinite continuance of the historical order, "this generation" was interpreted to mean either "the race of mankind" or "the company of the faithful." …**Did Jesus expect the end** *within the lifetime* **of those who heard him speak? It seems quite *certain* that the early church so understood him.**
Peake's Commentary A.S. Peake p.794 [#71]	In [Matthew] 16:28, Matthew made it clear that **some of the *first* disciples** would **live to see the Parousia**. He reinforces it here [Mt 24:34], following Mk 13:30-2
The NIV Matthew Henry Commentary p.131 [#72]	v. 34; there are those ***now alive***, who shall see Jerusalem destroyed.

Matthew 24:34
Generation: "γενεα"

Quotes

Pastor Chuck Smith Calvary Chapel 	*As a rule*, a <u>GENERATION</u> in the Bible lasts ***40 YEARS***. The children of Israel journeyed in the wilderness for 40 years until that generation died. **Future Survival** p.17 [#44]
	I believe that the generation of 1948 is the <u>LAST</u> generation. Since a generation of judgment is **FORTY YEARS**… I believe the Lord could come back for His Church… <u>ANY TIME BEFORE</u> **1981** (1948+40 – 7 = 1981). **End Times** p.35 [#250]
The Life of Jesus Critically Examined David Strauss p.587 [#76]	…the word genea… was put to the ***torture***…
Jesus And The Last Days George Murray pp.443-444 [#153]	It was Reimarus who drew attention to the **illegitimacy** of interpreting <u>GENEA</u> in these ways, and he drew the corollary that if the saying relates to the parousia, <u>**it sets the end time within the bounds of the first-generation church**</u>. The phrase "this generation" *should* cause no difficulty for interpreters. While admittedly *genea* in earlier Greek meant birth, progeny, and so race, in the sense of those descended from a common ancestor, in the LXX [Septuagint] it most frequently translated the Hebrew term ***dor***, meaning age, age of humankind, or generation in the sense of **contemporaries**. The expression "this generation" is often found on the lips of Jesus in the Gospels, but rarely elsewhere in the NT. In sayings attributed to Jesus the term appears to have a twofold connotation: on the one hand it **always** signifies his <u>contemporaries</u>, and on the other hand it always carries an implicit criticism.
The Quest of the Historical Jesus Dr. Albert Schweitzer p.240 [#36]	…and He was to **come**, moreover, ***within the lifetime** of the generation to which He had proclaimed the nearness of the Kingdom of God*.
Dr. Wm Lane Craig, Lecture attended by author at Hope Chapel, Hermosa Beach, CA, Jan 11 1999 8:33 PM.	"<u>**Two generations**</u> past the time of Jesus lands you in the 2nd Century."
Atheism Explained David Steele p.151 [#231]	A generation, in biblical terms, (Hal) Lindsey assures us, means around **forty years**. Quite a number of Evangelical Christians, apparently influenced by Lindsey, expected the Rapture in **1988**. [40 years from the founding of Israel]

Matthew 24:34

Generation: "γενεα"

	Quotes (con't)
Last Days Madness Gary DeMar p.114 [#34]	*No future generation* of Jews is meant here.
The Parousia Stuart Russell pp.84-85 [#33]	Next, our Lord sums up with an affirmation calculated to **remove <u>every</u> vestige of doubt** or uncertainty- "Verily I say unto you, this generation shall not pass, till all these things be fulfilled." One would **reasonably** suppose that *after* a note of time so clear and express there could not be room for controversy. Our Lord Himself has settled the question. **Ninety-nine persons in every hundred would undoubtedly understand His words as meaning that the <u>predicted</u> catastrophe would fall <u>within</u> the limits of the lifetime of the *existing* generation.** Not that all would probably live to witness it, but that most or many would. There can be <u>**no question**</u> that this would be the interpretation which the **disciples** would place upon the words…His coming… would come to pass *before* the *existing* generation had wholly passed away, and **within** the limits of their own lifetime.
Blaming Jesus for Jehovah Dr. Robert Price pp.108-109 [#203]	But it (the Second Coming) didn't happen. Furthermore, **there is no use in waiting for it still to happen.** You see, Jesus did **NOT** say, "*Someday, some century, some millennium, I plan to return.*" No, his promise included a **STATUTE OF LIMITATION**: "THIS generation shall not pass away," and "There are some standing here," and "You will not have finished going through the towns of Israel until…" Oy vey. …You can quote all the supposedly fulfilled prophecies you want, but that's not going to change the **fact** that **Jesus didn't return on schedule.** Jesus' ONLY **falsifiable** teaching has in fact BEEN **FALSIFIED.** He was a first-century Harold Camping.
The Decline & Fall of the Roman Empire Edward Gibbon p.276 [#73]	It was universally believed [in the primitive church] that the **end of the world** and the kingdom of heaven were <u>**at hand**</u>. The <u>**near**</u> approach of this wonderful event had been <u>**predicted**</u> by the apostles; the tradition of it was preserved by their earliest disciples; and those who understood in their literal sense the discourses of Christ himself were <u>**obliged**</u> to expect the second and glorious coming of the Son of Man in the clouds **before that GENERATION was totally extinguished** which had beheld his humble condition upon the earth…
Apocalypse of The Gospels Milton Terry pp.34-38 [#120]	But what ought to settle the question of time *beyond* all controversy is the most **emphatic declaration**: "This generation shall **not** pass away until all these things be accomplished." These words are *clearly* intended to answer the disciples' question, "**<u>When</u>** shall these things be?" …The words immediately preceding them show the **absurdity** of applying them to *another* generation than that of the apostles: "When YE see these things coming to pass, know YE that he is nigh, even at the doors. The teaching of Jesus was **<u>emphatic beyond all rational question</u>** that *that* generation should not pass away before *all* those things of which they inquired should be fulfilled.

	Quotes (con't)
God's Problem Dr. Bart Ehrman [#232]	Jesus believed… that God was **ABOUT TO DO SOMETHING** about it- soon- **WITHIN HIS OWN GENERATION**. (p.205) And when is the end of the age to come? …When will the judgment day arrive? When will the dead be raised? For apocalypticists the answer was clear and compelling: It will happen **VERY SOON**. It is **RIGHT AROUND THE CORNER**. It is **IMMINENT**. (p.218) For John, the wrath of God was **SOON** to appear… The ax is **ALREADY** "lying at the root of the trees." In other words, it is **READY TO BEGIN, NOW**. Jesus thought it would be **VERY SOON**, before "this generation passes away," **BEFORE HIS DISCIPLES "TASTE DEATH."** (p.224) Nearly every generation of Jesus' followers, from day one until now, has had its self-styled prophets- there are many on the scene today- who believed they could predict that the end, this time, really was **IMMINENT**. (p.225) The resurrection of Jesus for Paul was not merely God's vindication of a good man. It was the clear sign that **THE EXPECTED, IMMINENT END OF HISTORY AS WE KNOW IT HAD COME, AND THAT HUMANKIND WAS LIVING IN THE VERY LAST DAYS**. (p.238)
The Case Against Christianity Dr. Michael Martin p.62 [#236]	In Matthew one sees signs that **DOUBTS ABOUT JESUS' SECOND COMING WERE STARTING TO BE EXPRESSED**. Matthew takes the apocalyptic discourse of Mark 13 and adds to it a number of parables and warnings. He urges his readers at great length to be watchful and ready (Matt. 24:37-25; 46). As Wells notes: "Such long and detailed emphasis of this single point can only mean that THE <u>NON-APPEARANCE</u> OF THE END had cause the Christians to whom Matthew was appealing to, to **WAVER** in their expectancy."
Four Views on the Book of Revelation Kenneth Gentry p.43-44 [#247]	In Matthew 24:34 Jesus holds the same expectancy as John [Book of Revelation]… he urges his hearers, as John does his own, to expect these judgments **IN THEIR OWN LIFETIMES**. …*How else could the New Testament express nearness more clearly*? As these verses so evidently show, dramatic divine judgments are **"SOON," "NEAR," "AT HAND," "AT THE DOOR," "PRESENT," "THE HOUR HAS COME," "THE TIME IS SHORT,"** "the wrath of God is coming," "the day is **APPROACHING**," "just a **LITTLE** while." These events are to occur in "this generation," **BEFORE** "some who are standing…taste death."

Matthew 24:34
Generation: "γενεα"

Quotes (con't)

The Life of Jesus Critically Examined David Strauss pp.583-584 [#76]	The **EXISTING GENERATION** would, by all that was true, **LIVE TO WITNESS IT**, though its more precise period was known to God only …Thus in these discourses Jesus announces that shortly (24:29)… and within the term of the **COTEMPORARY GENERATION** (v.34) he would visibly make his second advent in the clouds, and **TERMINATE** the existing dispensation. Now [the 1840's] as it will soon be eighteen centuries since the destruction of Jerusalem, and an equally long period since the generation cotemporary with Jesus disappeared from the earth …his visible return and the end of the world… have **NOT** taken place. The Announcement of Jesus appears so far to have been ## ERRONEOUS . …No promise throughout the whole scriptures… is on the one hand more **DEFINITELY EXPRESSED**, and on the other, has turned out more # FLAGRANTLY FALSE than this, which yet forms one of the main *pillars* of Christianity. …(not) a mere error, but a **PREMEDITATED DECEPTION** on the part of the apostles.
Jesus: Apocalyptic Prophet of The New Millennium Dr. Bart Ehrman [#240]	He (Jesus) assures his hearers that **ALL THESE THINGS** will take place **WITHIN THEIR OWN GENERATION** (Matt. 24-25; Mark 13; Luke 21). (p.131) Jesus expected that this cataclysmic end of history would come **in his own generation**, at least during the **lifetime** of his disciples. (p.x)
Reasonable Faith Dr. Wm Lane Craig p.211 [#130]	It is true that the vibrant hope for a quick return of Christ gradually faded as the Church moved into its second **GENERATION**.
The Prophecy of Matthew 24 Thomas Newton p.47 [#251]	…the words "immediately after the tribulation of those days" show, evidently, that he is **NOT** speaking of any **DISTANT** event, but of something **IMMEDIATELY CONSEQUENT** upon the tribulation before mentioned, and that must be the destruction of Jerusalem.

	Lexicons, Dictionaries, Commentaries, Quotes **Matthew 24:34** **Generation: "γενεα"**	
colspan=3	*Genea ≠ Race*	

Matthew Douglas Hare p.281 [#140]	Some have argued, for example, that "this generation" refers not to Jesus' contemporaries but to **the Jewish nation** or to **the church**. The linguistic evidence in favor of such proposals is _**not**_ impressive. Since some of Jesus' contemporaries were still alive when the first gospel was penned, this prediction had not yet been falsified.
The Gospel According to Saint Matthew Alan M'Neile pp.354-355 [#86]	34. The truth illustrated by the parable is now stated plainly. "This generation" *cannot* mean: ▪ The Jews as a people ▪ Believers in Christ ▪ The (future) generation that will experience these things. It *must be* the particular generation of Jews **to whom**, or **of whom**, the words were spoken… It is *impossible* to escape the conclusion that **Jesus, as Man, expected the End *within the lifetime* of His contemporaries.**
The Broadman Bible Commentary Clifton Allen p.221 [#85]	The meaning of "this generation" is much disputed. Efforts like those of Jerome, to make it mean <u>the Jewish race</u>, or of Origen and Chrysostom, to refer it to <u>all Christians</u>, are **arbitrary** and are to be **rejected**. "This generation" refers to the *contemporaries* of Jesus.
Critical and Exegetical Handbook to the Gospel of Matthew Heinrich Meyer p.426 [#141]	Ver. 34. Declaration to the effect that all this is to take place before the generation then living should pass away. The **well-nigh absurd** (…**unreasonable**…**imaginary**) manner in which it has been attempted to *force* into the words η γενεα αυτη such meanings as: ▪ The Creation ▪ The Human Race ▪ The Jewish Nation ▪ The Class of Men Consisting of *My* Believers ▪ The Generation of the Elect Now in Question ▪ The Future Generation Which is to Witness Those Events …[The Second Coming] is to occur **during the lifetime of the generation then existing**…
The Gospel According to Matthew R.T. France p.346 [#87]	Those who interpret this passage as referring to the parousia must therefore either conclude that it **proved to be untrue**, or that "this generation" does **not** here carry its normal meaning. It has, for instance, been taken to mean ▪ The Jewish **race** ▪ Unbelieving Judaism It is **unlikely** that such an **improbable** meaning for the noun would have been suggested at all **without the constraint of apologetic embarrassment!** Nor can "all these things" easily be taken to **exclude** the events described in the immediately preceding verses. On the natural understanding of this verse either **Jesus was WRONG** (or Matthew has misunderstood him) or the discourse has not yet taken up directly the question of v. 3b…

Matthew 24:34

Generation: "γενεα"

Genea ≠ Race (con't)	
A Commentary on The Gospel According to St. Matthew Floyd Filson p.257 [#89]	Jesus states that **_before_** his generation ends **_all_** the preparatory events described will occur. Thus the end, the coming of the Son of Man, will come within a generation. Attempts to translate γενεα as: ▪ Human race ▪ Jewish race and interpret Jesus to say that the human race or Jewish race will still exist on earth when the end comes, are **MISGUIDED**; the word refers to **the generation living <u>when</u> Jesus spoke**… Matthew certainly understood "all these things" to refer to **the end of history**.
Hard Sayings of the Bible F.F. Bruce & Etc. pp.445-448 [#144]	This has been regarded as **a hard saying**… some other interpretation, they say, will **_have to_** be placed on "this generation." The word is sometimes used in the sense of "**race**," so perhaps, it is suggested, the point is that the Jewish race or even the human race, will not pass away before the Second Advent. **Plainly the idea that <u>the human race</u> is meant cannot be entertained**; every description of that event implies that human beings will be around to witness it, for otherwise it would have no context to give it any significance. Nor is there much more to be said for the idea that **the Jewish race** is meant; there is **no hint** anywhere in the New Testament that the Jewish race will **cease to exist** _before_ the end of the world. **_In any case, what point would there be in such a vague prediction? It would be as much as to say, "At some time in the indefinite future all these things will take place."_**… Jesus' hearers could have understood him to mean only that "all these things" would take place within _**their**_ generation… the phrase itself _**always**_ means "the generation _now_ living."
Bible Commentary Vol. 1 p.144 [#70]	The similar language of [Matthew] ch. x.23, xvi.28, seems to require us here to translate the word γενεα as meaning "generation," **_not_**, as it is **_sometimes_** rendered, "<u>race</u>" or "<u>people</u>". The former [i.e. generation] is the **_usual_** meaning.
The Imperial Bible Dictionary Patrick Fairbairn p.352 [#61]	It has been maintained by some…that in one passage—"Verily I say unto you, this generation shall not pass till all these things be fulfilled," (Mat xxix.34), our Lord identified **_generation_** with **the Jewish race**; and meant in the passage referred to that _the Jews as a people should still have a separate and outstanding existence, when the prophetic outline given by our Lord should have reached its complete fulfillment._ But this is a **very _forced_** explanation; and not a **_single_** example can be produced of an entirely **_similar_** use of the word. <u>**Whatever**</u> difficulties may hang around the interpretation of that part of Christ's discourse, it is **impossible** to understand by _the generation that was not to pass away_ anything _**but**_ the <u>existing</u> race of men living at the time when the word was spoken.

	Genea ≠ Race (con't)
The Great Tribulation David Chilton p.3 [#126]	The Lord Jesus declared that "this generation"—the people *then* living—would *not* pass away before the things He prophesied took place. The question is, *do you believe Him?* Some have sought to <u>get around</u> the force of this text by saying that the word generation here **really means <u>race</u>**, and that Jesus was simply saying that *the Jewish race would not die out until all these things took place*. Is that true? **I challenge you: Get out your concordance and look up <u>every</u> New Testament occurrence of the word <u>generation</u> (in Greek, genea) and see if it <u>ever</u> means "race" in <u>any</u> other context**. Here are all the references for the Gospels… Not <u>one</u> of these references is speaking of the entire Jewish race over **thousands** of years; **all** use the word in its **normal sense** of the sum total of those living at the same time. It **always** refers to **contemporaries**. (In fact, those who say it means "race" tend to acknowledge this fact, but explain that the word *<u>suddenly changes its meaning</u>* when Jesus uses it in Matthew 24! We can smile at such a transparent *<u>error</u>*, but we should also remember that this is very serious. We are dealing with the Word of the living God.)
Blaming Jesus for Jehovah Dr. Robert Price pp.112-113 [#203]	Starting with the Mark 13 [a parallel passage] "this generation will not pass away" prediction, is it possible that Jesus really meant "this *race*"? Well, the Greek word genea does sometimes mean that, but it cannot mean it in this context. The Jewish nation will not go extinct, or be wiped out, before the Second Coming of Christ. Such a theme is otherwise CONSPICUOUSLY ABSENT from the rest of the discourse. If this is what Jesus meant, it is certainly **ODD** that the question of Jewish survival should pop up here, out of nowhere, and just as quickly vanish.
Apocalypse of The Gospels Milton Terry p.34 [#120]	The various meanings which, under the **pressure** of a **dogmatic [crisis]**, have been put upon the phrase **"<u>this generation</u>"** must appear *in the highest degree* **absurd** to an <u>unbiased</u> critic. It has been explained as meaning: ▪ The Human Race (Jerome) ▪ The Jewish Race (Dorner, Auberlen) ▪ The Race of Christian Believers (Chrysotom, Lange)
The Parousia Stuart Russell p.85 [#33]	It is contended by many that in this place the word γενεα (genea) should be rendered "**race, or nation;**" and that our Lord's words mean no more than that <u>the Jewish race or nation should not pass away</u>, or perish, until the predictions which He had just uttered had come to pass… It is true, no doubt, that the γενεα, like most others, has different shades of meaning, and that *sometimes*, in the Septuagint and in classic authors it *may* refer to a nation or a race. But we think that it is demonstrable *without any shadow of doubt* that the expression "this generation" so often employed by our Lord, *<u>always</u>* refers solely and exclusively to His **contemporaries**, the Jewish people of His *own* period.

Matthew 24:34

Generation: "γενεα"

Genea ≠ Race (con't)	
The Quest of the Historical Jesus Dr. Albert Schweitzer p.22 [#36]	The saying of Christ about the generation which should *not* die out before his return *CLEARLY FIXES THIS EVENT AT NO VERY DISTANT DATE.* But since Jesus has not yet appeared upon the clouds of heaven, 'these words must be **strained into meaning**, not *that* generation, but the Jewish people. Thus by *exegetical art* they are saved forever, for the Jewish race will *never* die out.'
Why I Became an Atheist John Loftus p.363 [#205]	Theologians have tried to construe the word "generation" in the passage to mean "**race**," as in *"this race of people will certainly not pass away until all these things have happened."* But that is not the obvious meaning, given the context. The Davidic dynasty, after all, was supposed to be an eternal one (2 Sam. 7:11-16; Ps 89:36-37), so **no Jewish person in earshot of Jesus would even consider that their RACE could ever pass away**. Edward Adams states it forthrightly: "It is virtually certain that 'this generation' means **THE GENERATION LIVING AT THE TIME OF UTTERANCE**. The time frame in this verse is thus the lifetime of Jesus' own contemporaries."
Why I Believed Kenneth Daniels pp.218-219 [#204]	Some have argued that Jesus' use of the word generation (genea in Greek) does not necessarily signify a generation as commonly understood, but that a secondary meaning of genea, namely, **race** (that is, the Jewish race)… This suggest **the unlikely possibility** that **all** *the scholars who produced the major English translations of the Bible… were incompetent in their ability to discern the true meaning of the word, despite their mastery of Greek and the textual context.* The term "race" simply **makes no sense** in this context. There is no expectation anywhere in scripture that the Jewish race will **EVER** cease to exist. Introducing such a timeframe in a prophecy clearly intended to place parameters on the timing of his return would be MEANINGLESS, **on a par with, "I'm going to return before the human race ceases to exist."**
Jesus' Proclamation of The Kingdom of God Johannes Weiss [#225]	Whatever uncertainty there may be as to the **EXACT** time of the Second Coming, it is only conceivable **WITHIN THE LIFETIME OF THE GENERATION AMONG WHICH JESUS WORKED**… the next ten, twenty, or thirty years. (p.91) He will return upon the clouds of heaven at the establishment of the Kingdom, and do so **WITHIN THE LIFETIME OF THE GENERATION WHICH HAD REJECTED HIM.** (p.130)

Genea- The Generation at That Time?

	Lexicons, Dictionaries, Commentaries, Quotes # Matthew 24:34 # Generation: "γενεα"
	"The Generation Alive at That Time" **Excuse**
Blaming Jesus for Jehovah Robert Price p.113 [#203]	A fall-back interpretation is that, though Jesus does mean "generation," he does not mean "this" generation as that of "some standing here," his contemporaries. Rather, he merely means that **WHATEVER** generation **happens** to be alive at the time of these events will not die till they, er, do in fact see them. That's a tautology, like saying "A bachelor is a man who hasn't gotten married yet." It's **ABSOLUTELY POINTLESS.** Come on, GET REAL!
The Gospel According to Saint Matthew Alan M'Neile pp.354-355 [#86]	34. The truth illustrated by the parable is now stated plainly. "This generation" *cannot* mean # The (future) generation that will experience these things. ...Jesus, as Man, expected the End *within the lifetime* of His contemporaries.
Matthew 24 Fulfilled John Bray p.216 [#158]	Many commentators **play around with** the word 'generation' (genea), and **thinking to *avoid embarrassment***, project its application to the generation which will *be* alive during the last days immediately preceding the Second Coming of the Messiah... such **VERBAL GAMES** are soon exposed as being *nothing* but ARMCHAIR GYMNASTICS.
Why I Believed Kenneth Daniels p.219 [#204]	This passage *only* means *anything* to its recipients if taken at **face value**: members of THIS generation, that is, Jesus' generation, not the Jewish race, and **NOT SOME FUTURE GENERATION** (the Greek has a word for "**that**" in opposition to "**this**," so if Jesus meant "**that**" generation he could easily have made it explicit) will still be alive when Jesus returns. This is all the more evident when we consider that Jesus directs his comments to his disciples in the second person, making inescapable the conclusion that his disciples were expected to witness "these things".
Critical and Exegetical Handbook to the Gospel of Matthew Heinrich Meyer p.426 [#141]	The **well-nigh absurd** manner in which it has been attempted to *force* into the words η γενεα αυτη such meanings as: <ul><li>The Creation</li><li>The Human Race</li><li>The Jewish Nation</li><li>The Class of Men Consisting of *My* Believers</li><li>The Generation of the Elect Now in Question</li><li>**THE FUTURE GENERATION WHICH IS TO WITNESS THOSE EVENTS**</li></ul>...[The Second Coming] is to occur during the <u>lifetime</u> of the generation then [in 33CE] existing...

Second Coming Due Within Lifetime of Caiaphas

Matthew 26:57-66

New American Standard Bible [#1]	57 And those who had seized Jesus led Him away to **Caiaphas, the high priest**, where the scribes and the elders were gathered together. 58 But Peter also was following Him at a distance as far as the courtyard of the high priest, and entered in, and sat down with the officers to see the outcome. 59 Now the chief priests and the whole Council kept trying to obtain false testimony against Jesus, in order that they might put Him to death; 60 and they did not find *any,* even though many false witnesses came forward. But later on two came forward, 61 and said, "This man stated, 'I am able to destroy the temple of God and to rebuild it in three days.'" 62 And the **high priest** [Caiaphas] stood up and said to Him, "Do You make no answer? What is it that these men are testifying against You?" 63 But Jesus kept silent. And the **high priest** said to Him, "I adjure You by the living God, that You tell us whether You are the Christ, the Son of God." 64 Jesus said to **him**, "***You*** [Caiaphas] have said it *yourself*; nevertheless I tell *YOU*, hereafter **YOU SHALL SEE** the Son of Man sitting at the right hand of power, and **COMING on the clouds of heaven**." 65 Then the <u>high priest</u> tore his robes, saying, "He has blasphemed! What further need do we have of witnesses? Behold, you have now heard the blasphemy; 66 what do you think?" They answered and said, "He is deserving of death!"

Commentaries & Quotes

The Historical Jesus & The Kingdom of God Richard Hiers pp.103-105 [#119]	His reference to the prospective appearance of the Son of Man indicates that He expected His mission and message to be vindicated **IN THE NEAR FUTURE**. The High Priest and His other accusers would "see the Son of Man sitting at the right hand of God". …At any rate, this promise- or warning- **WAS NOT, IN FACT, FULFILLED.** …He expected that the priests and others before whom he stood would **themselves** soon be on trial before the Son of Man. …the High Priest and his fellow accusers would **soon** be in for the surprise of their lives!
Jesus, Interrupted Dr. Bart Ehrman p.51 [#233]	The high priest asks Jesus if he is the "Messiah, the Son of the Blessed one" (Mark 14:61), and Jesus gives a straightforward reply, "I am. And you will see the Son of Man seated at the right hand of Power and coming with the clouds of heaven (Mark 14:62). In other words, **in the NEAR FUTURE** God would be sending a cosmic judge of the earth, in fulfillment of the predictions of the Old Testament (Daniel 7:13-14). In fact, is was **so near** that **the high priest himself would see it happen**. [But] what if it **doesn't** happen? What if the high priest were to die before the Son of Man arrived? Wouldn't that *invalidate* Jesus' claim?

Second Coming Due Within Lifetime of Caiaphas
Matthew 26:57-66
Commentaries & Quotes (con't)

Jesus: Apocalyptic Prophet of The New Millennium Dr. Bart Ehrman p.131 [#240]	At Jesus' trail before the Sanhedrin… Jesus boldly states to the high priest, "You will see the Son of Man seated at the right hand of power and coming with the clouds of heaven" …That is, **THE END WOULD COME AND**
	THE HIGH PRIEST WOULD SEE IT.
	Luke, writing many years later, after the high priest was long **dead** and **buried**, *CHANGES* the saying: "from now on the Son of Man will be seated at the right hand of the power of God" (Luke 22:69). No longer does Jesus predict that the high priest himself will be **ALIVE** when the end comes.

Second Coming Due Within Lifetime of Caiaphas

Matthew 26:57-66 (con't)

Archaeology

Jesus looked Caiaphas straight in the eyes and made a FALSE PROPHECY. Jesus promised that Caiaphas would LIVE to see his Second Coming. Caiaphas did not, and as insane as it seems, some Christians have argued that therefore, rather than their Jesus be proven a liar, Caiaphas must STILL be alive 2000 years later.

But Caiaphas is no longer alive. He died, not having seen Jesus' Second Coming. And the proof of his death is his tomb carved into the rocks that was discovered in the early 1990's and made the cover of Biblical Archaeology Review. This is rock-hard evidence that what Jesus prophesied to Caiaphas turned out to be FALSE, thus making Jesus a

FALSE Prophet.

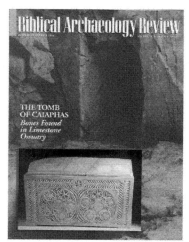

Biblical Archaeology Review
September / October 1992
Vol. 18   Number 5

The Second Coming Before You Die

Mark 9:1

NASB [#1]	And Jesus was saying to them, "Truly I say to you, there are some of those who are <u>STANDING HERE</u> who will **NOT TASTE DEATH** until they see the kingdom of God after it has come with power."
God's Word [#166]	He said to them, "I can **GUARANTEE** this truth: Some people who are standing here will **NOT** die until they see God's kingdom arrive with power."
Easy to Read Version [#163]	Then Jesus said, "**BELIEVE ME** when I say that **SOME** of you people **STANDING HERE** will see God's kingdom come with power **BEFORE YOU DIE**."

Commentaries & Quotes

God's Problem Dr. Bart D. Ehrman [#232]	What happens to an apocalyptic worldview when the expected apocalypse never comes? In Mark's Gospel Jesus indicated that some of his disciples "**WILL NOT TASTE DEATH**" before they see the "Kingdom of God having come in power" (Mark 9:1). Even though he says that no one knows the precise "day or the hour," he does indicate that **THE END OF ALL THINGS** is sure to come "**BEFORE** this generation passes away" (Mark 13:30). (p.255) Everyone who has **ever** made a prediction of this sort- **every single one of them**- has been absolutely and incontrovertibly **wrong**. (p.260)
Jesus, Interrupted Dr. Bart D. Ehrman [#233]	(Mark 1:15 "The time has been fulfilled; the kingdom of God is near.") Jesus' teaching in Mark is apocalyptic: "The time **HAS BEEN** fulfilled" implies that this current evil age, seen on a time line, is almost over. The end is almost **WITHIN SIGHT**. "The Kingdom of God is **NEAR**"... For Mark's Jesus, this kingdom is **SOON TO COME**. As he tells his disciples at one point, "Truly I tell you, some of those standing here will not taste death **BEFORE** they see the Kingdom of God having come in power" (Mark 9:1); later he tells them, after describing the cosmic upheavals that would transpire at the end of the age, "Truly I tell you, this generation will **NOT** pass away before all these things take place" (Mark 13:30). (pp.77-78) Jesus, in short, taught that the Son of Man was **SOON** to arrive from heaven in judgment... And when would this judgment come? **IN THE DISCIPLES' OWN LIFETIME**. ...That this view fits in a first century Palestinian context is **CLEAR TO <u>EVERY</u> HISTORIAN** of the period. Jesus was not alone in proclaiming the end of this age and the **IMMINENT** appearance of the Son of Man. Other Jewish prophets had **SIMILAR** apocalyptic messages... (p.160)

Before You Die	
Mark 9:1	
Commentaries & Quotes (con't)	
Jesus: Apocalyptic Prophet of The New Millennium Dr. Bart D. Ehrman p.x [#240]	Jesus is best understood as a first-century Jewish apocalypticist. This is a shorthand way of saying that Jesus fully expected that **THE HISTORY OF THE WORLD AS WE KNOW IT (WELL, AS HE KNEW IT) WAS GOING TO COME TO A SCREECHING HALT,** that God was **SOON** going to intervene in the affairs of this world, overthrow the forces of evil in a cosmic act of judgment, **DESTROY HUGE MASSES OF HUMANITY,** and abolish existing human political and religious institutions. All this would be a prelude to the arrival of a new order on earth, the Kingdom of God. Moreover, Jesus **EXPECTED** that this cataclysmic end of history would come **IN HIS OWN GENERATION,** at least during the **LIFETIME** of his disciples.
God Without Dogma Hugo Fruehauf p.222 [#248]	Since the Second Coming of Christ has obviously **NOT** happened yet, theologians do **HANDSTANDS** to **TALK THEIR WAY AROUND** the phrases "this generation" and "some standing here will not taste death until…" What does the everyday believer do with it? One approach is to **FORGET** about it and leave the mystery to God.

Second Coming Due
Within Their Lifetime
Mark 13:1-37

1 And as He was going out of the temple, one of His **disciples** said to Him, "Teacher, behold what wonderful stones and what wonderful buildings!"

2 And Jesus said to him, "Do **you** see these great buildings? Not one stone shall be left upon another which will not be torn down."

3 And as He was sitting on the Mount of Olives opposite the temple, **Peter** and **James** and **John** and **Andrew** were questioning Him **privately**,

4 "Tell **us**, _when_ will _these things be_, and _what_ will be <u>the</u> sign _when_ all _these things_ are going to be fulfilled?"

5 And Jesus began to say to **them**, "See to it that no one misleads **you**.

6 "Many will come in My name, saying, 'I am _He!'_ and will mislead many.

7 "And when **you** hear of wars and rumors of wars, do not be frightened; _those things_ must take place; but _that is_ not yet the end.

8 "For nation will arise against nation, and kingdom against kingdom; there will be earthquakes in various places; there will _also_ be famines. These things are _merely_ the beginning of birth pangs.

9 "But be on **your** guard; for they will deliver **you** to _the_ courts, and **you** will be flogged in _the_ synagogues, and **you** will stand before governors and kings for My sake, as a testimony to them.

10 "And the gospel must first be preached to all the nations.

11 "And when they arrest **you** and deliver **you** up, do not be anxious beforehand about what **you** are to say, but say whatever is given **you** in that hour; for it is not **you** who speak, but _it is_ **the Holy Spirit**.

12 "And brother will deliver brother to death, and a father _his_ child; and children will rise up against parents and have them put to death.

13 "And **you** will be hated by all on account of My name, but **_the one who endures to the end_**, he shall be saved.

14 "But when **you** see the abomination of desolation standing where it should not be (let the reader understand), then let those who are in Judea flee to the mountains.

15 "And let him who is on the housetop not go down, or enter in, to get anything out of his house;

16 and let him who is in the field not turn back to get his cloak.

17 "But woe to those who are with child and to those who nurse babes in those days!

18 "But pray that it may not happen in the winter.

19 "**FOR THOSE DAYS WILL BE A** _TIME OF_ **TRIBULATION SUCH AS HAS NOT OCCURRED SINCE THE BEGINNING OF THE CREATION WHICH** G**OD CREATED, UNTIL NOW, AND NEVER SHALL**.

20 "And unless the Lord had shortened _those_ days, no life would have been saved; but for the sake of the elect whom He chose, He shortened the days.

21 "And then if anyone says to **you**, 'Behold, here is the Christ'; or, 'Behold, _He is_ there'; do not believe _him;_

22 for false Christs and false prophets will arise, and will show signs and wonders, in order, if possible, to lead the elect astray.

23 **"But take heed; behold, I have told you everything in advance.**

24 "But in those days, after that tribulation, the sun will be darkened, and the moon will not give its light,

25 and **THE STARS WILL BE FALLING FROM HEAVEN**, and the powers that are in the heavens will be shaken.

26 "And then they **WILL SEE THE SON OF MAN COMING IN CLOUDS** with great power and glory.

27 "And then He will send forth the angels, and will gather together His elect from the four winds, from the farthest end of the earth, to the farthest end of heaven.

28 "Now learn the parable from the fig tree: when its branch has already become tender, and puts forth its leaves, you know that summer is near.

29 "Even so, **you** too, when **you** see these things happening, recognize that He is near, *right* at the door.

30 **"TRULY I SAY TO YOU, *THIS* GENERATION WILL NOT PASS AWAY UNTIL ALL THESE THINGS TAKE PLACE.**

31 "Heaven and earth will pass away, but My words will not pass away.

32 "But of that day or hour no one knows, not even the angels in heaven, nor the Son, but the Father *alone.*

33 "Take heed, keep on the alert; for **you** do not know when the *appointed* time is.

34 *"It is* like a man, away on a journey, *who* upon leaving his house and putting his slaves in charge, *assigning* to each one his task, also commanded the doorkeeper to stay on the alert.

35 "Therefore, be on the alert--for **you** do not know when the master of the house is coming, whether in the evening, at midnight, at cockcrowing, or in the morning--

36 lest he come suddenly and find **you** asleep.

37 "And what I say to **you** I say to **all**, 'Be on the alert!'"

Mark 13:1-37 NEW AMERICAN STANDARD BIBLE [#1]

Mark 13:1-37

Commentaries & Quotes

Why I Believed Kenneth Daniels p.223 [#204]	A skeptic could hardly ask for a more # OBJECTIVE FALSIFICATION of *ANY* religion: the religion's leader prophesies a globally identifiable series of events **with a specified time period**, but the events do *NOT* take place within that time period.
Mythology's Last Gods William Harwood p.341 [#222]	All three synoptic gospels put a TIME LIMIT ON JESUS' SECOND COMING. However, by the time Mark was written 40 years had passed and *still* he had not returned... Mark accordingly recorded a prophecy... that he would be crowned king of an independent Judea **within the lifetime of the persons listening to him preach**. ...John, who wrote after Jesus' time limit had expired, not surprisingly **left it out**.
The Historical Jesus & The Kingdom of God Richard Hiers p.15 [#119]	Jesus was certain that the Kingdom of God would come soon, at the latest **WHILE SOME OF THOSE ABOUT HIM WERE STILL ALIVE**.
Why I Became an Atheist John Loftus p.24 [205]	Failed predictions of Jesus' return have become # SUCH AN EMBARRASSMENT for Christians that there is now a movement to embrace **Preterism**, which is the belief that Jesus returned to earth to reign from Jerusalem in a spiritual sense around 70 EC.
Resurrection: Myth or Reality? John Shelby Spong [#223]	Primitive Christians (thought) that they lived **at the end of history**, that the dawn of God's eschatological kingdom was **about to occur**. (p.57) Like so many of the first generation of Christians, these people expected the **imminent return** of Jesus from heaven. (p. 121) All this would happen **before** this (first century) generation had passed away. (p.188)
Jesus, Interrupted Dr. Bart Ehrman p.81-82 [#233]	For many historical critics it makes sense that John, the Gospel that was written last, no longer speaks about the **imminent** appearance on earth of the Son of Man... In Mark, Jesus predicts that **the end will come right away**, during his own **generation, while his disciples are still alive** (Mark 9:1; 13:30). By the time John was written, probably from 90 to 95 CE, that earlier generation had died out and most if not all the disciples were already **dead**. That is, they died **before** the coming of the kingdom....[In the Gospel of John] no longer is the kingdom coming to earth. The kingdom is in **heaven**. ...This is a **very different** teaching from what you find in Mark.

Mark 13:1-37	
Commentaries & Quotes (con't)	
The Case Against Christianity Dr. Michael Martin pp.61-62 [#236]	Another allegedly surprising aspect of the New Testament story, if Jesus' historicity is called into question, is his pronouncement about his **imminent** Second Coming. In Mark 13:30 Jesus says… "this generation will **not** pass away"… and in Mark 9:1 he says … "some standing here who will **not** taste death…" Since these sayings turned out to be **false**, why, it may be asked, would they appear as part of the Jesus myth?
The Bible Handbook pp.194-195 [#238]	Nearly 2,000 years have elapsed, and it is still **UNFULFILLED**, although Christ himself most emphatically declared that it should be **COMPLETELY** fulfilled **WITHIN THE <u>LIFETIME</u> OF THE GENERATION THEN LIVING**. …the prophet of Nazareth stands a convicted **IMPOSTOR**. The prophecy was exceedingly useful in its day, because it <u>terrified</u> people into the arms of the Church; now it remains on record as a **GIGANTIC FALSEHOOD**. …These passages… show clearly that Christ's coming… was to take place **DURING THE LIFETIME OF <u>THEN-EXISTING</u> PERSONS**. …he [Jesus] stands ignominiously <u>condemned</u> as a **FALSE PROPHET**

Mark 13:1-37 (con't)

My Comments

Peter, James, John and Andrew- all Apostles, are privately questioning Jesus regarding the end times. Jesus responds by telling them, these four Apostles, what they themselves will be **alive to see and witness** for themselves, and if they "endure to the end" (v. 13) they'll be saved, thus guaranteeing all these events have a first century due date, for how could these Apostles "**endure**" (**i.e. stay alive**) to something several thousand years in the future? Jesus was *not* directing his comments to folks a thousand years in the future. If one follows the "you's" they can see that all the events described by Jesus were promised to be eye-witnessed by these first century Apostles:

- False Christs
- Wars
- Persecutions
- Gospel preached to every corner of the Earth
- Abomination of Desolation
- Time of Tribulation
- Sun will be darkened
- Moon will go dark
- The stars in the sky will fall to Earth
- The Second Coming of Jesus in "great glory"
- The worldwide rapture of the saints

All of these items were prophesied by Jesus to happen within the lifetime of the four Apostles he spoke to in 33CE. The stars falling to Earth? False prophesy. The worldwide rapture of the saints? Another false prophecy. And the biggest prophecy of all, the Second Coming of Jesus? It's actually the biggest FALSE prophesy of the lot. And just like murders make one a murderer, false prophecies make one a false prophet. Jesus, based on the evidence, was a false prophet.

Luke 13:24-29

	Within the Lifetime of Those Who Dined with Jesus
	Luke 13:24-29
NASB [#1]	24 "Strive to enter by the narrow door; for many, I tell you, will seek to enter and will not be able. 25 "Once the head of the house gets up and shuts the door, and you begin to stand outside and knock on the door, saying, 'Lord, open up to us!' then He will answer and say to you, 'I do not know where you are from.' 26 "Then you will begin to say, '**We ate and drank *in Your presence*, and You taught in our streets'** 27 and He will say, 'I tell you, I do not know where you are from; DEPART FROM ME, ALL YOU EVILDOERS.' 28 "There will be weeping and gnashing of teeth there when you see Abraham and Isaac and Jacob and all the prophets in the kingdom of God, but yourselves being cast out. 29 "And they will come from east and west, and from north and south, and will recline at the table in the kingdom of God.
	My Comments

This scenario of Jesus, twist as you might, will not match up with the traditional Christian heaven. In the Christian heaven, sinners will *not* be milling around the outside, striving to get in, banging on doors like it's Noah's ark or something. However, this scenario *does* fit a physical, literal "New Jerusalem" located in Israel, with walls that have doors that can be banged on, and locations outside the walls to mill about, along with visitors from all over the world coming to visit. That makes sense.

What also makes sense (in Jesus' time frame, at least) is that all this will happen **within the lifetime** of those men who made his life miserable. This fits in well with all of Jesus' other promises to set up his kingdom within the lifetime of other First Century men. Here, Jesus is talking about people who broke bread with him, ate with him, drank with him, in short- people who were alive at the same time as him. Jesus says all this partying was going on in his presence, i.e. First Century. It is also said that Jesus "taught in our streets". This means the physical Jesus of the First Century. All of these points securely lock the (predicted) timespan of Jesus' Second Coming into the First Century.

Second Coming Due Within Their 1st Century Lifetime

ALL is on the Verge of Taking Place

Luke 21:5-36

5   And while some were talking about the temple, that it was adorned with beautiful stones and votive gifts, He said,

6   "As for **these things** which **you** are looking at, the days will come in which there will not be left one stone upon another which will not be torn down."

7   And **they** questioned Him, saying, "Teacher, when therefore will **these things** be? And what will be **the** sign when **these things** are _**about**_ to take place?"

8   And He said, "See to it that **you** be not misled; for many will come in My name, saying, 'I am He,' and, 'The time is at hand'; do not go after them.

9   "And when **you** hear of wars and disturbances, do not be terrified; for these things must take place first, but **the end** does not follow immediately."

10   Then He continued by saying to **them**, "Nation will rise against nation, and kingdom against kingdom,

11   and there will be great earthquakes, and in various places plagues and famines; and there will be terrors and great signs from heaven.

12   "But _**before**_ all these things, they will lay their hands on **you** and will persecute **you**, delivering **you** to the synagogues and prisons, bringing **you** before kings and governors for My name's sake.

> **Apostles' Persecution & End Times: Same Era**
> Almost an exact parallel of what was promised the Apostles in the Gospel of John. This indicates that Jesus here, too, is speaking _only_ to the Apostles, with no one else in mind.
>> They will make _**you**_ outcasts from the synagogue, but an hour is coming for everyone who kills _**you**_ to think that he is offering service to God. (John 16:2 [#1])

13   "It will lead to an opportunity for **your** testimony.

14   "So make up **your** minds not to prepare beforehand to defend **yourselves**;

15   for I will give **you** utterance and wisdom which none of your opponents will be able to resist or refute.

> **Promises Specific to The Apostles**
> This clearly indicates that Jesus was giving directions to his Apostles, and no one else, as this is what was specifically promised to his Apostles, and them only, in the Gospel of John:
>> But the Helper, the Holy Spirit, whom the Father will send in My name, He will teach _**you**_ all things, and bring to _**your**_ remembrance all that I said to _**you**_. (John 14:26 [#1])

But when He, the Spirit of truth, comes, He will guide *you* into all the truth. (John 16:13 [#1])

16   "But **you** will be delivered up even by parents and brothers and relatives and friends, and they will put some of **you** to death,

17   and y**ou** will be hated by all on account of My name.

18   "Yet not a hair of **your** head will perish.

19   "By **your** endurance **you** will gain your lives.

20   "But when **you** see Jerusalem surrounded by armies, then recognize that her desolation is at hand.

21   "Then let those who are in Judea flee to the mountains, and let those who are in the midst of the city depart, and let not those who are in the country enter the city;

22   because *these* **are days of vengeance**, in order that *all things which are written may be fulfilled*.

"These Are The Days" = 1st Century
The "these days" clearly refers to the era of Jerusalem being sacked by Titus around 70 AD. And in "these days" what will be fulfilled? "*All things* which are **written**." The word "all" indicates that there will not be anything left to fulfill after this time. Therefore, since "all things which are written" are due to be fulfilled in the 1st Century, then "all things" concerning the 2nd Coming must *also* be fulfilled within the 1st Century as well. And therefore, there are no "gaps" or "delays" that could postpone Jesus' Second Coming past this First Century era. "All things" = "all things".

"Times of the Gentiles"
This "all things" would also, by *necessity*, include the so-called "Times of the Gentiles" indicated elsewhere in the New Testament:

> "Repent therefore and return, that your sins may be wiped away, in order that times of refreshing may come from the presence of the Lord; and that He may **send Jesus**, the Christ appointed for you, whom heaven must receive until *the* period of restoration of all things about which God spoke by the mouth of His holy prophets from ancient time.
> (Acts 3: 19-21 NASB [#1])

> For I do not want you, brethren, to be uninformed of this mystery, lest you be wise in your own estimation, that a partial hardening has happened to Israel until the **fulness of the Gentiles** has come in; and thus all Israel will be saved..
> (Romans 11:25, 26 NASB [#1])

> And they will fall by the edge of the sword, and will be led captive into all the nations; and Jerusalem will be trampled under foot by the Gentiles until the **times of the Gentiles** be fulfilled. (Luke 21:24 NASB [#1])

> *Whatever* Jesus may have meant by the "times of the Gentiles", however confusing or controversial that expression may be, one thing is crystal clear: *whatever it was, it was due to be done, finished, and completed within the 1ˢᵗ Century*. As Jesus himself said, "*these* [First Century days] are days of vengeance, in order that *all things which are written may be fulfilled.*"

23   "Woe to those who are with child and to those who nurse babes in those days; for there will be great distress upon the land, and wrath to this people,

24   and they will fall by the edge of the sword, and will be led captive into all the nations; and Jerusalem will be trampled under foot by the Gentiles until **the times of the Gentiles** be fulfilled.

25   "And there will be signs in sun and moon and stars, and upon the earth dismay among nations, in perplexity at the roaring of the sea and the waves,

26   men fainting from fear and the expectation of the things which are coming upon the world; for the powers of the heavens will be shaken.

27   "**And then they will see the Son of Man coming in a cloud with power and great glory**.

28   "But *when* these things *begin* to take place, straighten up and lift up **your** heads, because **your** redemption is drawing *near*."

> ### From Beginning ⇒ End: Within a Single Lifetime
> Whenever these events may *begin* to take place, their *conclusion* (i.e. "redemption" i.e. the Second Coming) is not far off. If *any* of these events happened within the era of the Apostles, *all* of these events happened within the era of the Apostles. We know for a fact that the Jewish temple was destroyed in 70 AD, and this one fact, if nothing else, locks everything else up into a 1ˢᵗ Century time frame.

29   And He told **them** a parable: "Behold the fig tree and all the trees;

30   as soon as they put forth leaves, you see it and know for yourselves that summer is now near.

31   "Even so **you**, too, when **you** **see** these things happening, recognize that the kingdom of God is

near.

32   "Truly I say to you, **THIS GENERATION** will not pass away until

ALL things take place.

33   "Heaven and earth will pass away, but My words will not pass away.

34   "Be on guard, that **your** hearts may not be weighted down with dissipation and drunkenness and the worries of life, and that day come on **you** suddenly like a trap;

35   for it will come upon all those who dwell on the face of all the earth.

36   "But keep on the alert at all times, praying in order that **you** may have strength to escape **ALL**

THESE THINGS that are **about** [Greek: Mello] to take place, and to stand before the Son of Man."

(Luke 21: 5-36 NEW AMERICAN STANDARD [#1])

> ### On The Verge of Happening
> Jesus tells his 1ˢᵗ Century Apostles that "**all** these things" (v.36) are *about* to take place. This word "about" is from the Greek word "mello" and means that which is *on the verge of happening*. This clearly indicate a 1ˢᵗ Century fulfillment is due for "**all** these things.". Please see the chart that follows.
>
> Jesus also tells his **APOSTLES** to pray to BibleGod so that **THEY** would have the strength to "**ESCAPE** all these things that are **AB`OUT** to take place." Need I point out that this statement is total nonsense, *unless* Jesus believed "all these things" would

take place *within* the lifetime of his Apostles? If "all these things" were *not* due to take place within that century, then why would they need to escape things that wouldn't even happen until thousands of years after these men had turned into dust? Clearly, the only option that makes sense is that "all these things" were due for fulfillment in their lifetime, in the First Century.

First Century: Jesus' Second Coming ABOUT TO Take Place

Luke 21:36	
New American Standard Bible [#1]	But keep on the alert at all times, praying in order that you may have strength to escape **all** these things that are **about to** take place, and to stand before the Son of Man.
Concordant Literal New Testament [#4]	…escape all these things which are **about to occur**…
The Modern Language New Testament [#13]	Pray… that you may have the strength to escape all those **impending** events…
New International Version [#16]	Pray that you may be able to escape all that is **about to** happen…
Young's Literal Translation [#3]	…all these things that are **about to** come to pass…
Darby Bible [#21]	…all these things which are **about to** come to pass…
Scholars Version [#11]	…all these things that are about to occur…
A Literal Translation of The Bible [#23]	…all these things which are **about to** happen…
Westcott & Hort [#7]	**Mello: "About To Occur"** agrupneite de en panti kairw deomenoi ina katiscushte ekfugein tauta panta ta **mellonta** ginesqai kai staqhnai emprosqen tou uiou tou anqrwpou The word used here for "**about to come to pass**" is **Mello**, which means on the verge of happening, on the point of fulfillment. As I heard it described once, think of a car teetering on the edge of a cliff, just before it makes it final plunge. THAT is how soon the Second Coming is promised to these people in 33 CE.

First Century: Jesus' Second Coming
ABOUT TO Take Place

Luke 21:36

Commentaries & Quotes (con't)

Blaming Jesus for Jehovah Dr. Robert Price p.107 [#203]	First, he (Jesus) has not returned to this earth by the deadline **he himself clearly set**... Jesus explicitly said to his followers that they could expect his return **within their lifetimes**, and it didn't happen.
Why I Believed Kenneth Daniels p.223 [#204]	A skeptic could hardly ask for a more **OBJECTIVE FALSIFICATION** of <u>ANY</u> religion: the religion's leader prophesies a globally identifiable series of events within a **specific** time period, but the events do **not** take place within that time period.
Leaving The Fold Ed Babinski p.393 [#206]	Much as I dislike to, I must in all honesty make a statement. By the records we have, which you and I have faithfully examined during these months of study, there can be no doubt that <u>**JESUS EXPECTED TO RETURN IN BODILY FORM**</u> in glorious appearance with an angelic escort <u>**BEFORE**</u> that generation of disciples to whom he was speaking passed away. But he did NOT return! So, young gentlemen, we are left with this dilemma, painful as it may be to face it. We are compelled to say that either Jesus was <u>**MISTAKEN**</u>, or the gospels are <u>**UNTRUSTWORTHY**</u>. Either alternative is terrible for a Christian. (Charles Francis Potter quoting Dr. Anderson of Newton Theological Seminary)
The Book Your Church Doesn't Want You To Read Tim Leedom p.126 [#207]	Moreover, he (Jesus) made solemn promises he <u>**FAILED TO KEEP**</u>. We can be as certain that Jesus taught the speedy coming of the kingdom as we can be of any matter in biblical studies. If Jesus had had his way... we and this world would not be here today. **The FIRST CENTURY would have been the LAST.** (A.J. Mattill)
Abingdon Bible Handbook p.332 [#216]	We learn from 1st Clement (c. A.D. 95) that **DOUBTING and QUESTIONING** of <u>Christ's return</u> was expressed in the church of that time.
The Interpreter's Bible: Vol VII p.153 [#42]	The stumbling block for conservative and liberal alike has been that the acceptance of the eschatological reading of the Gospels seem to mean that **JESUS WAS MISTAKEN** at an important point.
The Case Against Christianity Dr. Michael Martin p.62 [#236]	In Luke we see **FURTHER SIGNS OF EMBARRASSMENT**. ...he attempts to portray Jesus as maintaining that the end of the world will come later than Mark specified. ...As **THE EVIDENCE OF A <u>FALSE PROPHECY</u> BEGAN TO MOUNT**, Christian writers began to either reassure the faithful or modify the myth. ...Their actions could well be simply groping attempts to **SAVE** the doctrine of the Second Coming in the light of evidence. ...However, in John, the doctrine of the Second Coming is **ELIMINATED**. By the time the author of John wrote, it was presumably **NO LONGER <u>CREDIBLE</u>** to attempt to save the doctrine of the Second Coming. Even a vague term like "generation" could only be stretched so far.

Luke 23:26-31

Second Coming & Other Disasters	
Due Within First Century	
Luke 23:26-31	
NASB [#1]	26 And when they led Him away, they laid hold of one Simon of Cyrene, coming in from the country, and placed on him the cross to carry behind Jesus. 27 And there were following Him a great multitude of the people, and of women who were mourning and lamenting Him. 28 But Jesus turning to them said, "Daughters of Jerusalem, stop weeping for Me, but weep for **yourselves** and for **your children**. 29 "For behold, the days are coming when they will say, 'Blessed are the barren, and the wombs that never bore, and the breasts that never nursed.' 30 "Then they will begin to say to the mountains, 'Fall on us,' and to the hills, 'cover us' 31 "For if they do these things in the green tree, what will happen in the dry?"

My Comments
Jesus here almost defines *for us* the concept of "GENERATION" in that, don't weep for Jesus (he'll be dead in a few hours), but rather weep for yourselves **& your kids**- that is, weep for those who will still be alive when the you-know-what hits the fan within the "**ONE GENERATION**" time limit.

John 21:21-23

colspan	**Jesus Anticipated His Second Coming Within Their Lifetimes**

Jesus Anticipated His Second Coming Within Their Lifetimes

John 21:21-23

NASB [#1]	Peter therefore seeing him said to Jesus, "Lord, and what about this man?" Jesus said to him, **"if I want him to remain until I come, what is that to you?** You follow Me!" This saying therefore went out among the brethren that that disciple would not die; yet Jesus did not say to him that he would not die; but only, "If I want him to remain until I come, what is that to you?"

Commentaries & Quotes

Word Biblical Commentary pp.411-412 [#212]	That the saying of v 22 circulated among the Johannine churches is evident from the reference to "the brothers," who understood it **AS A PROMISE** from the Lord that **the Beloved Disciple would <u>survive</u> till the Parousia**. ...the <u>IMMINENT</u> expectation of the coming of Christ in the <u>FIRST GENERATION</u> Church was fostered in some minds by the continuance of the Beloved Disciple into old age. Surely the Lord was to come BEFORE he, the last of the original disciples, should die!
The Parousia Stuart Russell p.137-138 [#33]	This language is very significant. It assumes as POSSIBLE that John **might live till the Lord's coming**. It does more; it suggests it as PROBABLE, though it does not affirm it as CERTAIN. They (the brethren) evidently concluded that **John would live to witness the Lord's coming**... Nor was this inference of "the brethren" so incredible a thing or so unreasonable as it may appear to many... He (Paul) spoke to the Thessalonians of **the possibility of their being ALIVE at the Lord's coming**... such an opinion (as John's & Paul's) would harmonize with our Lord's express teaching respecting the nearness and coincidence of His own coming, the destruction of Jerusalem, the judgment of Israel, and the close of the age. ...all these events, according to Christ's declaration, **LAY WITHIN THE PERIOD OF THE <u>EXISTING</u> GENERATION.**
Last Days Madness Gary DeMar p.59 [#34]	Peter certainly understood that Jesus' coming was <u>NEAR</u>. He specifically asked whether John would be alive when Jesus came.

My Comments

It should be obvious by now where in the heck these Apostles could have gotten such an idea that Jesus would be back within their lifetime. Jesus *__himself__* had put this idea into their minds over & over- he planted the seed, and made sure it was often watered. The Apostles had listened to Jesus say, on more than one occasion, how he would return "in power" before his generation died off. What the Apostles questioned Jesus about here, can only be explained given that background. This is one more piece of evidence that Jesus *promised to return within that generation then alive, because that's what Jesus himself believed!* As for this attempt at "spin control" by the author of John, probably made years after the last of "this generation" died off, it smacks of Clintonian logic ("it all depends on what 'is' is") in its perverse delight in splitting hairs.

Judgment Day: So Close Just Wait For It

1st Corinthians 4:3-5

New International Version [#16]	I care very little if I am judged by you or by any human court; indeed, I do not even judge myself. My conscience is clear, but that does not make me innocent. It is the Lord who judges me. Therefore **judge <u>nothing</u> before the appointed time;** **WAIT** till the Lord comes. He will bring to light what is hidden in darkness and will expose the motives of men's hearts. At that time each will receive his praise from God
Weymouth [#2]	Therefore form no premature judgements, but WAIT UNTIL THE LORD RETURNS. He will both bring to light the secrets of darkness and will openly disclose the motives that have been in people's hearts; and then the praise which each man deserves will come to him from God.
The Amplified New Testament [#9]	So do not make any hasty or premature judgments before the time when the Lord comes again…
Smith & Goodspeed [#12]	Do not form any premature judgments, therefore, **but <u>WAIT</u> until the Lord comes back**…

Commentaries & Quotes

Who Tampered With The Bible Patricia Eddy p.224-225 [#237]	The first Christians… were characterized, as a group, with the overwhelming belief in the **imminent return of Jesus** heralding the apocalypse and the **end of the world**. …How, then, did the Christian notion of the imminent end of the world arise? …This belief was based upon the original calculations of the arrival of the end of the world based on clues provided in the book of Daniel. …Depending upon the dates chosen for the rebuilding of Jerusalem and the rebuilding of the Temple, various years in the first century A.D. were to be the end of the world. This era was one of fevered expectation by the Jewish people… The expectation of the imminent end of the world. …The **Essenes** *ALSO* believe they were living in **the last days** of the world… They were not only preoccupied with the coming apocalypse, they were **obsessed** by it.
Lost Christianities Dr. Bart Ehrman p.45-46 [#209]	Paul appears to have expected that he, too, was **living at he end of the age** and that God would soon intervene in a cataclysmic act of judgment, to be brought on by Jesus himself… For these people, there was **never** going to be a long haul. **The end was coming soon**, and the best one could do was prepare for it.
God Without Dogma Hugo Fruehauf p.219 [#248]	Since he (Paul) EXPECTED CHRIST TO RETURN IN HIS LIFETIME, it raises the possibility that Paul never INTENDED to instruct a church in the ensuing generations. This scenario is virtually impossible for a Christian to imagine, based on a nearly 1,700 year church tradition. This, however, may very well be the reality for the following very compelling reasons: 1) The ABSENCE of "God-appointed" apostles, prophets, teachers etc. in the church. 2) The lack of genuine first century type spiritual gifts… 3) The fact that Christ's Second Coming was EXPECTED in the first century church CE, with NO PROVISIONS MADE FOR A SUBSEQUENT CHURCH. …Paul states that he expected Christ to RETURN IN HIS LIFETIME and that he would be ALIVE in the FLESH at the time all believers are taken up to meet Christ in the air.

Judgment Day: So Close Just Wait For It

1st Corinthians 4:3-5 (con't)

My Comments

They are told to avoid any petty judgments against each other in the local legal system, seeing how the judge of the entire Universe was due any minute to commence JUDGMENT DAY}

- Do not complain, brethren, against one another, that you yourselves may not be judged; behold, **THE Judge is standing <u>right at the door</u>**. (James 5:9 NASB [#1])
- <u>**Before long**</u>, He will <u>**judge**</u> the world in righteousness (Acts 17:31 Weymouth's [#2])
- But when he dealt with the subjects of justice, self-control, and **the judgement which was <u>soon to come</u>**, (Acts 24:25 Weymouth's [#2])

Also, note that they are told to "<u>**wait**</u> until the Lord returns". Obviously, you'd only be told to WAIT for something that would happen within your lifetime- not something hundreds or thousands or billions of years past your death. The Second Coming was due any minute now, within their lifetime, and so close they could just wait for it. They waited, as they were told to do. They waited until they all died. And it never arrived as promised.

Jesus Due Back Soooo Soon...

No Time To Get Married!

1st Corinthians 7:26-31

New American Standard Bible [#1]	But this I say, brethren, **the time has been <u>shortened</u>**, so that <u>**from now on**</u> those who have wives **should be as though they had none**; and those who weep, as though they did not weep; and those who rejoice, as though they did not rejoice; and those who buy, as though they did not possess; and those who use the world, as though they did not make full use of it; for **the form of this world is passing away.**
The Living Bible [#31]	...our remaining time is **very short**... for the world in its present form will **soon** be gone.
Smith & Goodspeed [#12]	The appointed time has grown **very short**...
International Standard Version [#159]	In view of the present crisis, I think it is prudent for a man to stay as he is. Have you been bound to a wife? **Stop trying to get free.** Have you been freed from a wife? ***STOP LOOKING FOR A WIFE***. ...This is what I mean, brothers: The time has been *shortened*. ***From now on***, those who have wives should live as though they had <u>**none**</u>... For *the world in its present form* ***IS*** passing away.
The Amplified New Testament [#9]	I think then, because of <u>**the impending distress**</u> that is even now setting in, it is well- expedient, profitable and wholesome- for a person to remain as he or she is. ...Are you free from a wife? **Do not seek a wife**. ...The appointed time has been **winding up** and has grown **very short**. ***FROM NOW ON***, let even those who have wives be as if they had none.
The New Testament in Modern English (Phillips) [#15]	My opinion is this, that amid all the difficulties of the present time you would do best to remain just as you are. Are you married? Well, don't try to be separated. Are you unattached? Then **DON'T TRY TO GET MARRIED**. ...All our futures are so <u>**foreshortened**</u>, indeed, that those who have wives should live, so to speak, as though they had none! ...every contact with the world must be as light as possible, for the present scheme of things is <u>RAPIDLY PASSING AWAY</u>.
Today's English Version [#14]	Considering the present distress, I think it is better for a man to stay as he is. Do you have a wife? Then don't try to get rid of her. Are you unmarried? Then ***<u>DON'T LOOK FOR A WIFE</u>***. ...<u>There is not much time left</u>, and from now on married men should live as though they were not married... For this world, as it is now, *will not last much longer*.

Commentaries & Quotes

Leaving The Fold Ed Babinski p.218 [#206]	Paul preached the time was so "short" that married Christian couples ought to **abstain from having sex** keeping themselves pure for their soon-returning savior.
The Incredible Shrinking Son of Man Dr. Robert Price p.107 [#210]	Because the present world is already passing into oblivion, one might as well **remain in the position he occupied** when he was called by God, practice business as usual. Any serious attempt to reform life with the world on the eve of destruction would be like **rearranging the furniture aboard the Titanic.**

1st Corinthians 7:26-31

Commentaries & Quotes (con't)

The Parousia Stuart Russell p.196 [#33]	"The time that remains is **short**." ...he knew that they were on the **VERGE** of a great catastrophe. ...the coming of the Lord... Alford correctly expresses the force of the expression, "the time is shortened henceforth, i.e. the interval between NOW and THE COMING OF THE LORD has arrived at an **EXTREMELY contracted period**."
The Interpreter's Bible, Vol X, 1953 pp.84-85 [#42]	We may believe that the apostle is trustworthy, and yet in this particular regard unfortunately **MISTAKEN**. ...The distress (refers to) the messianic woes which were to precede the end. ...Since the age is supposed to be drawing **NEAR TO ITS CLOSE**, and since the event is expected to bring great disorders upon the world, he holds that it is far better for believers to keep life as simple and as free from complications as possible. ...We know that ### PAUL WAS WRONG in his estimate of the **nearness** of the "end of the age." ...In the **BRIEF** interval that remains, believers are to be unconcerned with outward affairs. ...The world is passing away (1 John 2:17); therefore it is the part of wisdom to become as little entangled as possible in its **TRANSIENT** affairs.
Forged Dr. Bart Ehrman [#234]	Or take a completely different idea, marriage. In 1 Corinthians 7 Paul is insistent that people who are single should try to remain single, just as he is. His reason is that **THE END OF ALL THINGS IS NEAR**, and people should devote themselves to spreading the word, **NOT TO ESTABLISHING THEIR SOCIAL LIVES**. (pp.99-100) But that's not what you find in the historical Paul. For the historical Paul, **THERE WAS NOT GOING TO _BE_ A LONG HAUL. THE END WAS COMING SOON**. (p.102)
Misquoting Jesus Dr. Bart Ehrman p.181 [#245]	He insisted that since "**the time is short**" (until the coming of the Kingdom) everyone should be content with the roles they had been given, and that **no one should seek to change their status**- whether slave, free, **married**, **single**, male, or female (1 Cor. 7:17-24)
The Kingdom of The Cults Dr. Walter Martin p.417 [#249]	When a well-respected Bible teacher and pastor reveals that he is predicating all of his plans on a **CERTAIN DATE** for the Lord's return, his trusting followers will likely do the same thing. They may forego school, **POSTPOSE MARRIAGE**, or **GIVE ALL OF THEIR MONEY AWAY** only to see the "near," "soon," and "any moment" return of Jesus never materialize.

Paul's First Century Advice of "<u>Don't Get Married</u>"
Applies Till Jesus Returns.
Christian- Has Jesus Returned? No? Then...
IT STILL APPLIES!

Paul, "inspired ambassador for BibleGod", advises that because of what was expected in their ***near*** future—the dramatic end of "the present scheme of things", Christian weddings should come to a complete halt, and those who already have wives should live as if they had none. This applied from the day Paul wrote it- to how far into the future? The answer is **"from now on"** as Paul says, until **whenever** Jesus may be returning. The New American Standard Version quotes Paul as saying that his advice given here is to apply "from now on". What does that mean? Well, according to Thayer's Greek English Lexicon of the New Testament, "Hereafter, for the future, henceforth 1 Co. vii. 29"   [#65] while The American Heritage Dictionary puts it "hence·forth adv. 1. **From this time forth**; from now on."

Seeing how Jesus <u>STILL</u> has not returned, it still applies! Paul even writes "**Stop looking for a wife!** according to the International Standard Version. Are present day Christians in compliance with this? Quite the opposite! They've made an entire **industry** out of church weddings. In fact, some churches, such as "Little Chapel of The Flowers" in Las Vegas, that's all they do- weddings. And it goes 100% against what Paul specifically wrote here.

This advice only makes sense to a movement that had good reason to believe that Judgment Day & the Second Coming would occur within their ***own*** era, to a movement that believed there was "not much time left." The fact that Paul's advice is ignored in our present era is evidence that modern Christians disagree strongly with Paul's "Holy Spirit inspired" eschatology.

Modern Christians pay LIP SERVICE to Paul as a true prophet, but by their DEEDS (ignoring his teachings on not getting married), they are calling him a LIAR.

Some Christians have quibbled regarding Paul's mentioning "the difficulty of the present time". They seem to think the prohibition against marriage was just till those "rough times" back then were over. The fact is, Paul taught that "those rough times" would be over **when <u>Jesus</u> returned**, as Paul says in the Today's English Version (#14), "this world as it is now (NOTE: this includes the "rough times" he mentioned), *will not last much longer*." The world would not last much longer, as it was soon coming to an end with the Second Coming. As that never came true, let's just all admit that Paul, like his Jesus, was also a false prophet.

"We Won't All Be Dead"
Therefore Jesus Due Back Within Their
First Century Lifetime

1st Corinthians 15:51-52

New American Standard Bible [#1]	Now I say this, brethren, that flesh and blood cannot inherit the kingdom of God; nor does the perishable inherit the imperishable. Behold, I tell you a mystery; *WE* shall **not all sleep**, but we shall all be changed, in a moment, in the twinkling of an eye, at the last trumpet; for the trumpet will sound, and the dead will be raised imperishable, and we shall be changed
Bible in Basic English [#20]	See, I am giving you the revelation of a secret: **we will not all come to the sleep of DEATH**, but we will all be changed.
Phillips Version [#15]	…**we shall not all die**, but suddenly, in the twinkling of an eye, every one of us will be changed… we who are STILL alive shall suddenly be utterly changed.

Commentaries & Quotes

The Parousia Stuart Russell p.208-209 [#33]	To whom does the apostle refer when he says "WE shall not all sleep" etc.? Is it to some hypothetical persons living in some distant age of time, OR is it of the Corinthians and himself that he is thinking? …When the apostle says "WE," he no doubt meant **THE CHRISTIANS OF CORINTH AND HIMSELF**. This conclusion Alford fully endorses: "We which are alive and remain until the coming of the Lord,-- IN WHICH NUMBER THE APOSTLE FIRMLY BELIEVED THAT HE HIMSELF SHOULD BE". …**It is to come to pass in their OWN DAY,** before the natural term of life expires.
God's Problem Dr. Bart Ehrman p.240 [#232]	That's why Paul call Jesus the "**FIRST FRUITS**" of the resurrection (1 Cor 15:20). This is an agricultural image: the first fruits were the crops brought in on the **FIRST** day of the harvest. Farmers would celebrate the event, in anticipation of going out and gathering in **THE REST OF THEIR CROPS**. And when would the rest of the harvest be gathered in? **RIGHT AWAY- NOT IN SOME DISTANT FUTURE**. By calling Jesus the first fruits, Paul was indicating that the rest of the resurrection was **IMMINENT**; it was to happen **RIGHT AWAY**.
Forged Dr. Bart Ehrman pp.106 [#234]	What most of the millions of people who believe that Jesus is coming back soon, in our lifetime, don't realize is that there have **ALWAYS** been Christians who thought this about their own lifetimes… in fact, in just about **EVERY CENTURY**. The one thing that all those who have ever thought this have had in common is that every one of them has been **DEMONSTRABLY AND IRREFUTABLY** *WRONG*.
God Without Dogma Hugo Fruehauf p.231 [#248]	Why was the church not raptured in the first century CE as **expected** by the believers of that time? We'll let God worry about this one.

1st Corinthians 15:51-52 (con't)	
Commentaries & Quotes (con't)	
The Historical Jesus & The Kingdom of God Richard Hiers pp.108 [#119]	**Paul** had been confident that it (The Kingdom of God) **WOULD COME IN THE COURSE OF HIS OWN LIFETIME** (1 Thess. 4:15-17; 1 Cor. 15:51f).
Lost Christianities Dr. Bart Ehrman p.118 [#209]	The apostle **Paul**, our earliest Christian author, believed that Jesus would return in judgment *in his own lifetime*.
My Comments	

Paul clearly says, to this group of people living in the first century, *that not everyone in their little group will have died off by the time of Jesus' Second Coming*. He says that not everyone alive at that time will die before this happens, but that everyone will "be changed". At the time of the coming, some will have died, some will still be alive, but every Christian- the dead AND the ones living then, when be instantly changed, "in the twinkling of an eye".

> **QUESTION**: Paul told the Christians **at <u>Corinth</u>** that "we (Paul & the Corinthians) shall not all sleep", i.e. not have all died off, before the Second Coming occurs. Did this prophecy turn out TRUE or FALSE?

Philippians 1:6

Can't "Perfect" Dead People		
Therefore Jesus Due Back While They Lived		
Philippians 1:6		
American Standard Version [#10]	Being confident of this very thing, that he who began a good work in you will **perfect it <u>until</u>** the day of Jesus Christ	
The New Testament in Modern English (Phillips) [#15]	I feel sure that the one who has begun his good work in you will **go on developing it <u>until</u>** the day of Jesus Christ.	
Today's English Version [#14]	And so I am sure that God, who began this good work in you, will carry it on until it is finished **<u>on</u>** the Day of Christ Jesus.	
Modern King James Version [#24]	being confident of this very thing, that He who has begun a good work in you **will perform it until the day of Jesus Christ.**	
The Amplified New Testament [#9]	And I am convinced and sure of this very thing, that He Who began a good work in you **will continue until the day of Jesus Christ—<u>right up to the time of His return</u>**—developing (that good work) and perfecting and bringing it to full completion in you.	
My Comments		
This "good work" that BibleGod has started in these First Century Christians, will be continued in them, **"right up to the time" that Jesus comes back**. This wording <u>demands</u> that these Christians, therefore, still be alive and "perfectable" at the time of the Second Coming. The perfecting was a PROCESS, that BEGAN, and CONTINUES in their lives, <u>until</u> Jesus returns to Earth.		

Philippians 3:20-21

Jesus Due Back While Their	
First Century Body Was Still Alive	

Philippians 3:20-21

NASB [#1]	For our citizenship is in heaven, from which also **we eagerly wait** for a Savior, the Lord Jesus Christ; who will **transform the body of our humble state into conformity with the body of His glory,** by the exertion of the power that He has even to subject all things to Himself.

Commentaries & Quotes

Lost Christianities Bart Ehrman p.141 [#209]	Paul imagined… the **brief interim** between Jesus' resurrection and his imminent return in glory.
God is Not Great C. Hitchens p.118 [#227]	He also promised his followers that he (Jesus) would reveal his kingdom *before* they came to the end of their own lives.
Jesus, Interrupted Dr. Bart Ehrman p.131 [#233]	(Paul) believed that Jesus' resurrection indicated that **the end of the age was near**. It would arrive any day, with the reappearance of Jesus from heaven; the **dead** would be raise and the **living believers would be transformed into immortal bodies…**

My Comments

You would not tell a group of people to wait around for the next ice age, or the sun to die of old age, or the heat death of the universe. You would only tell a group of people to **WAIT for something that's due to happen within their lifetime.** Therefore, Paul was telling these people that Jesus would be back within their lifetimes, **something they could WAIT for,** to transform their LIVING EARTHLY BODIES.

For Them to Await Rescue by Jesus
Means Jesus Due Back Within Their Lifetime

1st Thessalonians 1:10

Young's Literal Translation [#3]	…and to **wait** for His Son from the heavens, whom He did raise out of the dead-- Jesus, who is **RESCUING US** *from* the anger that is coming.
New International Version [#16]	and to **wait for his Son** from heaven, whom he raised from the dead-- Jesus, who **rescues us** from the coming wrath.
New Revised Standard Version [#17]	and to **wait for his Son** from heaven, whom he raised from the dead--Jesus, who **rescues us** from the wrath that is coming.
Weymouth's [#2]	and to **await the return** from Heaven of His Son, whom He raised from among the dead--even Jesus, **our Deliverer from God's coming anger**.
The Amplified New Testament [#9]	And (how you) *look forward to and await the coming of His Son from heaven*, Whom He raised from the dead, Jesus Who *personally rescues and delivers **US*** out of and from the wrath (bringing punishment) which is coming (upon the impenitent)…

Commentaries & Quotes

Jesus, Interrupted Dr. Bart Ehrman p.156-158 [#233]	Jesus' followers could expect this kingdom to arrive **SOON**—in fact, **IN THEIR LIFETIME**. It would be brought by a cosmic judge of the earth, whom Jesus called the Son of Man… When the Son of Man arrived there would be a **JUDGMENT** of the earth, in which the wicked would be destroyed but the righteous rewarded. Those who were suffering pain and oppression now would be exalted then.. it was to happen **VERY SOON**. …it will happen **WITHIN JESUS' OWN GENERATION**.

My Comments

Some things to point out here, and I apologize for being redundant, but the verses that DEMAND a First Century date of fulfillment are numerous. In this particular passage, Jesus is predicted to be rescuing **THEM** (Christians alive in 51 CE) from some cosmic disaster that's obviously due **WITHIN** THEIR LIFETIME, for if it wasn't due within their lifetime, there'd be no need to rescue them. One does not rescue people from disasters that won't even take place until thousands of years past their lifetime.

Can't Be	"*Alive & Remaining*" If Already "*Dead & Gone*" (Jesus Due Back Within The 1ˢᵗ Century)	
1st Thessalonians 4:15-17		
New American Standard Bible [#1]	For this **we** say to you by the word of the Lord, that **we who are alive, and <u>remain until the coming of the Lord</u>**, shall not precede those who have fallen asleep. For the Lord Himself will descend from heaven with a shout, with the voice of *the* archangel, and with the trumpet of God; and the dead in Christ shall rise first. Then **we who are alive and <u>REMAIN</u>** shall be caught up together with them in the clouds to meet the Lord in the air, and thus we shall always be with the Lord.	
Weymouth's [#2]	For this we declare to you on the Lord's own authority--that **we who are alive and <u>CONTINUE ON EARTH UNTIL</u>** the Coming of the Lord, shall certainly not forestall those who shall have previously passed away… Afterwards we who are alive and are still on earth will be caught up in their company amid clouds to meet the Lord in the air.	
Smith & Goodspeed [#12]	51CE} For we can assure you… that those of **us** who will **STILL BE LIVING** when the Lord comes… then those of us who are still living will be caught up…	
New International Version [#16]	According to the Lord's own word, we tell you that **we who are still alive**, who are left till the coming of the Lord, will certainly not precede those who have fallen asleep…After that, **we who are <u>STILL ALIVE</u> and are left will be caught up** together with them in the clouds to meet the Lord in the air. And so we will be with the Lord forever.	
Concordant Literal New Testament [#4]	For this we are saying to you by the word of the Lord, **that we, the living, who are <u>SURVIVING TO</u> the presence of the Lord**…	
Commentaries & Quotes		
The New Testament in Modern Speech Ernest H. Cook p.553 [#214]	The pronouns 'we' and 'you' cannot, as a rule, be used to the total exclusion of the persons speaking or immediately addressed. Therefore here (v. 15) and in verse 17 Paul implies that THE RETURN OF THE LORD JESUS WOULD TAKE PLACE **IN THE LIFETIME** OF SOME OF THE **FIRST READERS** OF THIS LETTER.	
The Historical Jesus & The Kingdom of God Richard Heirs p.108 [#119]	Paul had been confident that it (the Second Coming) would come **in the course of his <u>own</u> lifetime**. (1TH 4:15-17; 1Cor 15:51f.).	
The Interpreter's Bible: Vol VII p.147 [#42]	This eschatological foundation of the teaching of Jesus is clearly indicated by our earliest traditions. THERE WERE THOSE STANDING IN JESUS' PRESENCE WHO <u>WOULD NOT TASTE OF DEATH</u> UNTIL IT CAME WITH POWER (Mark 9:1; 13:30); **that was certainly also Paul's understanding** (1 Cor. 15:51; 1 Thess 4:15).	

Can't Be "*Alive & Remaining*"
If Already "**Dead & Gone**"

1st Thessalonians 4:15-17

Commentaries & Quotes (con't)

The Parousia J. Stuart Russell pp.160&167 [#33]	The author of the epistle (1 Thessalonians) (is) looking for the day of judgment to take place **in his own time** or near to it. The legitimate inference from the words of St. Paul in ver. 15, 'we who are **alive** and remain unto the coming of the Lord,' is that he anticipated it as possible, and even **probable**, that **his readers and himself would be ALIVE** at the coming of the Lord. Such is the natural and obvious interpretation of his language. Dean Alford (author of a Greek Testament) observes, with much force and candor,--- 'Then, BEYOND QUESTION, **HE HIMSELF EXPECTED TO BE ALIVE**, TOGETHER WITH THE MAJORITY OF THOSE TO WHOM HE WAS WRITING, **AT THE LORD'S COMING.** For we cannot for a moment accept the evasion of Theodoret and the majority of ancient commentators (that the apostle does not speak of himself personally, but of those who should be living at the period), but we must take the words in their only plain grammatical meaning, that 'we which are alive and remain' are a class distinguished from 'they that sleep' by being yet in the flesh when Christ comes, in which class by prefixing 'we' he includes his readers and himself." The early church, and even the apostles themselves, **expected their Lord to come again in that very generation**. St. Paul himself shared in that expectation...
Bible Review Dr. Marcus Borg p.16 [#118]	The widespread New Testament references to the second coming of Christ tell us that many early Christians thought they were living in "the last days." Paul, in his early letters, **SEEMS TO HAVE EXPECTED TO LIVE UNTIL THE SECOND COMING**; this is the most obvious way to read 1 Thessalonians 4:13-18 and 1 Corinthians 15: 51 & 52... In short, the texts tell us that many early Christians believed that the second coming of Jesus would occur **IN OR NEAR THEIR TIME.** And to say the OBVIOUS, # THEY WERE # WRONG
Porphyry's Against The Christians ~350 CE pp.69-70 [#241]	And there is more to **PAUL'S LYING**: He very clearly says, "WE WHO ARE ALIVE." For it is now THREE HUNDRED YEARS since he said this and NOBODY- not Paul and not anyone else- has been caught up in the air. It is high time to let Paul's confusions rest in peace!

Can't Be "*Alive & Remaining*" If Already "**Dead & Gone**"

1st Thessalonians 4:15-17

Commentaries & Quotes (con't)

Jesus: Apocalyptic Prophet of The New Millennium Dr. Bart Ehrman p.17 [#240]	Our earliest surviving Christian author is the apostle Paul, who wrote his extant letters even prior to the New Testament Gospels of Matthew, Mark, Luke, and John. …Like so many Christians who lived in the centuries since, Paul was **CONVINCED** that **THE END WOULD COME IN HIS OWN GENERATION**. …Paul speaks about the **IMMINENT** end of the age to be brought by Jesus' return. This is the first letter to the Thessalonians, written probably in **49 CE**, fewer than twenty years after the death of Jesus. …What has long struck scholars of the New Testament is that… Paul appears to understand that **HE HIMSELF WILL BE ONE OF THESE LIVING WHEN JESUS RETURNS**. It would have been easy enough for him to talk about "**THOSE**" who are alive if he did not imagine himself to be one of them.
Forged Dr. Bart Ehrman pp.106-107 [#234]	Paul himself thought the end was **COMING IN HIS LIFETIME**. Nowhere is this more clear than in one of the letters we are sure he wrote, 1 Thessalonians. …When he converted these people, Paul had taught them that **THE END OF THE AGE** was **IMMINENT**, that they were **SOON** to enter the kingdom when Jesus returned. …Read the verse (1st Thess. 4:17) carefully: **PAUL EXPECTS TO BE ONE OF THE ONES WHO WILL STILL BE ALIVE WHEN IT HAPPENS**. …There seems to be a fundamental disparity between the teachings of 1 and 2 Thessalonians, which is why so many scholars think that 2 Thessalonians is not by Paul.
Beyond The End Times John Noe p.180 [#253]	Their "whole spirit, soul and body" (physical, *soma* bodies) would be "kept blameless (until) the coming of the Lord. …If they all **died** without receiving Paul's promise, **AND THEIR BODIES WEREN'T KEPT BUT DECAYED IN GRAVES**, hasn't his inspiration failed, too?

My Comments

Around 51 CE Paul flat out states to Christians living in Thessalonica that some of them will be **SURVIVING TO** the Second Coming, that some WILL BE "STILL LIVING" when Jesus returns: "we who are ALIVE and CONTINUE ON EARTH **until** the coming of the Lord…" (Weymouth's [#2]). Unless some want to advocate that some of these folks are still walking around, the Second Coming is now about 1,900 years overdue.

Jesus Due w/i Lifetime
Before Their Souls Separate From Their Bodies

1st Thessalonians 5:23

New American Standard Bible [#1]	Now may the God of peace Himself sanctify you entirely; and may your **spirit** and **soul** and **body** *be preserved complete*, without blame at the coming of our Lord Jesus Christ.
Philip's [#15]	May you be kept in soul and mind and **body** in spotless integrity **UNTIL** the coming of our Lord Jesus Christ.
The Living Bible [#31]	May your spirit and soul and **body** be kept **strong** and blameless **UNTIL** that day when our Lord Jesus Christ comes back again.
Weymouth [#2]	And may God Himself who gives peace, make you entirely holy; and **may your spirits, souls and *bodies* be preserved *complete* and be found blameless at the Coming of our Lord Jesus Christ.**
The Amplified New Testament [#9]	…and may your spirit and soul and **body** be **preserved sound and complete** (and found) blameless **AT** the coming of our Lord Jesus Christ…

Commentaries & Quotes

The Parousia J. Stuart Russell p.170 [#33]	If any shadow of a doubt still rested on the question whether St. Paul believed and taught the incidence of the Parousia in his own day, this passage would dispel it. No words can more **CLEARLY** imply this belief than this prayer that the Thessalonian Christians **might not die before the appearing of Christ**. Death is the **DISSOLUTION** of the union between body, soul, and spirit, and the apostle's prayer is the spirit, soul, and body might "**ALL TOGETHER**" be preserved in sanctity **TILL** the Lord's coming. **This implies THE CONTINUANCE OF THEIR CORPOREAL (I.E. PHYSICAL) LIFE until that event.**

My Comments

Paul expects Jesus to have returned well before all of these folks have grown feeble with age and/or died. He expects their bodies to "be preserved sound and complete". The time spans alluded to in this verse do not allow their bodies to have rotted away into dust. The Second Coming is, again, promised & prophesied to First Century Christians within their lifetime, and again, the prophecy turned out to be false.

Relief & Vengeance w/i Their Lifetime Via 2nd Coming

2nd Thessalonians 1:6-8

The New International Version [#16]	6 God is just: He will pay back trouble to **those** who trouble **you** 7 *and* give **RELIEF** to you who are troubled, and to us as well. This will happen **when** the Lord Jesus is revealed from heaven in blazing fire with his powerful angels. 8 He will punish those who do not know God and do not obey the gospel of our Lord Jesus.
Today's English Version [#14]	God will do what is right: **he will bring suffering on those who make you suffer**, and he will **give RELIEF to <u>you</u>** who suffer and to us as well. *He will do this* **WHEN** *the Lord Jesus appears from heaven with his mighty angels*, with a flaming fire, to punish those who reject God…
The New English Bible [#25]	It is surely just that God should balance the account by sending trouble to **those** who trouble **you**, and **RELIEF** to you who are troubled, and to us as well, **when** our Lord Jesus Christ is revealed from heaven with his mighty angels in blazing fire.

Commentaries & Quotes

The Parousia J. Stuart Russell pp.171-172 [#33]	The apostle comforts them with the prospect of deliverance at the appearing of the Lord Jesus, which would bring rest to them and retribution to their enemies… The apostle seems not to anticipate the "rest" of which he speaks until the Parousia, "when the Lord Jesus shall be revealed from heaven" etc. It follows that the rest was conceived by St. Paul to be *very near*… It will be observed that it is not said that **death** is to bring them rest, but "the apocalypse" of the Lord Jesus from heaven: a clear proof that **the apostle did not regard that apocalypse as a distant event**.
The Prophecy of the Destruction of Jerusalem Nisbett (1787 AD) p.19 [#157]	…their sufferings would be but of **short continuance**; that they who were the chief sources of their present troubles, would ere long be deprived of the power of injuring them, as they had hitherto done, and in a word, that the promised coming of their Lord was **at hand**, to <u>take vengeance on (their persecutors).</u>
Texts Explained F.W. Farrar p.178 [#215]	**All the apostles believed that the day was near**… and their watchword was "Maranatha the Lord is near".

My Comments

Paul, around 51 CE, promises these Christians that when Jesus comes back, Jesus will "**bring suffering on those who make you suffer**", and then Paul locks in the time frame for this: "when the Lord Jesus **appears from heaven with his mighty angels**", i.e. at the **Second Coming**. Therefore, **Jesus is prophesied as coming within the lifetime of the folks causing the pain**. This never happened. The torturERS and the torturEES have since long ago turned to dust, with no Second Coming in their lifetime.

Notice also the word "relief" that Paul uses. "Relief" implies that the sufferings will still be happening right up to the moment Jesus creates a sonic boom with his re-entering the atmosphere. And once Jesus has landed, he's supposed to quickly rescues these Christians by kicking the butts of their persecutors. The word "relief" **demands** a First Century fulfillment within the lifetime of the folks who first read this letter from Paul.

"Obey Till Jesus Comes" =
Jesus Coming Within Timothy's Lifetime

1st Timothy 6:14-15

The New International Version [#16]	14 to **keep this command** without spot or blame *UNTIL* the appearing of our Lord Jesus Christ, 15 which God will bring about in his own time-- God, the blessed and only Ruler, the King of kings and Lord of lords,
Today's English Version [#14]	...OBEY YOUR ORDERS AND KEEP THEM FAITHFULLY <u>UNTIL</u> the Day when our Lord Jesus Christ will appear.
The New English Bible [#25]	...obey your orders irreproachably and without fault <u>UNTIL</u> our Lord Jesus Christ appears.

My Comments

Paul does not even <u>***consider***</u> the possibility that Jesus might return way beyond the era of the lifetime of his young assistant Timothy. If he had had even the faintest notion that it would end up being 2000+ years later, then he would have obviously phrased his command thusly:

"...keep the commandment... **until you die** $\underline{OR}$ until the appearing of our Lord."

This is certainly how modern preachers would say it to their flocks. But Jesus had prophesied that "this generation shall not pass away" and Paul & others back then made the mistake of trusting what Jesus had promised. The fact is it was physically **impossible** for Timothy or anyone else to have kept on doing ANYTHING, till such and such a time, IF that "such and such" a time was thousands of years in the future. Imagine a drill sergeant ordering a cadet to do pushups for 1,000 years. They would label him insane.

So once again, we have a text that *ONLY* makes sense *if* the Second Coming was prophesied to occur **within the <u>LIFETIME</u> of the person being ordered** to do "such and such" till Jesus comes.

Revenge via Judgment Day
Due Within 1st Century
via The 2nd Coming
Patience... The Lord Is Coming

James 5:1-9

New International Version [#16]	1 Now listen, **you rich people**, weep and wail because of the misery that **is** coming upon **_you_**. 2 Your wealth has rotted, and moths have eaten your clothes. 3 Your gold and silver are corroded. Their corrosion will testify against you and eat your flesh like fire. You **_have_** hoarded wealth **in the _last_ days**. 4 Look! The wages you failed to pay the workmen who mowed your fields are crying out against you. The cries of the harvesters have reached the ears of the Lord Almighty. 5 You have lived on earth in luxury and self-indulgence. **You have fattened yourselves in <u>the day of slaughter</u>.** 6 You have condemned and murdered innocent men, who were not opposing you. 7 **Be patient, then, brothers, _until_ the Lord's coming. See how the farmer waits for the land to yield its valuable crop and <u>how patient he is</u> for the autumn and spring rains.** 8 You too, be patient and stand firm, **because** the Lord's coming is **near**. 9 Don't grumble against each other, brothers, or you will be judged. **The Judge is standing _at the door!_**
The Amplified New Testament [#9]	8 ...for the coming of the Lord is **_very_** near.
Weymouth [#2]	8 So you also must be patient: keeping up your courage; for the Coming of the Lord is now **close at hand**.
New American Standard Bible [#1]	8 ...for **the coming of the Lord is <u>at hand</u>**.

My Comments

In this passage, maybe written around 80 CE, James is telling these Christians that the rich, who are now bothering them, are **soon** to be "slaughtered" (Good News! They're all going to DIE!!!), and that these Christians are to be patient "**until** the Lord's coming", because he is so near he is "**standing at the door**".

These Christians, alive in 80 CE, could only continue being **PATIENT** for as long as they were yet **ALIVE**. Once they are **DEAD**, as Solomon said, "they know nothing", and can no longer be patient, eager, happy, sad whatever. Telling them to "be patient" until the sun explodes in a super nova makes no sense. Therefore **these verses clearly assume the Second Coming to be**

WITHIN THEIR LIFETIME.

Revenge Within First Century via The 2nd Coming
Patience... The Lord Is Coming

James 5:1-9

My Comments (continued)

➢ The rich "have hoarded wealth in the last days."
➢ One can only hoard wealth when one is living.
  ➢ **Therefore, they must have been living "in the last days."**

➢ The rich have fattened themselves for "the day of slaughter."
➢ In order to be *slaughtered*, they must first still be *alive*.
  ➢ **Therefore, "the day of slaughter" must take place while they are still alive, i.e. within their lifetime.**

➢ The Christians are told to "be patient <u>until</u> the Lord's coming."
➢ One can only be patient while one is still <u>alive</u>.
  ➢ **Therefore, "the Lord's coming" is assumed to take place within their lifetime.**

➢ The Christians are to emulate the patience of farmers.
➢ Farmers plant with the expectation of <u>seeing</u> a harvest <u>within</u> their lifetime.
  ➢ Therefore, these 1st Century Christians were led to believe they could expect a "harvest" of hope within their own lifetime- the harvest being the Second Coming of Christ.

Compare what James writes-
  Don't grumble against each other, brothers, or you will be judged. The **Judge** is standing *<u>at the door</u>!* (James 5:9 NASB [#1])
To what Paul writes-
  Don't make complaints against one another in the meantime, my brothers... The **judge** himself is *<u>already at the door</u>*. (1ˢᵗ Cor 4:15 Phillips Version [#15])
One is almost a carbon copy of the other. And what they are **both** trying to communicate to the Christians of the First Century is that, seeing how Jesus is sooooo close to returning, and Jesus is <u>THE JUDGE</u>, it would make sense to let Jesus solve your petty lawsuits one against the other, rather than trying to solve them amongst yourselves.

Needless to say, the implication is that Jesus' return would happen **within** their lifetime, in time to solve their current legal problems, rather than after they'd long since been dead, making any such legal problems a moot point.

Commentaries & Quotes

Last Days Madness Gary DeMar p.314 [#34]	How could James have told his readers to "be patient... *<u>until</u>* the coming of the Lord" if the Lord's coming was not within their lifetime? James bases his call for patience upon the fact that the Lord's coming *<u>was</u>* near, near for those who first read his letter.
	    "James clearly believed, as other of his time did, that the coming of Christ was **imminent**. Since, then, *there is not long to wait*, his plea for patience is greatly reinforced."
	                    (quoted by DeMar from *The Epistle of James*, Leslie Mitton, Eerdmans, Grand Rapids, MI, 1966, pages 186-187)

1st Peter 2:12

	Second Coming Within Lifetime of
	First Century Gentiles
	1st Peter 2:12
Bible in Basic English [#20]	Being of good behaviour among the Gentiles; so that though they say now that you are evil-doers, they may see your good works and **give glory to God when he comes** to be their judge.
	My Comments

These Pagans, neighbors to the 1st Century Christians, will be giving "glory to God when he comes" so obviously they must be able to **SEE** his coming with their eyeballs so as to know **WHEN** to "give glory." In order to **see** the 2nd Coming of Jesus, they must therefore be **ALIVE** and on the EARTH to be able to look up and **SEE** Jesus coming on the clouds in the sky. If these non-Christians were already **dead**, then, per standard Christian theology, they would not be around on the Earth with eyeballs in order to witness, first hand, the coming of Jesus as it happens in the sky. Therefore, the 2nd Coming is assumed to take place before these 1st Century people died off from old age.

1st Peter 4:5

	Judgment Day: Within Their Lifetime
	1st Peter 4:5
Weymouth [#2]	But they will have to give account to Him who **stands ready** to pronounce **judgement** on the **living** and the **dead**.
Young's Literal Translation [#3]	…who shall give an account to Him who is **ready to judge** living and dead
American Standard Version [#10]	…who shall give account to him that is **ready to judge** the **living** and the **dead**.
The Emphasized New Testament [#5]	…who shall render an account unto him who is holding in **readiness** to judge **living** and dead.
	Commentaries & Quotes
Luke and the Last Things [#35] p.42	On this verse Hampden-Cook remarks that "the living" refers to "those who were **alive at the time this letter was written**; an indication that Peter expected the Second Advent to take place in the **lifetime** of his contemporaries."
The Parousia [#33] p.304	(this) can by no means refer to any but an almost ***immediate*** event.

The 2nd Coming:
w/i the Lifetime of Those Who Pierced Him

Revelation 1:7

Weymouth [#2]	**He is coming** in the clouds, and every eye will <u>see</u> Him, and **so will <u>those who pierced Him</u>**; and all the nations of the earth will gaze on Him and mourn. Even so. Amen.
New International Version [#16]	Look, he is coming with the clouds, and every eye will see him, *even those who pierced him*…
New Life Version [#174]	See! He is coming with the clouds. **Every** eye will see Him. **Even the men who <u>killed him</u> will see him**…

These are the men who killed Jesus in 33 CE. His Second Coming is prophesied to occur <u>within their lifetime</u>. It didn't. This prophecy turned out to be false.

Revelation 1:7 (con't)

My Comments

"Those that pierced him"	John, the claimed author of <u>Revelation</u> also wrote <u>The Gospel of John,</u> in which is found the story of Jesus, dead on the cross, being pierced: Accordingly **the soldiers** came and broke the legs of the first man and also of the other who had been crucified with Jesus. Then they came to Jesus Himself: but when they saw that He was already dead, they refrained from breaking His legs. **One of the soldiers, however, made a <u>thrust at His side with a lance</u>, and immediately blood and water flowed out.** (John 19:32-34 Weymouth [#2])
The "Spiritual Eyes" Excuse	## THE "SPIRITUAL EYES" EXCUSE *Some Christians have attempted to explain away Revelation 1:7 by claiming the soldiers could still see Jesus' return "with spiritual eyes" even thousands of years after their death, and thus Jesus need not return within their lifetime. This is easily refuted in several ways.*
	<u>Assertions ≠ Evidence</u> The attempt to spiritual*ize* this passage via spiritual *eyes* is just another case of Christian "logic" in action. Outside of their inability to explain this passage, there is no reason to "spiritualize" it away. There is *no evidence*, other than their mere *assertions*, that within this passage John is talking of a *spiritual* coming in *spiritual* clouds visible only with *spiritual* eyes. And to teach such nonsense is enough to invite a *spiritual* boot up one's *spiritual* wazoo. The text says "eyes" and normal interpretive pricinples demand that, unless within the verse there is good reason to the contrary. "Eyes" should be taken in its normal sense; it is the *living*, not the dead, who are promised to see this event (Mt 24:30)
	<u>Dead Soldiers Not Resurrected In Time To See Second Coming</u> According to their own theories about future resurrections, these soldiers will not even be around to witness the Second Coming as it is occurring. Most Christians can stop fighting amongst themselves over the Second Coming long enough to agree with the following sequence based upon 1st Corinthians 15:23} • Jesus returns to Earth. • THEN at some point in time Jesus resurrects Christians. • THEN at a further point in time Jesus resurrects anyone else. Thus, according to their own theory, dead Christians AND dead sinners would not even have been resurrected yet in time to see with their "spiritual eyes" Jesus arriving on a cloud. The only way the "spiritual eyes" excuse can work is if everyone gets resurrected *before* the Second Coming even happens, so they can be standing around gawking into the sky as it unfolds.

My Comments

The "Spiritual Eyes" Excuse (con't) 	**The Dead See Nothing** Some Christians, realizing the shortcomings shown above, dreamed up another "explanation." This time they claimed that the dead soldiers, without being resurrected, would somehow wtihin their state of being dead "see" the Second Coming as it occurs. However, this is easily answered by their own Bible: The living are conscious that death will come to them, but **the dead** are not conscious of *anything*… (Ecclesiastes 9:5 Bible in Basic English [#20]) Thus, yet another "explanation" meets a dead end. **These Soldiers Will Have No Body After Death** Christian theory teaches that only Christians will be given bodies (and thus somewhere to put eyes in, with which to see) in the resurrection. These soldiers, however, as *non*-Christians, are nowhere promised a "new body" (1 Cor 15). *Assuming* these soldiers *were* resurrected before Jesus returned (so they could be in a position to *see* his return), where is the verse that says NON-Christians will be given a new body, with eyes, to see Jesus returning??? **Leads To Gnosticism** If you grant that non-physical "spiritual eyes" can see Jesus' return, then Gnostics can grant a "spiritual, non-physical" Jesus rising from the dead with a ghostly-type body not of flesh & bones. Thus you've opened an even *BIGGER* can of worms for *orthodox* Christians, according to Luke 24:39 and 1st John 4:2 and 3.

Quotes

Bible Review Marcus Borg [#118]	The notion that these texts refer to *our* time or some *future* time has other very serious difficulties. It means, for example, that the central message of the Book of Revelation was *not* meant for the people to whom it was written, but for whatever generation lives in the last days. **That would be odd: John of Patmos wrote to seven Christian communities in Asia Minor telling *them* that Christ was coming soon, but the message wasn't meant for *them*.**
Four Views on the Book of Revelation Ken Gentry [#247]	What is more, the terms appear **FREQUENTLY** in Revelation, showing John's urgent emphasis on temporal expectancy. We find *tachos* ("SOON") in 1:1; 2:16; 3:11; 22:6,7,12,20 and (we find) *engys* ("NEAR") in 1:3; 3:10; 22:10… John emphasizes **THESE TWO CLEAR TERMS** with similar meanings, thereby preempting any confusion among his readers regarding **WHEN** the prophecies will occur. …John himself positively asserts that the events are **NEAR IN HIS DAY**. Consequently, they must lie in our **DISTANT** past. (pp.41-42) John's reference to Christ's piercing demands a first-century focus if the theme is to be relevant and true, for those who pierced him are now long since deceased. (p.48) Revelation specifically claims to relate events "**SHORTLY** to come to pass," in that "the time is **AT HAND**." *WHY NOT ACCEPT JOHN'S STATEMENTS AT FACE VALUE?* (p.92)

"Hold On To The End!!!"
(And "The End" Is Promised Within Their Lifetime)

Misc. Verses

1st Cor 1:7-8 Weymouth [#2]	So that there is no gift of God in which you consciously come short **while patiently waiting for the reappearing of our Lord Jesus Christ**, who will also **keep you** steadfast **to the very End**, so that you will be free from reproach on the day of our Lord Jesus Christ.
2nd Cor 1:13-14 NASB [#1]	For we write nothing else to you than what you read and understand, and I hope <u>you will understand</u> **until the <u>end</u>**; just as you also partially did understand us, that we are your reason to be proud as you also are ours, in **the day of our Lord Jesus**.
1st Thess 1:10 NIV [#16]	…and to **wait for his Son** from heaven
1st Tim 6:14 TEV [#14]	…**obey your orders** and keep them **faithfully** <u>until</u> the Day when our Lord Jesus Christ will **appear**.
Heb 3:6 Weymouth [#2]	But Christ was faithful as a Son having authority over God's house, and we are that house, **if we hold firm to the End** the <u>boldness</u> and the <u>hope</u> which we boast of as ours.
Heb 3:14 NRSV [#17]	For we have become partners of Christ, if only we **hold our first confidence firm to the end.**
Heb 6:11 Darby [#21]	But we desire earnestly that each one of you shew the same diligence to the full assurance of hope **unto the end**.
1st John 2:28 Berkeley [#13]	And now, dear children, <u>remain</u> in Him so that *when* he appears <u>we</u> may have confidence and may not <u>shrink in shame</u> **from Him at His coming.** *<u>Note:</u> Can't "shrink in shame" if dead, therefore, expected within their lifetime.*
Rev 2:5-26 NIV [#16]	**Only <u>HOLD ON</u>** to what you have *<u>until I come</u>*. To him who overcomes and **does my will** *<u>to the end</u>*, I will give authority over the nations…

Commentaries & Quotes

The Jesus Party Hugh Schonfield [#202]	For the Jewish people the time was perhaps the strangest in the history of any nation, dominated as it was by the ***obsession*** that this was the **climax of human history**, the closing phase of an age-old struggle between the forces of Light and Darkness. (p.16) To understand the times of which we are writing… we have continually to remind ourselves that for multitudes in the Holy Land **these were the Last Times… the sands were fast running out in the hourglass of destiny**. Ahead lay Judgment Day, and beyond it the bliss of the Kingdom of God on earth. (p.23)

My Comments

None of these verses make sense if the Second Coming was due to happen several thousand years in the distant future. They can't be expected to "understand *UNTIL* the end" unless they've *SURVIVED* "until the end". People can't "patiently **wait**" for something thousands of years beyond their lifetime. You can't "obey your orders & keep them **until** the day" if said day is 10 BILLION years in the future. One can't do God's will "to the end" if THAT END is 5 billion years in the future. It.Is.Impossible. All of these verses clearly rely on the prophecies placing the Second Coming within the First Century.

"The Glory ABOUT TO Be Revealed"

Romans 8:18-25

New Revised Standard Version [#17]	18 I consider that the sufferings of this present time are not worth comparing with the glory *__about to be__ revealed to us. 19 For the creation waits with eager longing for the **revealing** of the children of God; 20 for the creation was subjected to futility, not of its own will but by the will of the one who subjected it, in hope 21 that the creation itself will be set free from its bondage to decay and will obtain the freedom of the glory of the children of God. 22 We know that the whole creation has been groaning in labor pains **until _now_**; 23 and not only the creation, but we ourselves, who have the first fruits of the Spirit, groan inwardly while **we wait for adoption, the redemption of our __bodies__**. 24 For in hope we were saved. Now hope that is seen is not hope. For who hopes for what is seen? 25 But if we hope for what we do not see, **we wait for it with patience**.
Weymouth [#2]	18 Why, what we now suffer I count as nothing in comparison with the glory which is ***soon to be** manifested in us.
The Emphasized New Testament [#5]	18 …the glory ***about to be** revealed toward us.
Concordant Literal New Testament [#4]	18 For I am reckoning that the sufferings of the current era do not deserve the glory ***about to be** revealed for us.
The Amplified New Testament [#9]	18 …the glory that is ***about to be** revealed to us and in us and for us…
The Emphasized New Testament [#5]	18 For I reckon that unworthy are the sufferings of the present season to be compared with the glory ***about to be** revealed toward us.
Young's Literal Translation [#3]	18 For I reckon that the sufferings of the present time *are* not worthy *to be compared* with the glory ***about to be** revealed in us.
Westcott & Hort [#7]	18 logizomai gar oti ouk axia ta paqhmata tou nun kairou proj thn ***_mellousan_** doxan apokalufqhnai eij hmaj

*Greek: Mello} In 58 CE, all of this was promised to be on the point of happening, about to occur, impending,

ON THE VERY **VERGE** OF TAKING PLACE.

My Comments

Besides the Greek word "mello" being used here, which clearly promises a First Century fulfillment for these prophecies, these Christians at Rome are told, in regards to the 2ⁿᵈ Coming, to "**wait for it with patience**". Had they known that 2,000 years in the future it STILL had not happened, do you think they would have still **WAITED WITH PATIENCE**? If Paul hadn't gotten the idea that Jesus was due back within their lifetime, he would have never asked these people to wait around for it with patience.

Romans 13:11-12

It Is Already The Hour... The Day Is At Hand	
Romans 13:11-12	
New American Standard Bible [#1]	And this *do,* knowing the time, that **it is already <u>the</u> hour** for you to awaken from sleep; for now salvation is nearer to us than when we believed. The night is almost gone, and **the day is <u>at hand</u>**. Let us therefore lay aside the deeds of darkness and put on the armor of light.
Weymouth [#2]	Carry out these injunctions because **<u>YOU KNOW</u> the critical period at which we** [i.e. Christians in 58 CE] **are living**, and that it is **<u>now</u>** high time, to rouse yourselves from sleep; for salvation is now nearer to us than when we first became believers. The night is far advanced, **and day is *<u>about to</u>* dawn**. We must therefore lay aside the deeds of darkness, and clothe ourselves with the armour of Light.
The Amplified New Testament [#9]	The night is far gone and **the day is almost HERE**.
Commentaries & Quotes	
The Interpreter's Bible pp.608-610 [#42]	In his earlier letters he (Paul) not only accepted the view that **the present age would terminate in the return of Christ**, but he also believed that the day of the Lord was **CLOSE AT HAND**. It was near enough to affect the decisions people made and the way they lived. ...In the awareness of living under IMMINENT divine judgment... This PRESENT AGE WAS PASSING AWAY, the new age was standing on the threshold. ...They believed in was NEAR AT HAND. ...The end was near and they knew it. Certainly it was not time for a "little folding of the hands to sleep". ...Critical events are ON THE **THRESHOLD**. ...That day had seemed IMMINENT when they first believed in Christ; but time had hurried on since then. Therefore it must now be nearer still. ...If we postulate that *the night is far spent*, the figure conveys the idea of something already NEAR AT HAND.

	The "New Age" Is Impending
	Ephesians 1:21
Concordant Literal New Testament [#4]	(Jesus is Lord)… not only in this eon, but also in that which is ***impending**.
Webster's Seventh New Collegiate Dictionary [#32]	***Impending**: threatening to occur soon : approaching. syn: ****imminent** ****IMMINENT** mean **_threatening to occur very soon_**. IMPENDING implies signs that keep one in suspense; IMMINENT emphasizes **the shortness of time before happening.**
Westcott & Hort [#7]	uperanw pashj archj kai exousiaj kai dunamewj kai kuriothtoj kai pantoj onomatoj onomazomenou ou monon en tw aiwni toutw alla kai en tw ***mellonti**

*Greek: Mello} Paul was promising to these Ephesians that "the new age", i.e. the Second Coming, was on the **POINT** of happening, **about** to occur, **IMPENDING** ("threatening to occur VERY soon), it was…

ON THE **VERGE** OF TAKING PLACE.

1st Timothy 4:8

	A New & Better Life is Coming... Soon!
	1st Timothy 4:8
Weymouth [#2]	Train yourself in godliness. Exercise for the body is not useless, but godliness is useful in every respect, possessing, as it does, the promise of Life now and of **the Life which is *soon* coming**.
Concordant Literal New Testament [#4]	…for bodily exercise is beneficial for a few things, yet devoutness is beneficial for all, having promise for the life which now is, and that which is *IMPENDING.
Westcott & Hort [#7]	h gar swmatikh gumnasia proj oligon estin wfelimoj h de eusebeia proj panta wfelimoj estin epaggelian ecousa zwhj thj nun kai thj **melloushj**

*GREEK: MELLO} On the point of happening, about to occur, **impending, *ON THE VERGE OF TAKING PLACE.*

IMPENDING: threatening to occur soon : approaching. syn: IMPENDING, IMMINENT mean *threatening to occur very soon*. IMPENDING implies signs that keep one in suspense; IMMINENT emphasizes the **shortness of time before happening. Websters Dictionary [#32]

1st Timothy 6:17-19

	Invest In Good Deeds
	Reap Your Heavenly Rewards
	Soon! Really Really Soon!!!
	1st Timothy 6:17-19
Concordant Literal New Testament [#4]	Those who are rich in the **current** eon be charging not to be haughty, nor yet to rely on the dubiousness of riches, but on God, Who is tendering us all things richly for our enjoyment; to be doing good acts, to be rich in ideal acts, to be liberal contributors, **treasuring up for themselves an ideal foundation for that which is** *IMPENDING, that they may get hold of life really.
Westcott & Hort [#7]	19 apoqhsaurizontaj eautoij qemelion kalon eij to *mellon ina epilabwntai thj ontwj zwhj

*Greek: Mello} The "New Age" (eon) was promised by Paul to be on the point of happening, about to occur, impending, *LITERALLY ON THE **VERGE** OF TAKING PLACE.*

103

Second Coming Within Sight

Hebrews 10:25

New International Version [#16]	Let us not give up meeting together, as some are in the habit of doing, but let us encourage one another-- and all the more as you see ***the Day*** approaching.

My Comments

Due to the "signs of the times" they could "see the day," that is, the Second Coming, as being right around the corner, within their grasp. Therefore, they were being told to encourage one another and not give up their meetings in the short meantime.

Commentaries & Quotes

The Parousia Stuart Russell p. 273 [#33]	"The day" means, of course, "the day of the Lord," the time of His appearing, the Parousia. It was now **at hand**; they could **SEE IT APPROACHING**. Doubtless the indications of its approach predicted by our Lord were apparent…
The Prophecy of the Destruction of Jerusalem N. Nisbett (1787 CE) pp.29-30 [#157]	They were now grievously persecuted by their unbelieving countrymen… but the day was **AT HAND**, things were so ripe for the **COMPLETION** of our Lord's **PROPHECIES** [which would include the **Second Coming**], that they saw by the **signs** of the times, that is was near approaching, which would put an end to their troubles. **TWO OR THREE YEARS** # AT THE MOST would find other employment for their adversaries… The day approaching in the 25th verse… meant the destruction of Jerusalem. [NOTE: The destruction of Jerusalem, in 70 CE, was THE major sign that the Second Coming was due to **IMMEDIATELY** follow. In other words, when you saw that, you'd better have your suit cases packed & ready to go.]
Beyond The End Times John Noe p.179 [#253]	In the Bible, "near" never means "far" nor does "far" mean "near." …For example, "as you see the day approaching" (Heb 10:25), and other statements like it, cannot be ignored, twisted, or lightly brushed aside. They are indicative of the nearness and certainty of the **Lord's return**. …**HOW COULD THEY "SEE THE DAY APPROACHING" IF IT WAS** *TWO MILLENNIA LATER?*

Short of Screaming

Fire!!!

Couldn't Have Gotten Their Attention Better To Make
"*NEAR*" Seem Any "*Nearer*"

Hebrews 10:37
Various Translations

Youngs Literal Translation [#3]	For yet a **very, VERY little**, He who is coming will come, and **will not tarry**.
American Standard Version [#10]	For **yet a very little while**, He that cometh shall come, and shall not tarry.
Bible in Basic English [#20]	**In a very little time** he who is coming will come; he will not be slow.
Darby [#21]	For yet a very little while he that comes will come, and **WILL NOT DELAY**.
New International Version [#16]	For in just a **very little while**, "He who is coming will come and will not delay.
Weymouth [#2]	For there is still but a **short time** and then 'The coming One will come and will not delay…'
Concordant Literal New Testament [#4]	For still **how very little**, He Who is coming will be arriving and **NOT DELAYING**.
The Amplified New Testament [#9]	For still a *little* while—a *very* little while—and the Coming One will come and He will not delay.
The New English Bible [#25]	**For soon, very soon**, in the words of Scripture, 'he who is to come will come; he will not delay.'
The Emphasized New Testament [#5]	For yet a little while- how short! how short! The Coming One will be here, and **WILL NOT TARRY**.

Hebrews 10:37 (con't)	
Commentaries & Quotes	
Expositor's Bible Commentary [#200]	The "very little while" points to a **quite short period**.
The Parousia Stuart Russell p. 274 [#33]	That coming was now at hand. The language to this effect is far more expressive of the nearness of the time in the Greek than in English: **"Yet a very, _VERY_ little while"** or, as Tregelles renders it, **"A little while, how little, <u>how little!</u>"** The duplication of the thought in the close of the verse—"will come, and **will <u>_not_</u> tarry**," is also indicative of the certainty and **speed** of the approaching event."

Revelation 6:9-11

Judgment Day: Wait Just a Little Longer!	
Revelation 6:7-11	
Today's English Version [#14]	I looked, and there was a pale-colored horse. Its rider was named **DEATH**, and **HADES** followed close behind. They were given authority over one forth of the earth, to **KILL BY MEANS OF WAR**, famine, disease, and wild animals. …Then the Lamb broke open the fifth seal. I saw underneath the altar the souls of those who had been **KILLED** because they had proclaimed God's word and had been faithful in their witnessing. They shouted in a loud voice, "Almighty Lord, holy and true! **How long** will it be until you <u>JUDGE</u> **the people on earth** and **punish** them for killing us?" Each of them was given a white robe, and they were told to rest **a _little while_ longer**, until the complete number of their fellow servants and brothers were killed, as they had been.
Commentaries & Quotes	
The God Delusion Dawkins p.302 [#230]	Some rapture Christians go further and actually yearn for nuclear war because they interpret it as the "Armageddon" which, according to their bizarre but disturbingly popular interpretation of the Book of Revelation, will hasten the Second Coming.
My Comment	
Seeing how the entire book of Revelation was promised to be fulfilled "any minute now" (Rev. 1:1,3), it follows that this section from the sixth chapter concerning the arrival of **JUDGMENT DAY** would also be due quick, fast, and in a hurry. The Apostle John prophesied to them that they'd only have to wait just "a little while longer" for Judgment Day to commence, and all these cataclysmic events listed be unleashed upon the Earth. John's prophesy turned out false. The Apostle John was a False Prophet.	

Kingdom of God Expected IMMEDIATELY

Luke 19:11

NASB [#1]	And while they were listening to these things, He went on to tell a parable, because He was near Jerusalem, and **they supposed that the kingdom of God was going to appear** <div align="center">***IMMEDIATELY**.</div>
The New Testament in Modern English (Phillips Version) [#15]	…the fact that he was nearing Jerusalem made them imagine that the kingdom of God was **ON THE *POINT OF APPEARING.**
Darby Bible [#21]	…he was near to Jerusalem and they thought that the kingdom of God was about to be ***IMMEDIATELY** manifested.
Disciples' Literal New Testament [#162]	…their thinking that the kingdom of God was <div align="center">**ABOUT TO APPEAR *AT-ONCE.**</div>

*Greek Word "Mello"} On the *POINT* of happening, *ABOUT* to take place, on the very *VERGE* of happening.

Commentaries & Quotes

NIV Study Bible Notes [#254]	They **expected** the Messiah to appear in power and glory and to set up his earthly kingdom, **DEFEATING ALL THEIR POLITICAL AND MILITARY ENEMIES.**

"Near, Soon, Any Minute Now!"

	More Misc. Verses	
Philippians 4:5	The Lord is **near**—He is coming ****SOON**.	Amplified [#9]
	The Lord is ****AT HAND**	RSV [#18]
Romans 16:20	And the God of *peace* will *****SOON** *crush Satan* under your feet.	NASB [#1]
Hebrews 9:11	But Christ appeared as a High Priest of the blessings that are ***SOON** to come	Weymouth [#2]
Hebrews 9:26	Instead now, when *all* ages of time are **NEARING** the end…	TEV [#14]
Hebrews 13:14	For we have no permanent city here, but we are longing for **the city which is *SOON** *to be ours*.	Weymouth [#2]
1st Peter 4:7	The end of **all things** is **NOW** ****close at hand**.	Weymouth [#2]
	And of *all* things *the end hath come* ****NIGH.**	Young's [#3]
1st Peter 4:17	****The time HAS COME** for judgment to begin…	TEV [#14]
1st Peter 5:1	the glory which is ***SOON** to be revealed.	Weymouth [#2]
	the glory ***ABOUT** to be revealed	Young's [#3]
1st John 2:17	the world **IS** passing away	NASB [#1]
Rev 1:1	The revelation given by Jesus Christ…(to) make known to His servants **certain events which MUST ***SHORTLY come to pass.**	Weymouth [#2]
Rev 1:3	Blessed is he who reads… the words of this prophecy… for **the time for its fulfillment is NOW **close at hand.**	Weymouth [#2]

* STRONG'S #3195 MELLO} to be *on the point of* doing or suffering something, on the very VERGE of happening.

** STRONG'S #1448 EGGIZO} to bring *near*, to join one thing to another, to draw or come near to, to approach, of times *imminent* and *soon to come to pass. On the point of doing, not long to wait.*

*** STRONG'S #5034 / #5036 TACHOS / TACHU} *quickness, speed, without delay. As quickly as possible. At once.*

"Near, Soon, Any Minute Now!" (con't)

More Misc. Verses

Rev 3:10-11	… I also will keep you from the hour of testing, that hour which is *about to come* upon the *WHOLE WORLD*, to test those who dwell upon the earth. **I am coming ***QUICKLY**…	NASB [#1]
Rev 22:6-7	And he said to me, "These words are faithful and true… the God of the spirits of the prophets, sent His angel to show to His bond-servants the things which must ***SHORTLY take place*. And behold, *I am coming ***QUICKLY*. Blessed is he who heeds the words of the prophecy of this book.	NASB [#1]
Rev 22:10-20	Make no secret, he added, of the meaning of the **PREDICTIONS** contained in this book; for **the time for their fulfillment is** *NOW* **close at hand**… I am coming ***quickly… **Yes, I am coming QUICKLY**.	Weymouth [#2]

* STRONG'S #3195 MELLO} to be *on the point of* doing or suffering something

** STRONG'S #1448 EGGIZO} to bring *near*, to join one thing to another, to draw or come near to, to approach, of times *imminent* and *soon to come to pass*

*** STRONG'S #5034 / #5036 TACHOS / TACHU} *quickness*, *speed*, *without delay*.

Commentaries & Quotes

The False Prophecies of Joseph Smith [#256]	Remember… according to Deuteronomy 18:20-22, it only takes **ONE FALSE PROPHECY** to make a prophet false, just as it only takes **one** murder to make a person a murderer.

"Near, Soon, Any Minute Now!" (con't)

Commentaries & Quotes

Last Days Madness Gary DeMar [#34]	This is nonsense. **"Soon" means "near in time,"** BEFORE the generation of the apostles who were with Jesus <u>**PASSED AWAY**</u>. Sound Bible interpretation cannot mean that "near" can mean "any moment" when nearly **two thousand years** have passed. (pp.172-173) Why use time markers that in ordinary speech mean <u>**CLOSE AT HAND**</u> if their real meaning **actually stretches time over centuries**? There is no need to be ambiguous about the meaning of "near," "shortly," and "quickly." Translators chose these English words because they convey the proper meaning of their Greek counterparts. (p.284) Every use of "**<u>near</u>**" or "<u>at hand</u>" in the New Testament means **close in relation to time or distance. There are no exceptions**. (p.287)
The Historical Jesus John Crossan pp.235 & 238 [#221]	(John the Baptist's) message was an announcement of **imminent apocalyptic intervention by God**.. Baptism and message went together as the only way to obtain forgiveness **before the fire storm came**. ...The eschatological Jesus is one who thought this was **IMMINENT**.
The Message from Patmos David Clark pp.22-23 [#226]	It would be stretching language to the **BREAKING POINT** to make "**SHORTLY**" mean <div align="center">**<u>SEVERAL</u> <u>THOUSANDS</u> <u>OF YEARS</u>**.</div>
The Interpreter's Bible Vol 7 p.153 [#42]	When the New Testament writers said "**soon**," they meant "soon" <u>**in relation to their own time.**</u>
Beyond The End Times John Noe pp.176-177 [#253]	As well as **TAKING JESUS AT HIS WORD**, we'd be well advised to take the New Testament writers at their word, too. *Bible scholars generally agree that every New Testament writer, all the Apostles, and members of the 1st century church expected that Christ's coming again, his return, parousia, **WOULD OCCUR WITHIN THEIR LIFETIME**.* ...If Jesus's Apostles and first disciples were **WRONG** or **MISGUIDED** in their Spirit-guided expectations of the Lord's return, **WHAT ELSE** might they have been mistaken about?

Brought To You As A Public Service by BibleGod & Son

Acts 17:30-31

	Judgment Day: Soon! *REALLY* Soon!!!		
	Acts 17:30-31		
Weymouth's [#2]	Those times of ignorance God viewed with indulgence. But now He commands all men everywhere to repent, seeing that He has appointed a day on which, ****BEFORE LONG***, He will **JUDGE** the world in righteousness, through the instrumentality of a man whom He has pre-destined to this work, and has made the fact certain to every one by raising Him from the dead."		
Young's Literal Translation [#3]	The times, indeed, therefore, of the ignorance God having overlooked, doth now command all men everywhere to reform, because He did set a day in which He is ***about to JUDGE the world** in righteousness, by a man whom He did ordain, having given assurance to all, having raised him out of the dead.'		
Concordant Literal New Testament [#4]	Forasmuch as He assigns a day in which He is ***about to be** judging the inhabited earth in righteousness by the Man...		
The Emphasized New Testament [#5]	Inasmuch as he hath appointed a day in which he is ***about to be** judging the habitable earth in righteousness...		
The Riverside New Testament [#108]	...since he has set a day in which he will ***_soon_** judge the world in justice...		
Westcott & Hort Greek Text [#7]	31 kaqoti esthsen hmeran en h ***mellei** krinein thn oikoumenhn en dikaiosunh en andri w wrisen pistin parascwn pasin anasthsaj auton ek nekrwn		

Judgment Day: Soon! *REALLY* Soon!!!

Acts 17: 30-31 (con't)

The New Testament Samuel Davidson [#213]	…he appointed a day in which he is ***ABOUT** to judge the world.
The Nestle Greek Text with a Literal English Translation [#6]	Because he set a day in which he is ***about to** judge the inhabited earth in righteousness…

*Greek: Mello} "Mello" means to be on <u>the point of happening</u>, about to occur, impending, about to do something,

ON THE LITERAL **VERGE** *OF TAKING PLACE.*

As one theologian described it, picture a car teetering on the edge of a cliff & about to fall.

Commentaries & Quotes

Who Tampered With The Bible p.172 [#237]	The preeminent expectation of the first Christians was that Jesus would return **imminently**, **END THE WORLD**, and punish their enemies… The expectation of an imminent return of Jesus allowed the earliest evangelists to **recruit converts swiftly** and spread Christianity over a wide geographical area rapidly. The evangelists preached that not only had Jesus risen from the dead, but that he was also expected to **RETURN** **DURING THEIR LIFETIMES** **TO END THE WORLD** and bring the last judgment.
Last Day's Madness, p. 147 [#34]	Such a position strips the Bible of meaning. "**Soon**" and "**near**" *cannot mean* an undetermined period of time.
The Parousia pp.153-154 [#33]	The words "he will judge" do not express a simple future, but a SPEEDY future… He is **ABOUT to judge, or will SOON judge**. This shade of meaning is NOT preserved in our English versions.

My Comments

In the human way of seeing things- and this WAS written BY a human FOR humans- in the human way of seeing things, something that is "about to happen" is due to happen way before 2,000 years, way before 200 years, and most certainly well within 100 years. There is <u>NO WAY</u> to explain this prophecy of Paul, other than to admit he got it wrong, thus making the Apostle Paul a false prophet.

	The Resurrection is On **The Verge** of Happening!
	Acts 24:15
Weymouth's [#2]	and having a hope directed towards God, which my accusers themselves also entertain, that ***BEFORE LONG** there will be a **resurrection** both of the righteous and the unrighteous.
Young's Literal Translation [#3]	having hope toward God, which they themselves also wait for, *that* there is ***about to be** a **rising again** of the dead, both of righteous and unrighteous.
Nestle Greek Text Interlinear [#6]	hope having toward God, which also themselves these expect, a resurrection to be ***about to be** both of just and of unjust.
A Literal Translation of The Bible [#23]	…a resurrection being ***about to be** of the dead, both of just and unjust ones.
Concordant Literal New Testament [#4]	…there shall be a **resurrection** which is ***impending** for both the just and the unjust.
American Heritage Dictionary [#8]	**im·pend** (¹m-pµnd") *v. intr.* **im·pend·ed im·pend·ing im·pends 1.** To be about to take place: *Her retirement is impending.*
Westcott & Hort Greek Text [#7]	elpida ecwn eij ton qeon hn kai autoi outoi prosdecontai anastasin ****mellein** esesqai dikaiwn te kai adikwn

*Greek: Mello} What Paul is PROMISING & PROPHESYING here, in his trial before the Roman Governor Marcus Antonius Felix, is that the RESURRECTION of all the dead in all of the world, followed by Judgment Day (see v. 25), is on the point of happening, it's about to occur, it is…

ON THE VERGE OF TAKING PLACE.

Judgment Day: On The Verge of Happening!

Acts 24:25

Weymouth's [#2]	But when he dealt with the subjects of justice, self-control, and **the JUDGEMENT which was *SOON to come**, Felix became **alarmed** and said, "For the present leave me, and when I can find a convenient opportunity I will send for you."
Young's Literal Translation [#3]	And he reasoning concerning righteousness, and temperance, and **the judgment that is *about to be**, Felix, having become afraid, answered, `For the present be going, and having got time, I will call for thee;'
A Literal Translation of The Bible [#23]	…the Judgment that is *about to be…
Concordant Literal New Testament [#4]	Now as he is arguing concerning righteousness, and self-control, **and the *impending judgment**, Felix became **affrighted**…
Westcott & Hort Greek Text [#7]	dialegomenou de autou peri dikaiosunhj kai egkrateiaj kai tou krimatoj tou ***mellontoj** emfoboj genomenoj o fhlix apekriqh to nun econ poreuou kairon de metalabwn metakalesomai se

*Greek: Mello} Around 55 CE, give or take a few years, Paul was on trial. During this trial he spoke of JUDGMENT DAY to the Roman Governor Felix, predicting it to be on the point of happening, just about to occur, impending,

ON THE **VERGE** OF TAKING PLACE.

This shook up the Governor so much that he had to end the trial early. A threatened "judgment day" thousands of years in his future would *not* have shaken him up nor ended the trial early. But this threat did. It shook him up because it was promised to occur maybe a week, maybe a month, certainly within a few years at the most. That shook the Governor up. The threat, as we all know now, turned out to be bogus. And two thousands years later, it's obviously an empty threat, and a worldwide joke.

"Anti-Christ" & 2nd Coming: First Century

2nd Thessalonians 2:1-8

The New International Version [#16]	1 Concerning **the coming of our Lord Jesus Christ** and our being <u>GATHERED TO HIM</u>, we ask you, brothers, 2 not to become easily unsettled or alarmed by some prophecy, report or letter supposed to have come from us, saying that the day of the Lord has already come. 3 Don't let anyone deceive you in any way, for that day will not come until **the rebellion** occurs and **the man of lawlessness** is revealed, the man doomed to destruction. 4 He will oppose and will exalt himself over everything that is called God or is worshiped, so that **he sets himself up in God's <u>temple</u>, proclaiming himself to be God.** 5 Don't you remember that when I was with you I used to tell you these things? 6 And now **you know what is holding him back**, so that he may be revealed at the proper time. 7 For the secret power of lawlessness is <u>ALREADY</u> at work; but <u>THE ONE WHO NOW HOLDS IT BACK</u> will continue to do so till he is taken out of the way. 8 And then the lawless one will be revealed, whom the Lord Jesus will overthrow with the breath of his mouth and destroy by the splendor of his coming.
The Amplified New Testament [#9]	4 Who opposes and exalts himself so proudly and insolently... even to his actually **taking his seat in the <u>temple</u> of God**, proclaiming that he himself is God.
New Revised Standard Version [#17]	3 Let no one deceive you in any way; for that day will not come unless **the rebellion** comes first and the lawless one is revealed, the one destined for destruction

Commentaries & Quotes

Last Days Madness Gary DeMar p.322-323 [#34]	In his description of the 'man of lawlessness,' Paul makes it clear that he had a **contemporary figure** in mind. First, he tells the Thessalonians that 'the mystery of lawlessness is *already* at work.' Second, the Thessalonians knew what was presently restraining the 'man of lawlessness': 'And you know what restrains him NOW'. Paul does not write, 'You know what *will* restrain him.'...Without ever being able to identify the 'man of lawlessness' **we can conclude that he appeared and disappeared IN THE FIRST CENTURY**. "He expects him to sit in the 'temple of "God,' which perhaps most naturally refers to **the literal temple in Jerusalem**, although the Apostle knew that the out-pouring of God's wrath on the Jews was close at hand, 1TH 2:16...Paul can have nothing else in view than what our Lord described as 'the abomination of desolation which was spoken of by Daniel the prophet, standing in the holy place' (Mt 24:15)." (DeMar, quoting Benjamin B. Warfield in "The Prophecies of St. Paul" in Biblical and Theological Studies, Presbyterian and Reformed, 1968, page 472)

"Anti-Christ" & 2nd Coming: First Century

2nd Thessalonians 2:1-8 (con't)

My Comments

Paul wrote this letter around 51 CE. At that time, the Jewish temple in Jerusalem was still very much a reality. When Paul prophesied that this "anti-Christ" would take a seat in this temple *before* the Second Coming could happen, it was a possibility. However, this temple ceased to exist about twenty years after Paul penned this letter, when Roman soldiers had it flattened. Wisely, none of the Second Coming prophesies in the New Testament that were penned *AFTER* the destruction of the temple mention this tidbit of "taking his seat in the temple".

Per what Paul wrote, Jesus must return **within the lifetime** of this "man of sin" in order to be able to "slay him." And this "man of sin" was *already* being restrained when Paul penned this, and therefore was a man (v. 3) alive in the First Century. This "man of lawlessness" is predicted to take "his seat in the temple". Seeing how the temple ceased to exist in 70 CE, this whole storyline, this prophecy, had to be fulfilled within the First Century, and **BEFORE** the destruction of the temple in 70 CE. But it was not, and that's a fact of history.

Paul clearly prophesied the "Second Coming of Jesus" to occur within the confines of the First Century, even before 70 CE. But we know for a fact that the world was **NOT** destroyed before 70 CE. And we know for a fact that "judgment day" did **not** occur before 70 CE. And thus we know for a FACT that these prophecies of the Parousia were **false**, making the Apostle Paul yet another false prophet mentioned in the New Testament.

"Last Days" = First Century

2nd Timothy 3:1-5

New American Standard Bible [#1]	But realize this, that **_IN_ THE LAST DAYS** difficult times will come. For men will be lovers of self, lovers of money, boastful, arrogant, revilers, disobedient to parents, ungrateful, unholy, unloving, irreconcilable, malicious gossips, without self-control, brutal, haters of good, treacherous, reckless, conceited, lovers of pleasure rather than lovers of God; holding to a form of godliness, although they have denied its power; and **AVOID** such men as these.

My Comments

Paul prophesied that "in the *LAST* days" certain men would be such and such. He then told Timothy to AVOID these "certain men." In order to **AVOID** these men, Timothy AND these men both had to be **ALIVE** at **THE SAME TIME**, that time being "the last days". Therefore, the "Last Days" happened within Timothy's lifetime which itself happened within the First Century. In other words, these "Last Days" are now, 2000 years later, ancient history, showing this to be yet another false prophecy.

	Judgment Day is About to Come
	2nd Timothy 4:1
Weymouth [#2]	I solemnly implore you, in the presence of God and of Christ Jesus who is *about to judge the living and the dead, and by His Appearing and His Kingship:
Young's Literal Translation [#3]	I do fully testify, then, before God, and the Lord Jesus Christ, who is *about to judge living and dead at his manifestation and his reign--
Darby Bible [#21]	I testify before God and Christ Jesus, who is *about to judge living and dead, and by his appearing and his kingdom,
A Literal Translation of The Bible [#23]	Then I solemnly witness before God and the Lord Jesus Christ, *He being *about to judge living and dead at His appearance* and His kingdom:
Concordant Literal New Testament [#4]	I am conjuring you in the sight of God and Christ Jesus, Who is *about to be judging the living and the dead, in accord with His advent and His kingdom.
The Emphasized New Testament [#5]	I adjure thee before God, and Christ Jesus- Who is *about to be judging living and dead…
Westcott & Hort [#7]	diamarturomai enwpion tou qeou kai cristou ihsou tou **mellontoj** krinein zwntaj kai nekrouj kai thn epifaneian autou kai thn basileian autou

*Greek: Mello} Supposedly the Apostle Paul wrote this to his young disciple Timothy in the 1st Century. Paul prophesied to Timothy that the Second Coming & Judgment Day was **on the point of happening**, about to occur, impending,

ON THE **VERGE** OF TAKING PLACE.

But it *wasn't* "on the verge" of happening, as we well know 2000 years later. I really think no one is stepping out on a limb to finally declare that Paul's First Century prophecy of the Second Coming being "**on the verge of taking place**" turned out to be a *false* prophecy, thus making Paul a False Prophet.

Judgment Day is About to Come	
James 2:12	
Concordant Literal New Testament [#4]	Thus be speaking and thus be doing, **as those** ***ABOUT TO BE JUDGED** by a law of freedom.
Young's Literal Translation [#3]	so speak ye and so do, **as *about by a law of liberty to be judged,**
The Emphasized New Testament [#5]	So be speaking, and so doing, as they who through means of a law of freedom are ***about to be judged.**
The NIV Interlinear Greek – English New Testament [#6]	So speak ye and so do ye as through a law of freedom **being** ***about to be judged.**
Westcott & Hort [#7]	outwj laleite kai outwj poieite wj dia nomou eleuqeriaj **mellontej** krinesqai

*GREEK: MELLO} "Mello" means to be on the point of happening, about to occur, impending, about to do something,

ON THE LITERAL *VERGE* OF TAKING PLACE.

Picture a car teetering on the edge of a **cliff**- it's ABOUT to take a fall. Thus by using the Greek word "mello", James was clearly **PROPHESYING** to his readers that **JUDGMENT DAY** was 100% due within just a few years, maybe even months- scout's honor! The prophecy turned out to be <u>FALSE</u>, making the Apostle James a false prophet.

Luke 12:54-56

All Signs Point to The First Century	
Luke 12:54-56	
New American Standard Bible [#1]	And He was also saying to the multitudes, "When you see a cloud rising in the west, immediately you say, 'A shower is ***coming*,**' and so it turns out. And when *you see* a south wind blowing, you say, 'It will be a hot day,' and it turns out *that way*. You hypocrites! You know how to analyze the appearance of the earth and the sky, but why do you not analyze this **<u>PRESENT</u>** time?

	2nd Coming Past Due: **Should Have _Already_ Happened**	
	1st Peter 3:22	
New American Standard Bible [#1]	(Jesus)… who is at the right hand of God, having gone into heaven, *after* angels and authorities and powers **had** been subjected to Him.	
The New International Version [#16]	(Jesus)… who **has** gone into heaven and **is** at God's right hand-- with angels, authorities and powers **in submission** to him.	
	My Comments	

Using the Bible to interpret the Bible, the above verse shows that the Second Coming should have already happened}

➤ Jesus will return **when** he abolishes **authorities** and **death**. *(1Cor 15:22-26)

  ➤ Jesus (1ˢᵗ Century) **has** already abolished **death**. **(2 Tim 1:10)
  ➤ Jesus (1ˢᵗ Century) **has** already abolished **authorities**. (1 Pet 3:22)
➤ THOSE CONDITIONS WERE ALL MET IN THE FIRST CENTURY, BUT JESUS NEVER SHOWED UP, THUS MAKING PETER & PAUL FALSE PROPHETS.

****

*For as in Adam all die, so also in Christ all shall be made alive. But each in his own order: Christ the first fruits, after that those who are Christ's **at His coming, then** *comes* **the end**, when He delivers up the kingdom to the God and Father, **when** He has abolished **all rule and all authority and power**. For He must reign *until* He has put *all* His enemies under His feet. The last enemy that **will be** abolished is **death**.   (1ˢᵗ Cor 15:22-26 NASB [#1])

But now has been revealed by the appearing of our Savior Christ Jesus, **who *abolished* **death**, and brought life and immortality to light through the gospel…   (2ⁿᵈ Tim 1:10 NASB [#1])

	The Last Time is _NOW_
	Jude 17-18
RSV [#18]	But you must remember, beloved, the **predictions** of the apostles of our Lord Jesus Christ; they said to you, "In the **LAST TIME there will be scoffers**…"
	My Comments

The "scoffers" Jude is complaining about who would be alive "**in the last time**," are the very same people who, in verse four, he said were _ALREADY_ living among the people who first received Jude's letter. Yet again, the "last time" is placed firmly within the First Century.

May/June   33 AD
"These Are The Last Days"

According to the <u>Book of Acts</u>, in the first official speech proclaiming Christianity to an unbelieving world, Peter explained to a crowd that the drunken behavior of his comrades was ***not*** the result of being **drunk**, oh no! It was *rather* a sign that "<u>the last days</u>" had already arrived. Peter explained-

But <u>*this*</u> **IS** <u>*that*</u> which hath been spoken through the prophet Joel:

And it shall be **in the <u>*last*</u> days**, saith God, I will pour forth of My Spirit…

Peter's *"<u>this</u>"* thus refers to the strange behavior going on, while his *"<u>that</u>"* refers to sure signs that indicate the last days have already arrived, and his *"is"* equates the two, thus proving (in Peter's "inspired" mind at least), that "the last days" had already arrived.

In the "Last Days"}

- BibleGod will pour forth his spirit
- People will prophesy
- People will see visions
- People will dream
- Great wonders and signs in the sky. & on the earth
- Blood & fire & vapor of smoke
- Sun turned into darkness
- Moon turned into blood
- Everyone who calls on the name of the lord shall be saved
- *THEN*… "the great and glorious <u>**day of the lord**</u> (i.e. The 2nd Coming) shall come"

Acts 2:15-21 New American Standard Bible   [#1]

Acts 2:15-17 ASV [#10]	For these are not drunken... But ***<u>this is that</u>*** which hath been spoken through the prophet Joel: And it shall be **in the <u>*last*</u> days**, saith God, I will pour forth of My Spirit upon all flesh…
Hebrews 1:1-2 KJV [#19]	God…hath in ***THESE*** **last days** spoken unto us by *his* Son.
1st Peter 1:20 Weymouth [#2]	He was pre-destined indeed to this work, even before the creation of the world, but **has been plainly manifested in *THESE* <u>last days</u>** …
James 5:3 NASB [#1]	Your gold and your silver have rusted; and their rust will be a witness against you… It is **in the last days** that you ***have*** stored up your treasure!
Rev 3:10-11 NASB [#1]	…the hour of testing, that hour which is ***about to come** upon the whole world… I am coming *****quickly**.
Rev 22:6-7 NASB [#1]	…sent His angel to show His servants the things which **must ***shortly take place**. And behold, I am coming *****quickly**.
Rev 22:10, 12, 20 NASB [#1]	Do not seal up the words of … this book, for **the time is **NEAR**… Behold, I am coming *****quickly**… Yes, I am coming *****quickly**.

*Greek: Mello} On the **VERGE** of happening, **ABOUT** to happen, Impending!

Greek: Eggizo/Engus} **On the point of doing, will happen SOON, not a long time to wait!

***Greek: Tachos/Tachu} As **QUICKLY AS POSSIBLE**, at once, **WITHOUT DELAY!!!**

1st John 2:18 NASB [#1]	Children, it is the **last *hour***... we **know** that **It is** **the** **last** # HOUR !! (NOTE: The letters of John, written in the 90's of the First Century, are some of the last books of the New Testament to be penned. And the prophesied "due date", the "countdown," has now gone from **days** to mere *hours*.)

Commentaries & Quotes

God's Problem Dr. Bart Ehrman p. 247 [#232]	But the sad reality is that I don't think the **Book of Revelation**... was written with us in mind. It was **written for people living in the AUTHOR'S own day**... It was anticipating that **THE END** would come in the **AUTHOR'S OWN TIME**. When the author of Revelation expected that the Lord Jesus "was coming soon" (Rev 22:20), he really meant "soon"—**not two thousand years later**.
James the Brother of Jesus Dr. Robert Eisenman [#235]	This last allusion, again incorporating the imagery of "Power" and applied to the **imminent return of Jesus** in Scripture, will not only be at the heart of James' Messianic proclamation in the Temple... (pp.362-363) James' **apocalyptic** proclamation in the Temple at Passover- presumably 62 CE, but possibly before too- of the **imminent coming of the Messiah** and the Heavenly Host with Power on the clouds of Heaven. (p.417) (Around 62 CE) in Hegesippus' account, the Scribes and Pharisees are constrained not only to recognize James' following "among the people" as a popular charismatic leader, but also to utilize it in damping down the **rampant Messianic agitation and expectation**. This picture of rampant, energized Messianism is borne out not only by Josephus' ascription of the final cause of the Uprising against Rome... (p.419) Eusebius, quoting from Hegesippus, now continues his description of the tumultuous events (around 62 CE): ...So the Scribes and the Pharisees made James stand... on the Pinnacle of the Temple... and he answered, shouting out loudly, "Why do you ask me concerning the Son of Man? He is now sitting in Heaven at the right hand of the Great Power and is **ABOUT TO COME** on the clouds of Heaven." (p.423)

"*These* Are The Last Days"

Commentaries & Quotes (con't)

The Case Against Christianity Dr. Michael Martin pp.117-118 [#236]	His ministry was **BASED ON AN ERROR**. But why not **admit** that Jesus was **MISTAKEN** and change Christian doctrine? …if **Jesus was** # WRONG about the nearness of Parousia or the Kingdom of God, he could have been mistaken that the Parousia or the Kingdom of God was coming at all. In addition, he might have been mistaken that one should turn the other cheek and love one's neighbor.
Who Tampered With The Bible Patricia Eddy p.116-117 [#237]	The earliest Christians believed in an **IMMINENT SECOND COMING** of Christ with an attendant **APOCALYPSE**. Not only did they believe this, they did so conspicuously, throwing the notion that the other residents of this world would die in the ensuing conflagration in their neighbors' faces. …their neighbors assumed that they simply **HATED** all humanity.

Jesus Made Mistakes

	## Jesus Wasn't Perfect ### He Made Mistakes
World's Last Night C.S. Lewis pp.97-100 [#74]	**Jesus' "Human" Side Goofed** But there is worse to come. "Say what you like" we shall be told*, "the apocalyptic beliefs of the first Christians have been **proved to be false**. It is clear from the New Testament that they all expected the Second Coming in their own **lifetime**. And, worse still, **they had a reason, and one which you will find very embarrassing. <u>Their</u> <u>Master</u> <u>had</u> <u>told</u> <u>them</u> <u>so</u>.** He shared, and indeed *created*, their ## <u>DELUSION</u>. He said in so many words, 'this generation shall not pass till all these things be done.' ## *And he [Jesus] was* # *WRONG.* He clearly knew no more about the end of the world than anyone else." It is certainly **the most <u>embarrassing</u> verse in the Bible**. …The one exhibition of **error** and the one confession of **ignorance** grow side by side. …The facts, then, are these: that Jesus professed himself (in some sense) **ignorant**, and within a moment **showed that he really *was* so**. …if he said he could be ignorant, **then <u>ignorant</u> <u>he</u> <u>could</u> <u>really</u> <u>be</u>**. …we ought to expect that the ignorance should at some time be actually displayed. *[NOTE: That is, told by a hypothetical Atheist. Lewis does not appear to disagree with what his Atheist is saying here. -MS]
A Commentary on the Revelation of John George Ladd p.22 [#154]	John, like the *entire* [early] Christian community, thought that the coming of the Lord was **NEAR**, when in fact *they were*  Our Lord *Himself* seems to **share this error** in perspective.

124

ANY Explanation Except *THAT* One

My Comments

In the gospels, when Jesus talks of the "Son of Man" coming within the lifetime of his Apostles, he is talking about his **Second Coming** and **Judgment Day**. He is *NOT*, I repeat, NOT talking about

- ➢ "The Mount of Transfiguration"
- ➢ "The Coming of the Spiritual Kingdom at Pentecost"
- ➢ "The Resurrection of the Savior from the Dead"
- ➢ "The Founding of the Church"
- ➢ "The Destruction of Jerusalem in 70 AD"
- ➢ "The Diffusion of Christianity in the World"
- ➢ "The Triumphant Historical Development of the Gospel"
- ➢ "The Powerful Influences of the Spirit of the Glorified Messiah as Extending Over the World"
- ➢ "The (invisible) Second Coming of Jesus in 70AD"
- ➢ "The (invisible) Destruction of The World"

Believe it or not, all these excuses have been presented, at one time or another, as "explanations" of what Jesus *"really"* meant in Matthew 10, Matthew 16, Matthew 24 etc. As you can see, these outlandish "explanations" are just wild attempts to **save the savior** from being labeled a false prophet, which is the simplest and most obvious explanation. It is easy to see from the desperation in these excuses that any explanation or nonsense will do, other than what Jesus clearly said on the subject of the Second Coming- that he would visibly return within the lifetime of his Apostles.

Just because theologians have managed to be creative enough to cough up these unlikely "explanations" that have a "one in a million chance" of being true, these hairbrained concocted "explanations" do NOT somehow cancel out the most **likely** conclusion: that Jesus said what he meant, and meant what he said. Many

The Three Shell Con Game

theologians, when dealing with the topic of the Parousia, like to bring up that there are **dozens** of contradictory "explanations" other than the obvious. They do this like a con man playing the old "THREE SHELL CON GAME," in order to leave everybody confused as to which shell the truth might actually be hiding under. They do all this to DIVERT ATTENTION away from the most obvious and simplest explanation, hoping to confuse people to the point where they just give up trying to understand it, and walk away muttering *"it's just another mystery above my pay grade."* The theologian's con game is to get everyone to think that all these "explanations" carry equal weight, and therefore we all can just forget about ever drawing a hard conclusion, and leave the matter up in the air. What they do NOT want people to do is to believe what Jesus actually DID promise, which is to return within the First Century. If people were to believe THAT, THAT would put THEM out of business, as the prophet they are trying to "sell" to everyone would have been exposed as a *FALSE* Prophet, and that's harder to sell.

Christian Dishonesty

The Quest of the Historical Jesus Albert Schweitzer p.20 [#36]	*There is no justification for TWISTING THIS ABOUT or explaining it away. *(Re: Matt 16:28, a Second Coming passage.)
The Jerome Biblical Commentary p.106 [#94]	The affirmation that "all these things" will happen in **this** generation is *clear*, and there is *no reason* to **alter** the meaning of the word "generation" from its usual sense except a fear that *the Scriptures may be in error if it is not so altered*.
The Parousia Stuart Russell [#33]	Often as our Lord reiterates the assurance that He *would* come in His kingdom, come in glory, come to judge His enemies and reward His friends, *before the generation then living on earth had wholly passed away*, there seems an almost invincible **repugnance** on the part of **theologians** to **accept** His words *in their plain and obvious* sense. They **persist** in supposing that He **must** have meant something else or something more. (p.136) Far, however, from *accepting* this decision of our Lord as final, the commentators have **violently resisted** that which seems the **natural** and **common-sense** meaning of His words. They have insisted that because the events predicted did *not* so come to pass in *that* generation, therefore the word generation **cannot** *possibly* mean, what it is *usually* understood to mean, the people of that particular age or period, the **contemporaries** of our Lord. ...It is the business of *grammarians* not to be apprehensive of possible **consequences**, but to settle the true meaning of words. Our Lord's predictions may be safely left to take care of themselves; it is for us to try to understand them. (p.84) As it stands, all is perfectly clear and intelligible; but **the exegesis of a theologian** can render it turbid and **obscure** indeed. (p.45)
Reasonable Faith Wm. Lane Craig, pp. 36-37 [#130]	… it's the Holy Spirit who gives us the **ultimate** assurance of Christianity's truth. Therefore, the **only** role left for argument and *evidence* to play is a *subsidiary* role. ...Should a conflict arise *between* the witness of the Holy Spirit [the "**Holy Ghost**"] to the fundamental truth of the Christian faith **and** beliefs based on argument and **evidence**, then it is the former [the "**Holy Ghost**"] which must take precedence over the latter [evidence and arguments], and not vice versa. ...*as long as reason* is a *minister* [i.e. **servant**] of the Christian faith, Christians should employ it. ...The Holy Spirit teaches us *directly* which teaching is really from God **AUTHOR'S NOTE:** Notice that objective, factual **evidence** which goes *against* what some inner voice ("Holy Spirit") tells the Christian, is to be *rejected*. Regardless of the amount or weight of evidence, he wants Christians to go with their feelings instead. Notice also the admission that, for the Christian, reason is *optional*, to be used "as long as" it supports his religion. When reason goes *against* his religion, it is reason that must go, *not* religion. With such an approach to evidence and reason, men would still be living in caves and barking at the moon. ************************ **AUTHOR'S NOTE**: Many years ago, while giving Dr. Craig the benefit of the doubt, I assumed when I first read these statements in his book "Reasonable Faith" that there was no way he could believe this. Surely, I thought, he couldn't have meant what was printed on the pages before me. So I went in person to hear him give a talk at Calvary Chapel in Costa Mesa, California, and afterwards spoke to him about these passages for about 20 minutes. The conclusion? On page 37 of my copy of his book, he willingly signed his John Hancock to these statements in the space I provided, to show that he still was of this mindset: *I still agree with what I wrote on page 36 & 37* *x William L. Craig* Date: *26 Aug 98*

Christian Dishonesty (con't)

Bible Review Marcus Borg August 1994 p.16 [#201]	But to mainline scholars, the transfer of these [eschatological] texts to a future time seems **unwarranted**. The *only possible justification* is the **claim** that the Bible is infallible and inerrant, and that *therefore* what it says about the end of the world will someday come to pass (for it *cannot* be wrong). Without this **assumption**, one would *never* think of transferring to *our* time these late first-century beliefs about the second coming.
Last Days Madness DeMar [#34]	*Every* Bible commentator **danced around the text** (of Mt. 24:34 "this generation")...not sound Bible interpretation. [p. 3] |||| The **time texts** are *made* to conform to an **already**-developed theological system. [p. 289] |||| A *literal* hermeneutic...is cleverly avoided... *when* it comes to the plain meaning of certain **time texts** that do **not** support his position. [p. 289]

Apocalypse of The Gospels
Milton Terry
p.34 [#120]
	The various meanings which, under the **pressure** of a **dogmatic [crisis],** have been put upon the phrase **"this generation"** must appear *in the highest degree absurd* to an **unbiased** critic. It has been explained as meaning:
	   ▪ The Human Race (Jerome)
	   ▪ The Jewish Race (Dorner, Auberlen)
	   ▪ The Race of Christian Believers (Chrysotom, Lange)

The Great Tribulation David Chilton p.3 [#126]	In fact, those who say it ["generation"] means "race" tend to acknowledge this fact, but explain that the word *suddenly changes its meaning* when Jesus uses it in Matthew 24! We can smile at such a transparent **error,** but we should also remember that this is *very serious*. We are dealing with the Word of the living God.
Matthew 24 Fulfilled John Bray p.216 [#158]	Many commentators **play around with** the word 'generation' (genea), and **thinking to *avoid embarrassment*,** project its application to the generation which will *be* alive during the last days immediately preceding the Second Coming of the Messiah... such **VERBAL GAMES** are soon exposed as being *nothing* but ARMCHAIR GYMNASTICS.
The Life of Jesus Critically Examined David Strauss p.587 [#76]	...the word *genea... was **put to the TORTURE,** that it might **cease** to bear witness against this [theology of gaps]. *"This generation (Greek: *genea) shall not pass away, until all these things take place"* (Jesus, Gospel of Matthew 24:34)
How To Defend The Christian Faith John R. Loftus [#218]	Professors in evangelical institutions are **NOT ALLOWED TO BE HONEST SCHOLARS**. That is a fact. They are not allowed to think and write freely. If they step out of line, **THEY ARE FIRED**. ..More than a few evangelical scholars have been fired. ...Because of these and other censorings, I consider honest evangelical scholarship a **RUSE**. There is no such thing. (p.78) Moses didn't write the first five books of the Bible... There are clear and obvious instances of **FORGED TEXTS THAT MADE IT INTO THE NEW TESTAMENT**. The Book of Jude is quoting as authoritative into scripture a **FORGED** text ("The Book of Enoch")! ...The four canonical gospels have names attached to them who did **NOT** write them. ...Modern Christians translators even **LIE** when translating from the original languages of these texts... She (Candida Moss, professor of New Testament at Univ. of Notre Dame) exposes the so-called Age of Martyrs as a **FICTION**... pious exaggerations... There is a fascinating and well-researched book called, what else, **LIARS FOR JESUS**. ...William Lane Craig is a **LIAR FOR JESUS**... he lied to win the debate. ...I would think if Christianity is true, then Christians wouldn't have to **lie for Jesus**. (pp.178-187) Typical Christian. Do or say **anything** that can be said in order to **save one's faith**. ...They are **not interested in the truth**. That's what a brain **overdosing on faith** does... The goal is clear. Try to find a way to **exonerate** God... (p.204 & 240)

Christian Dishonesty (con't)

The Five Gospels p.1 [#11]	American biblical scholarship retreated into the closet. The fundamentalist mentality generated a **CLIMATE OF INQUISITION** that made honest scholarly judgments **DANGEROUS**.
Forged Dr. Bart Ehrman [#234]	I want my readers to think more deeply about the role of **LIES** and **DECEPTION** in the history of the Christian religion. I want to show the irony in the fact that lies and deception **HAVE HISTORICALLY BEEN USED TO ESTABLISH THE "TRUTH"**. I want my readers to see that there may be **FORGERIES** in the New Testament. (pp.170-171) So once more we have one of the great ironies of the early Christian religion: some of its leading spokespersons appear to have had **NO QUALMS ABOUT <u>LYING</u>** in order to promote the faith, to practice **DECEPTION** in order to establish the truth. (p.178) The <u>**VAST MAJORITY**</u> of these apostolic books [in early Christianity] were in fact **FORGED**. Christians intent on establishing what was **RIGHT** to believe did so by telling **LIES**, in an attempt to **DECEIVE THEIR READERS** into agreeing that they were the ones who spoke the truth. (p.218) Whoever added the **FINAL TWELVE VERSES OF MARK** did not do so by a mere **SLIP OF THE PEN**. …The use of **DECEPTION** to <u>**PROMOTE THE TRUTH**</u> may well be considered one of the most unsettling ironies of the early Christian tradition. (p.250)
The Case Against Christianity Dr Michael Martin p.119 [#236]	One must conclude that the Second Coming doctrine of Orthodox Christianity is **mistaken** and that the only reason it continues to be maintained today is that apologists have reinterpreted Scripture in an **IMPLAUSIBLE** way in order to SAVE CHRISTIANITY FROM REFUTATION.
Treatise on The Gods H.L. Mencken p.230-231 [#239]	Says Cardinal Newman in his "Apologia Pro Vita Sua": "The Greek Fathers thought that, when there was a *justa causa*, **AN UNTRUTH NEED NOT BE A LIE.**" Augustine… himself freely **SUPPRESSED INCONVENIENT FACTS**, and so did Eusebius, the father of church history. Eusebius specialized in accounts of martyrdoms, and **INVENTED** many of the fantastic stories that are still believed. Jerome, one of the most high-minded of the Fathers, was convinced that is was **PERFECTLY PROPER TO EMBELLISH THE FACTS** when they seemed insufficient to enforce a godly point, and defended the custom by showing that • Origen • Eusebius • Methodius • Cyprian • Minutius Hilary had followed it. He even added (the Apostle) Paul, whose arguments against the Jews had been **FULL OF QUOTATIONS DISCREETLY STRETCHED**.

Christian Dishonesty (con't)

Jesus: Apocalyptic Prophet of The New Millennium Dr. Bart Ehrman [#240]	Some Christians have refused to take the teachings of Jesus at **FACE VALUE**, denying that his words could **MEAN** what they say. (p.18) If we were to tally up these data to this point, we'd have a fairly compelling subtotal. **EARLY TRADITIONS** record apocalyptic teachings on the lips of Jesus. Later traditions generally **MUTE** this emphasis. And the latest of our early sources **EXPLICITLY ARGUE <u>AGAINST</u> IT**. I'd say we have a trend. (p.132) The **EARLIEST** souces that we have consistently ascribe an **APOCALYPTIC** message to Jesus. This message **BEGINS TO BE MUTED** by the end of the first century (e.g. in Luke), until it **VIRTUALLY DISAPPEARS** (e.g. in John), and begins, then, to be explicitly **REJECTED** and spurned (e.g. in Thomas). It appears that when the end **NEVER DID ARRIVE**, Christians had to take stock of the fact that Jesus said it would and **<u>CHANGED HIS MESSAGE</u>** accordingly. You can hardly blame them. (p.134)
The True Believer Eric Hoffer p.76 [#242]	It is the true believer's ability to "**SHUT HIS EYES AND STOP HIS EARS**" to **FACTS** that do not deserve to be either seen or heard which is the source of his unequaled fortitude and constancy. He cannot be frightened by danger, nor disheartened by obstacle, **NOR BAFFLED BY CONTRADICTIONS**, because he **DENIES THEIR EXISTENCE**. **Strength of faith... manifests itself _not_ in moving mountains, but in _NOT SEEING_ mountains to move.**
Evolving Out of Eden Price & Suominen p.112 [#243]	James Barr once pointed out how Bible inerrantists are by no means literalists, though they would like to think they are. No, Barr says, inerrantists will resort to any **HARMONIZATION**, any **FIGURATIVE**, any **STRAINED INTERPRETATION**, in short, any non-literal interpretation of a difficult text to make the text seem inerrant.
Twilight of The Idols Friedrich Nietzsche p.166 [#244]	Buddhism makes no promises but **keeps them**; Christianity makes a thousand promises but **keeps _none_**.
Forgery in Christianity Joseph Wheless [#246]	Many spurious books were **forged** in the earliest times of the church." (p.xxviii) The greatest zealots in religion, or the leaders of sects and parties, whatever purity or principles they **pretend** to, have seldom scrupled to make use of a commodious **lie** for the advancement of what they call the **truth**. (p.xxviii) The Fathers laid down... that **pious frauds** were justifiable and even laudable. (p.xxix)

Christian Dishonesty (con't)

My Comments

When I originally started my study of The Second Coming, I had a basic trust of Christian scholars. By the time I finished, that trust had evaporated. Many Christian scholars and clergymen, I have learned, have been more than willing, even eager, for the past 2,000 years, to lie, deceive, and mis-direct people, all in order to preserve their jobs, and save their "savior" Jesus. But maybe all this lying should have been expected; after all, they have only been continuing the examples of Jesus & his Apostles, who falsely prophesied (i.e. flat out lied) about The Second Coming time & time again.

When Anybody Else But Jesus...

...makes false prophecies,
Christians *CRUCIFY* them.

The way Christians would have it, no other sacred cows, except *their* sacred cows, are allowed to make false prophecies without being crucified. What Christians so **LOUDLY** condemn in other religions like the Mormons and the Jehovah Witnesses, is SILENTLY CONDONED- and excused- within their own. Christians being hypocrites- imagine that!

A perfect example of this is the Christian ministry known as "Saints Alive." This ministry, founded by Ed Decker, specializes is skewering the Christian offshoot religion commonly known as Mormonism. It seems that Rev. Ed is upset that the Mormons have been making **false prophecies**. "How dare they! That's our gig!" (Just kidding.) But it does seem that when *other* false prophets make false prophecies, the Christian scholars conveniently "remember" how to use a dictionary. What Ed Decker doesn't seem to notice, though, is that the Mormons are repeating, almost word for word, the *same* catch phrases and slogans found within the New Testament, so when Ed condemns the Mormon's Joseph Smith he's also, without knowing it, condemning his own Jesus.

This information listed here is from the online essay: "**And It Didn't Come To Pass: A Shocking Look At The So-Called Prophecies of Joseph Smith**" by Ed Decker and William Schnoebelen. The essay was originally found about 10+ years ago or so at the following WEB site:
http://www.saintsalive.com/mormonism/falseprophetjs.htm

For an edited version of that older website which, among other things, has removed the embarrassment of condemning Joe for his "generation" comment, see the bibliography [#256].

New Testament Prophecies By Jesus & Co.	Equivalent Mormon Prophecies By Joseph Smith	Saints Alive Web Page Bashing Mormon Prophecies while Ignoring Similar Bible Prophecies
Jesus Christ: 1st Century All these things (end of world, Second Coming, Judgment Day) would happen **within that generation**, "**before the people now living [33 AD] have all died**." Mt 24:34 TEV [#14]	**Joseph Smith: 1800's** A certain temple would be built by the "**generation then living**" and "**during *that* generation**" (para. 2)	**Ed Decker: 1991 AD** "Allowing the widest possible latitude of **100 years** for a *generation*, that still leaves the prophecy *unfilled*..." (para. 2) "No one is now left alive from that generation... That generation has passed by before the end of the 19th century." (para. 30)
New Testament: 1st Century The Lord is **near**—He is coming **soon**. He is **about to be** judging the inhabited earth in righteousness by the Man... Phil. 4:5 Amp. [#9] & Acts 17:30-31 CLNT [#4]	**Joseph Smith: 1832 AD** Some Old Testament prophecies were "**about to be fulfilled**" and were "**soon to be**" fulfilled. (para. 4)	**Ed Decker: 1991 AD** "More than 165 years have passed...Joseph Smith sure got [his] dates *wrong*!" (para. 4)

When Anybody Else But Jesus... (con't)

New Testament: 1st Century	Joseph Smith: 1832 AD	Ed Decker: 1991 AD
"So you also, when you see all these signs, may be sure that **He is near**--at *your very door*.." Matt 24:33 NASB [#1]	"The… dreadful day of the Lord is **near**, **even at the doors**." (para. 14)	"Over **150 years** have passed, and that "dreadful day of the Lord" has not come. **Another failed prophecy!**" (para. 14)
New Testament: 1st Century And this do, knowing the *time*, that **it is already *the hour*…** Romans 13:11 NASB [#1]	**Joseph Smith: 1832 AD** "Prepare ye the way of the Lord… for the **hour** of his coming is **nigh**." (para. 28)	**Ed Decker: 1991 AD** "This prophecy was given nearly **160 years ago**, and has still not occurred. That is **stretching the meaning of the word 'nigh' to the breaking point!**" (para. 28) "Any *reasonable reading* of the words **'nigh'** and **'soon'** would indicate Smith was prophesying the coming of the Lord *in his lifetime*." (para. 48)
New Testament: 1st Century "…there are some of those who are standing here **who shall not taste death** *until* they see the *Son of Man* coming in His kingdom." Matt 16:28 NASB (#1)	**Joseph Smith: 1832 AD** "Were I to prophesy, I would say the end [of the world] would come… in <u>forty</u> years. There are those of the rising generation ***who shall not taste death*** till Christ comes." (para. 41)	**Ed Decker: 1991 AD** "Obviously, **none** of the 'rising generation' ever saw Jesus' coming… A century has passed since that date; and **Smith's prophecy lies dead and buried** along with that 'rising **generation**.'" (para. 41) "Another ***blatantly false prophecy!***" (para. 46)

My Comments

CHRISTIANS- PRACTICE WHAT YOU PREACH: STOP BEING HYPOCRITES

You are not to be as the hypocrites… (Matthew 6:5 NASB [#1])

Woe to you, scribes and Pharisees, hypocrites… (Matthew 23:13, 14, 15, 23, 25, 27, 29 NASB [#1])

You hypocrites! (Matthew 15:7; 22:18; Luke 12:56; 13:15 NASB [#1])

You, then, who teach others, do you not teach yourself? You who preach against stealing, do you steal? You who say that people should not commit adultery, do you commit adultery?

(Romans 2: 21, 22 NIV [#16])

****

HYPOCRISY: CONDEMNING AS FALSE THE "PROPHET" JOSEPH SMITH WHEN ALL HE'S DONE IS REPEAT ALMOST VERBATIM WHAT THE "PROPHET" JESUS PROPHESIED.

WHEN YOU CONDEMN *JOE*

YOU'VE CONDEMNED *JESUS*

RAILING AGAINST FALSE PROPHECY IN *OTHER* RELIGIONS WHILE IGNORING IT WITHIN YOUR *OWN* = *HYPOCRISY*

When Anybody Else But Jesus... (con't)

Commentaries & Quotes

Blaming Jesus for Jehovah Dr.Robert Price pp.108-109 [#203]	Christians don't mind poking fun (to put it mildly) at Jehovah's Witnesses for setting a series of dates for the predicted Second Coming of Christ. It was scheduled for 1914, with no visible result. Several recalculations were no more accurate. **Mainstream Christians, while shaking their heads at the follies of these sectarians, are suffering from a far more <u>SERIOUS CASE OF</u> AMNESIA**. It never occurs to them that their **OWN** religion suffered **the very same ghastly embarrassment** at the very beginning. That's when their Christ predicted he would revisit the earth *before* the generation of his contemporaries had passed away. The gospels have him making this obviously failed prophecy not just **ONCE**, but **SEVERAL** times... If words mean ANYTHING, these passages ALL depict Jesus predicting his return **well before the close of the first century A.D.** Looked at the calendar lately?
Why I Believed Kenneth Daniels p.218 [#204]	As a believer I had often heard evangelicals **making fun** of Jehovah's Witnesses for their **failed prophecies** of Jesus' return, yet I was for many years effectively oblivious to **the SAME problem** in the New Testament.

	Ethics for La La Land
	Follow These Teachings of Jesus & You'll Be Broke, Homeless, & Miserable Within a Year- *Guaranteed!*
Luke 14:26 NASB [#1]	If anyone comes to Me and does not *HATE his own father and mother and wife and children… he cannot be My disciple. ------------------------------------- *NOTE: For any who've been told that "hate" doesn't mean "hate" in this verse, please consult the "Happy Father's Day" page in my website: http://jcnot4me.com/page16.html
The Gospel of Matthew NASB [#1]	Everyone who looks at a woman with lust for her has already committed adultery with her in his heart. If your right eye makes you stumble, **TEAR IT OUT** and throw it from you." (Mt 5:28-29) **DO NOT RESIST AN EVIL PERSON**; but whoever slaps you on your right cheek, turn the other to him also. (Mt 5:39) If anyone wants to sue you and take your shirt, **LET HIM HAVE YOUR COAT ALSO**. (Mt 5:40) **GIVE** to him who asks of you, and <u>**DO NOT TURN AWAY**</u> from him who wants to **BORROW** from you. (Mt 5:42) **DO NOT STORE UP FOR YOURSELVES TREASURES ON EARTH**… (Mt 6:19) **DO NOT BE WORRIED ABOUT YOUR LIFE**, as to what you will eat or what you will drink… Look at the birds of the air, that they do not sow, nor reap nor gather into barns, and yet your heavenly Father feeds them. Are you not worth much more than they? (Mt. 6:25-26) So **DO NOT WORRY ABOUT TOMORROW**; for tomorrow will care for itself. Each day has enough trouble of its own. (Mt. 6:34)
1st Cor 7:26-31 Today's English Version [#15]	…are you **unmarried**? Then **DON'T LOOK FOR A WIFE** …there is **not much time left**… this world… **will not last much longer!!!**
	Commentaries & Quotes
Treatise on The Gods H.L. Mencken p.233 [#239]	The ethical teachings of Jesus did not long survive the <u>ABANDONMENT</u> of hopes for the Second Coming. …they soon collided, not only with immediate human needs, but also with the eternal nature of man, and so they had to be **modified**. So long as it was believed that the end of the world was **at hand** it all was well enough to be <u>POOR</u> and humble, but when years of uncertainty began to stretch ahead, every man of any prudence had to take thought for his own security, and that of his family. Thus the Beatitudes were discreetly **FORGOTTEN**, and the immemorial game of dog-eat-dog was resumed.

134

Ethics for La La Land

Commentaries & Quotes (con't)

Merriam-Webster Online Dictionary [#254]	**Interim Ethics:** *An interpretation of the ethical teachings of Jesus as principles enunciated for governing the conduct of the disciples during the ANTICIPATED* BRIEF **span** *of time BEFORE the coming of the second advent & the passing of the terrestrial world.*
The Quest of the Historical Jesus Albert Schweitzer p.400-401 [#36]	…notice how they have **WEAKENED DOWN** His imperative world-contemning [i.e. contempt for the world] demands upon individuals, that He might not come into conflict with our ethical ideals, and might tune **HIS** denial of the world to our **ACCEPTANCE** of it. Many of the greatest sayings [of Jesus from the gospels] are found lying in a corner like explosive shells from which the charges have been removed. …If we have known Christ after the flesh, yet henceforth **KNOW WE HIM NO MORE**.
Jesus: Apocalyptic Prophet of The New Millennium Dr. Bart Ehrman p.244 [#240]	From the historical perspective that I've tried to maintain here, what is clear is that the **APOCALYPTIC JESUS** we've uncovered is a far cry from the Jesus many people in our society today know. The Jesus of history, contrary to modern "**common sense**" …was **NOT** a proponent of "**FAMILY VALUES**." He urged his followers to **ABANDON** their homes and **FORSAKE** families for the sake of the Kingdom that was soon to arrive. He didn't encourage people to pursue fulfilling careers, make a good living, and work for a just society for the **LONG HAUL**; for him, there wasn't going to *be* a **LONG HAUL**. The **END OF THE WORLD** as we know it was **ALREADY AT HAND**. …People should sacrifice **EVERYTHING** for his coming.
The Search for The Twelve Apostles Wm. McBirnie p.15 [#37]	The early Christians **did not really have a sense of building a movement FOR THE AGES.** To them the Return of Christ might well be expected during their **GENERATION**. They certainly spoke of it often, so they must have looked for the Return of Christ **DAILY**- at first.

Ethics for La La Land (con't)

My Comments

Most modern day Republican Evangelical Christians are completely repulsed by these Haight-Asbury hippy ethics of their Jesus. They silently all agree & believe these commands of Jesus are better off ignored, and at least that's one belief they actually practice. Maybe these rules made sense if you thought the end of the world would happen before the end of the year, but seeing how the Second Coming is about 2,000 years overdue now, I don't think any Christians on Earth are losing sleep worrying about ignoring Jesus' commands here. Similarly, they also ignore Paul's advice in 1st Corinthians 7:26-31 to forego marriage due to the Second Coming being just a few months or a couple years away. For most Christians, common sense about marriage and money overrules anything Jesus and Paul might have said.

The fact that modern Christians are perfectly comfortable ignoring & explaining away these crystal clear commands of Jesus shows that they agree these commands do not apply to them. In essence, by their actions, they are in agreement that the early church anticipated the end of the world and in that context these rules made sense, they don't make sense any more. It's sort of like if you are on the sinking Titanic- there would be a whole different ethic going on- and rearranging the deck chairs, while a perfectly good idea on a non-sinking Titanic, is a complete waste of time and effort on a sinking Titanic. The fact that Jesus and Paul made these harsh rules shows they thought their ship was sinking, and as we all know now, they were wrong. The ship wasn't sinking, there was no Second Coming, and the world went on as usual.

For those Christians who would disagree with me on this, I challenge them- put the commands of Jesus and the "you can trust me" (1 Cor 7:25) advice of Paul into action. Let's explore the real-world impact on modern Christians with faith enough to follow these parts of the Bible...

> **GOUGE OUT YOUR EYES:** *Every Christian husband in the country would be blind by the time his 10th anniversary rolled around.*
> **TURN THE OTHER CHEEK:** *The USA would have been conquered, eh, by Canada, and Ottawa would be the capital, you bet!*
> **GIVE ANYTHING IF ASKED:** *Every single Christian would be flat broke, and every single non-Christian would be laughing all the way to the bank.*
> **DON'T SAVE ANY MONEY:** *Christians would have no bank accounts or retirement plans, and no money saved. They would all be perpetually flat broke.*
> **DON'T WORK FOR FOOD OR SHELTER:** *Christians would quit their jobs & loose their homes & just sit around and wait for BibleGod to feed & house them.*
> **DON'T PLAN AHEAD:** *No planning for the future- no career planning, no social security, no pensions, no planning to go to college to have a better life in the future.*
> **DON'T GET MARRIED:** *Were all Christians nowadays to follow this advice, along with their "no pre-marital sex" obsession, within a couple generations the Christian religion would pretty much cease to exist as the last of them died off from old age.*
> **HATE YOUR MOTHER:** *This one would make celebrating Mother's Day in church quite challenging. "If everyone will now please reach around and slap your mama!"*

In short, modern Christians would have brought upon themselves inancial and social ruin unseen in human history. The fact they ignore Jesus & Paul on **ALL** of these ethics shows that, deep down inside at least, they realize that Jesus & Paul were way off, mistaken, in error. Maybe these teachings made sense to Jesus & Paul because they thought the world was going to end in a few months or a couple years, but that never happened. And those "interim ethics" are now obsolete.

The "Gap" or "Delay" Theory

The Christian theory known as **dispensationalism** attempts to explain why Jesus, if he really was the Jewish messiah, didn't show up in the First Century in his 2nd Coming & end the world, as predicted throughout the New Testament and in the Old Testament book of *Daniel*, chapter nine. To explain this failure of prophecy, they claim a "gap" or "parenthesis" or "delay" of unknown duration was invisibly penciled into the schedule by BibleGod, who didn't bother telling anyone else about this.

To picture this "Delay Theory," imagine a man named Jaycee walks into a Toyota dealership and signs a car loan, promising to repay it within four years. Well, more than four years pass, the loan remains unpaid, the account gets turned over to a collection agency. Jaycee pens an explanation to Bruno of the collection agency that,

> "Yes, I will repay the bank within four years as promised. However, without telling the bank, I had 'inserted a gap' of unknown length into the four-year payback schedule on my own copy of the loan contract. Therefore, *when* the loan *actually* gets paid off", JC explains, "nobody knows. It may be next month, next year, within this generation, or even a thousand generations from now. Thank you for your understanding. Yours Truly, Jaycee."

Almost everybody, except Christians with a dispensational axe to grind, can clearly see that Jaycee has **DEFAULTED** on the loan and is legally **IN THE WRONG**. If this were to go before a jury, Jaycee would be found guilty, and no amount of theological hair splitting would get him off.

****

Does the New Testament have any evidence that a "gap" or "delay" exists in the cosmic timetable of BibleGod? Just the opposite- in several places it clearly shows that no such gaps or delays are even **allowable**. Those that dishonestly postulate these imaginary delays do so only to **save the savior's** fractured reputation as a prophet. For them, **situational ethics** kicks in, and the "end" of saving the savior's reputation, justifies the "means" of lying. For more on this, see the chapter "Christian Dishonesty."

Luke 12: 45-46	"But if that slave says in his heart, '**My master will be a long time in coming**,' [Side Note} Literally: "is **DELAYING TO COME**"] and begins to beat the slaves, *both* men and women, and to eat and drink and get drunk; the master of that slave will come on a day when he does not expect *him,* and at an hour he does not know, and **will cut him in pieces**, and assign him a place with the unbelievers. New American Standard [#1]
	But if that slave says to himself, '**My master is *DELAYED* in coming**,' and if he begins to beat the other slaves, men and women, and to eat and drink and get drunk... New Revised Standard Version [#17]
Hebrews 10:37 NIV [#16]	For in just a *very* **little while**, He who is coming will come and # *will **not** delay*.
Matthew 24:48 NRSV [#17]	But if that ***WICKED*** slave says to himself, 'My master is *delayed*,'...

The "Gap" or "Delay" Theory (con't)

Luke 18:6-8 NRSV [#17]	And the Lord said, "Listen to what the unjust judge says. And will not God grant justice to his chosen ones who cry to him day and night? ***Will he <u>delay</u> long in helping them?*** I tell you, he will QUICKLY grant justice to them. And yet, when the Son of Man comes, will he find faith on earth?"
2nd Peter 3:9 Darby Bible [#21]	**The Lord does *not* delay his promise** [to come again], as some account of delay, but is longsuffering towards you, not willing that any should perish, but that all should come to repentance.
Rev. 6:10-11 Weymouth [#2]	And now in loud voices they cried out, saying, "**How long**, O Sovereign Lord, the holy One and the true, **dost Thou <u>DELAY</u> judgment** and the taking of **vengeance** upon the inhabitants of the earth for our blood?" And there was given to each of them a long white robe, and *they were bidden to wait patiently for **a short time longer**,* until the full number of their fellow bondservants should also complete--namely of their brethren who were soon to be killed just as they had been.

Commentary & Quotes

The Prophecy of the Destruction of Jerusalem Nisbett (1787 AD) pp.14-15 [#157]	And farther to express his coming as *very near*, he declares [Matthew, chapter 24] verse 34, "Verily I say unto you, This generation shall not pass, till all these things be fulfilled." Upon which Bishop Newton thus expresses himself: "It is to me a wonder how *any* man can refer **part** of the foregoing discourse to the destruction of Jerusalem, and **part** to the end of the world, or **any** other distant even, when it is here said, so positively, in the conclusion; ***All these things*** shall be fulfilled in **this** generation. It seemeth as if our Saviour was aware of some **misapplication** of his words, by adding **yet GREATER** force and emphasis to his affirmation, verse 35, "Heaven and earth shall pass away, but my words shall not pass away."
Matthew 24 Fulfilled John Bray pp.132-133 [#158]	But I ask, could Jesus be accused of being so *reckless* with His own **use of language** that He would **equate** the word "**immediately**" with a period of time extending hundreds (maybe **thousands**) of years into the future? I hardly think so. Milton Terry said: "But we can find **no word or sentence** which appears designed to impress anyone with the idea that the destruction in question and the parousia would be **far separate** as to time. The one, it is said, will ***immediately*** follow the other, and ***all*** will take place ***before*** that generation shall pass away." (Milton S. Terry, Biblical Hermeneutics, note on p. 439) Still later, Terry said: "We are driven, then, by **every sound principle of hermeneutics**, to conclude that Matt xxiv, 29-31, must be included within the time-limits of the discourse of which it forms an essential part, and **cannot** be legitimately applied to events **far separate** from the final catastrophe of the Jewish State." (same, p. 449) ...No matter ***what*** we think (or know) ***will*** happen in the future, it is not ours to insert them into these passages and thereby change the ONE meaning that Jesus was expressing to His disciples.

The "Gap" or "Delay" Theory (con't)

Commentary & Quotes

Matthew 24 Fulfilled John Bray p.216 [#158]	Even my post-tribulational, premillennial friend Henry Hudson, editor of Echoes of the Ministries… acknowledges the *very obvious meaning* of this word "**GENERATION**" in [Matthew, chapter 24] verse 34. He says: "Many commentators play around with the word 'generation' (genea), and ***thinking to avoid embarrassment***, project its application to the generation which will *be* alive during the last days immediately preceding the Second Coming of the Messiah… such **verbal games** are soon exposed as being **nothing but armchair gymnastics**. The word is generally used to signify a people belonging to a particular period of time, or more loosely, to a period of time defined by what might be considered as an average life span of a man."
What Happened in A.D. 70? Edward Stevens pp.18-19 [#252]	The Olivet Discourse Cannot Be Divided: …Luke 17 discusses the same events as Matthew 24, however there is **not a hint that two different time periods** are under consideration. …Luke's account **cannot be divided** into the same two groups of events. Notice on the chart above [shown in the book, not shown here] how Luke records the same events as Matthew, but in a different order. …**both Matthew and Luke speak of the same events which would all happen in the same time period**… the "generation" alive when He spoke those words, **THE GENERATION FROM AD 30-70**.

The Loose Canon Theory

"The Apostles Misunderstood Jesus and thus Didn't *Teach* What Jesus *Taught*"

Some teach that the Apostles possibly got "carried away" in their excitement over the 2nd Coming, and in their incompetence or innocent enthusiasm either *scrambled* what Jesus had said, or *went beyond* what Jesus had *authorized* them to say. Either way, it is claimed they ended up writing things that Jesus would not have authorized. The New Testament claims otherwise. It claims a Jesus who authorized his Apostles to be his <u>SPOKESMEN</u> on earth, receive fresh revelation and guidance "into all truth" as the need arose. In short, the New Testament claims that the Apostles spoke with the **full authority** of a **living** Jesus **directing** their teachings from above in **real time**.

Per The Bible}

The Apostles *Taught* What Jesus *Told Them* To Teach
The Apostles Taught via Direct "Divine Inspiration"

1st Th 4:15 Weymouth [#2]	15 For **this** <u>*we*</u> declare to you <u>on the Lord's own authority</u>
World's Last Night C.S. Lewis p. 98 [#74]	It is clear from the New Testament that they all expected the Second Coming in their own **lifetime**. And, worse still, **they had a reason, and one which you will find very embarrassing.** <u>Their</u> **Master** <u>had</u> **told** <u>them</u> **so.** He shared, and indeed *created*, their *delusion.* (*Lewis was "quoting" from an imaginary Atheist, but does not disagree with what is said, thereby signifying approval.*)
Gal. 1:11-12 NASB [#1]	…the gospel which was preached by me [the Apostle Paul] is *not* according to man. For I <u>**neither**</u> received it from man, <u>**nor**</u> was I taught it, but I received it through a *revelation* of Jesus Christ.
John 16:13 NASB [#1]	But when He, the Spirit of truth, comes, He will guide you into **ALL** the truth; for He will not speak on His own initiative, but whatever He hears, He will speak; and **He will disclose to you** what is to come.

The Apostles Were *Put In Charge* By Jesus Himself

John 15:16 NASB [#1]	You [Apostles] did not choose Me, but I chose you, and appointed you…
1 Cor. 12:28 NASB [#1]	And *God* **has appointed** in the church, *first* Apostles, second prophets…
Mt. 16:19 NASB [#1]	I will give you [the Apostle Peter] the keys of the kingdom of heaven; and whatever you shall bind on earth shall have been bound in heaven…
John 20:23 Amplified [#9]	Now, having received the **Holy Spirit** and being <u>**led and directed by Him**</u>, if you [Apostles] *forgive* the sins of anyone, *they are forgiven*; if you *retain* the sins of anyone, **they are retained**.
Mark 3:13-15 NASB [#1]	And He went up on the mountain and summoned those whom <u>*He Himself*</u> wanted, and they came to Him. And <u>*He appointed twelve*</u> [Apostles], so that they would be with Him and that He could send them out to preach, and to have *authority* to cast out the demons.
John 17:18 NASB [#1]	As You sent *Me* into the world, *I also have sent them* [the Apostles] into the world.
Titus 2:15 NASB [#1]	These things speak and exhort and reprove with <u>***all***</u> authority. Let <u>***no one***</u> disregard you.

The Loose Canon Theory (con't)

The Apostles Were The Very *Foundation* of the Church

Ep. 2:20 NASB [#1]	Having been built upon the **FOUNDATION** of the **APOSTLES** and **PROPHETS**, Christ Jesus Himself being the chief corner stone.
Rev. 21:14 NASB [#1]	[Describing "The New Jerusalem"]: And the wall of the city had twelve foundation stones, and on them were the names of the twelve **APOSTLES** of the Lamb.

Per 1st Corinthians 14:9 Jesus Would Have Made Sure His Apostles Understood Him

1 Cor. 14:9 Living Bible [#31]	In the same way, if you talk to a person in some language he doesn't understand, how will he know what you mean? You might as well be talking to an empty room

2nd Peter 3:3-14

Christian Math: 1 = 1000

New American Standard Bible
[#1]

1 This is now, beloved, the second letter I am writing to you in which I am stirring up your sincere mind by way of reminder,

2 that you should remember the words spoken beforehand by the holy prophets and the commandment of the Lord and Savior *spoken* by your apostles.

3 Know this first of all, that **in the last days** mockers will come with *their* mocking, following after their own lusts,

4 and saying, **"Where is the promise of His coming?** For *ever* since the fathers fell asleep, all continues just as it was from the beginning of creation."

5 For when they maintain this, it escapes their notice that by the word of God *the* heavens existed long ago and *the* earth was formed out of water and by water,

6 through which the world at that time was destroyed, being flooded with water.

7 But the present heavens and earth by His word are being reserved for fire, kept for **the day of judgment** and destruction of ungodly men.

8 *But do not let this one fact escape your notice, beloved, that with the Lord one day is as a thousand years, and a thousand years as one day.*

9 **The Lord is <u>not slow</u>** about His promise, as some count slowness, but is patient toward you, not wishing for any to perish but for all to come to repentance.

10 But **the day of the Lord** will come like a thief, in which the heavens will pass away with a roar and the elements will be destroyed with intense heat, and the earth and its works will be burned up.

11 Since all these things are to be destroyed in this way, what sort of people ought you to be in holy conduct and godliness,

12 **looking for and hastening the coming of the day of God**, on account of which the heavens will be destroyed by burning, and the elements will melt with intense heat!

13 But according to His promise we are looking for new heavens and a new earth, in which righteousness dwells.

14 Therefore, beloved, since **you look for these things**, be diligent to be found by Him in peace, spotless and blameless.

2nd Peter 3:8

Introduction

Hermeneutics 101

Jesus was direct, Peter circumspect.
One exception doesn't negate a rule.
Don't let a single tree obscure the forest.
Jesus spoke plain true, Peter allegorical goo.
Jesus set the stage, Peter re-wrote the last page.
One passage obscure doesn't override a hundred clear.
Jesus wrote a one-time play, Peter ran it a thousand days.
One verse of *dubious* origins doesn't negate dozens from *known* origins.
Modern Christians ignore the LOG in 2nd Peter, to fawn over a splinter in Matthew 24:34
Who are you going to believe? Jesus who made the **prediction**, or Peter's apocalyptic **fiction**?

Any who wish to appeal to a questionable epistle which has a questionable verse, which may show Jesus due back within several thousand years, you must **first** explain the **dozens** of explicit passages in non-questionable epistles which show **otherwise**.

2nd Peter 3:8 → Why Does This Sound *Sooooo* Familiar???

"But do not let this one fact escape your notice brethren, for it depends on what the meaning of the word **'is'** is, beloved. For with the Lord one day **is** as a thousand years, if **'is'** means **is** and never has been that **is** not- that **is** one thing. And a thousand years, as I have testified before this Grand Jury, and I'd like to testify again, *is* **as one day**, if **'is'** really **is**."

---Saint Wm. Jefferson Clinton

2nd Peter 3:3-14

My Comments

Know this first of all, that **in the last days** mockers will come with *their* mocking, following after their own lusts, and saying, **"Where is the promise of His coming?** For *ever* since the fathers fell asleep, all continues just as it was from the beginning of creation."   2nd Peter 3:3-4 NASB [#1]

The (Broken) Promise of His 2nd Coming	The 2nd Coming that Jesus promised, found within the gospel stories, only showed the world he couldn't *keep* his promises. Jesus' promise to return "within that generation" of 33 AD had now, decades later, come back to haunt & taunt his remaining followers.
	Knowing how Christians are, for year after year they had probably, using this promise, threatened many people into joining their religion. These converts knew full well the threat of imminent destruction the "Prince of Peace" had promised to unleash upon the world. Jesus' mistake, however, had been to put an "expiration date" on his promise to return.
	Judging by the complaints, that "expiration date" had come and gone. Jesus had promised to return before his Apostles had all died off; before "that generation" of 33 AD faded into history. Apparently, by the time this letter was written, the "due date", the Apostles, and Jesus' reputation as a prophet had all expired, thus allowing many Christians to leave their religion in good conscience.
Internal Evidence #1 Peter Didn't Write "2nd Peter"	**"Where is the promise of his coming? For ever since the fathers fell asleep..."** Jesus had *promised to return before the people of his generation died off, especially before all of his Apostles- the **fathers of the churches- had died off. Well, those men all died off, and Jesus had not yet returned. This apparently led some to ask a reasonable question: *"Where is the promise of his coming? For ever since the fathers died..."*
	At the time this question was asked, Peter was either **alive**, or Peter was **dead**.
	If Alive: If the Apostle Peter were ALIVE, a comment claiming that all the Apostles were dead would NOT have come up.

	If Dead: If Peter had already been dead for decades, an epistle from Peter (i.e. 2nd Peter) that had been written a few months previous to their receiving it, would not have existed. Why? because *dead people don't write letters!*
	Therefore, alive or dead, something was amiss. And what was amiss, and missing, was an authentic book called "Second Peter" actually written by Peter himself. The only reasonable explanation is that at the time the question was asked, Peter *must* have been dead (this explains the question), and therefore the question's response must have been a forgery (this explains 2nd Peter).
	*Mt 16:28; 24:34 **1Cor 4:15; 3:1-9

2nd Peter 3:3-14

My Comments (con't)

Know this first of all, that **in the last days** mockers will come with *their* mocking, following after their own lusts, and saying, **"Where is the promise of His coming?** For *ever* since the fathers fell asleep, all continues just as it was from the beginning of creation."   2nd Peter 3:3-4 NASB [#1]

Internal Evidence #2 **Peter Didn't Write** **"2nd Peter"**	*If* the author of this letter had been Peter himself, he would have pointed to his own *existence* as being <u>*the*</u> best counter-argument to show that the "<u>this generation</u>" of Jesus' promise, had not yet passed away, and Jesus had not yet turned into a false prophet; thereby showing the mockers to be wrong. Peter himself would have been his own best proof. He'd have only to point to himself (or any living Apostle), to jerk the rug out from under all the mockers. Yet not one word is mentioned in this letter using this line of reasoning as a defense. It is not even attempted. Instead, the author of 2nd Peter goes into a convoluted contorted distorted argument regarding the very nature of time itself. The obvious conclusion is that 2nd Peter was NOT penned by the *Apostle* Peter. By the time 2nd Peter *had* been penned, it was common knowledge the Apostles *had* all passed on (as the mockers so willingly pointed out). This explains the existence of the mockers, as well as the NON-existence of the best counter-argument the author of 2nd Peter (had he *been* Peter) could have used- himself.
Internal Evidence #3 **Peter Didn't Write** **"2nd Peter"**	• The author of 1st Peter admitted "the end of all things is **at hand**."* • The author of 1st Peter also admitted his *current* era was "**in** these last times." ** • Therefore, the author of 1st Peter authored 1st Peter in "the last times." *(1st Peter 4:7) **(1st Peter 1:20) • The author of 1st Peter authored 1st Peter in "the last times." • 2nd Peter was written *after* 1st Peter. • Therefore, even more so, 2nd Peter was written in the era of "the last times." • 2nd Peter was written in the era of "the last times." • 2nd Peter writes about mockers being a problem in the era of "the last times." • Therefore, mockers were a problem in the same era that 2nd Peter was being written. • Mockers were a problem in the same era that 2nd Peter was being written. • Mockers pointed out that the Apostles had already all died off before. • Therefore, the Apostles had already all died off before 2nd Peter was written. And thus 2nd Peter could not have been written by an Apostle, such as the **Apostle** Peter, because all of the Apostles were <u>**DEAD**</u> by then.

2nd Peter 3: 3-14

My Comments (con't)

Know this first of all, that **in the last days** mockers will come with *their* mocking, following after their own lusts, and saying, **"Where is the promise of His coming?** For *ever* since the fathers fell asleep, all continues just as it was from the beginning of creation."   2nd Peter 3:3-4 NASB [#1]

Internal Evidence #4
Peter Didn't Write
"2nd Peter"

- The author of 2nd Peter believed "the last days" had *already* commenced.
- The author wrote that in "the last days" mockers would come.
- Therefore, the mockers and the author lived in the same era.

- The mockers lived in the same era as the author.
- Jesus had promised to return AFTER *Jerusalem had been destroyed but BEFORE the **generation of 33 AD had passed away. The mockers believed Jesus had broken his promise.
- Therefore, the mockers, living in the same era as the author of 2nd Peter, believed *the generation* of 33 AD had *already* passed away, and Jerusalem had *already* been destroyed.
                                  *(Lk 21:6) **(Mt 24:34)

- The mockers, living in the same era as the author of 2nd Peter, believed the generation of 33 AD had *already* passed away, and Jerusalem had *already* been destroyed.
- In 70 AD, Jerusalem was destroyed. By 73 AD, the generation of 33 AD would have been considered gone, one Biblical generation being equal to about 40 years.
- Therefore, the mockers could not have commenced with their mocking at any time before 73 AD.

- The mockers could not have commenced with their mocking at any time before 73 AD.
- The author of 2nd Peter wrote in the present tense regarding these mockers. (2P 3:5)
- Therefore, the author of 2nd Peter penned 2nd Peter sometime *after* 73 AD.

- 2nd Peter was penned sometime *after* 73 AD.
- The Apostle Peter died years *before* that, in *67 AD.
- Therefore, the Apostle Peter could ___not___ have written 2nd Peter.
                *The Search for The Twelve Apostles p. 67 [#37]

- The Apostle Peter could not have written 2nd Peter.
- Therefore, somebody else wrote 2nd Peter and signed Peter's name to it.
- Therefore, 2nd Peter is a forgery.

- 2nd Peter is a forgery.
- Christians should reject forgeries.
- Therefore, Christians should reject the "1,000 Year" claim, it being a part of this forgery.

And thus, 2nd Peter carries no weight in the argument and should be ignored.

2nd Peter 3:3-14

My Comments (con't)

1 Day ≠ 1000 Years? Then Jesus Broke His Promise ☞	Christians can claim poetic license all they want. The fact remains that one day does *NOT* equal one thousand years, any more than one dollar equals one thousand. BibleGod or not, anyone who borrows a $1,000 from you today, with the *PROMISE* to pay it back **tomorrow**, had better hand back the full $1,000 and on time. If they instead hand you some cockamamie excuse about paying you back in a month or whatever, they have broken their promise. This isn't rocket science, it's common sense and honesty. An *HONEST* man (or god) does *NOT* on his own re-write a contract or promise *AFTER* it is signed. If he does so, that is known as *FRAUD*. Jesus *promised* (and verses 4 and 9 confirm that it was indeed a promise) to return… when? **Before** the generation living in 33 AD died off. For him to deliver **anything less**, whatever the convoluted excuse, is nothing but fraud and broken promises. If this verse had been written by the Apostle Peter, inspired by a holy spirit from BibleGod, this verse alone is enough to prove your BibleGod an untrustworthy liar. And as a liar, he could very well promise anything, including an "eternity in heaven" yet deliver only a thousand day stay, using similar "logic" as in this verse.
1 Day = 1000 Years **= Backpedaling** ☞	From 1889 onward, the Jehovah Witnesses *predicted that Jesus would return to Earth and set up his kingdom in 1914. When 1914 came and went, it was obvious to all a mistake had been made. Rather than admit an error, they came up with the lame excuse that Jesus had indeed returned to Earth in 1914- but nobody saw him because he was *invisible!!!* This dishonest backpedaling worked well enough, as the movement survives unto this day. In similar fashion, when Jesus failed to return within the time limit he himself allotted, the early Christians came up with an excuse to "explain" the prophetic failure of their god to their pagan neighbors. What they dreamed up was almost as good as an invisible Jesus: they **rewrote the dictionary**. They claimed that a day no longer means a day. A day *now* means a thousand years. And this explains why Jesus didn't show up!!! Of course, like the Jehovah Witnesses, nobody comes up with these lame excuses until *after* the fact, which is why it is called **backpedaling**. 　　　　　*The Time Is At Hand* [#255] Charles T. Russell,

My Comments (con't)

> In the same way, if you talk to a person in some language **he doesn't understand**, how will he know what you mean? You might as well be talking to an **empty room...** God is *not* the author of confusion...
>
> 1 Cor 14:9&33   [#31 & #19]

An intelligent being would know that to communicate with Earthlings, one must speak the language of Earth, including using human systems of time measurement.

For example, if a year is defined as the amount of time it takes a planet to revolve around its sun, a year on Earth is *not* the same length of time as a year on Pluto. Picture two beings, born at exactly the same time: one on Pluto, the other on Earth. By the time the Plutonian has reached his *first* birthday (i.e. Pluto has circled once around the sun), the Earthling would have gone thru *248* birthdays, as Pluto takes 248 *Earth* years to circle the Sun.

If, therefore, a Plutonian were to take out a four-year car loan on Earth, it is obvious that a common system of time measurement must first be agreed upon. If not, the Earth bank might be waiting 992 Earth years for the re-payment of what they thought was a simple four year loan!!! The potential for confusion is evident.

According to the Bible, BibleGod is not the author of confusion. Therefore BibleGod, when speaking to humans, should be intelligent enough to use human terms of time measurement, and not "heavenly" ones. Therefore, when BibleGod says one year, he would mean one EARTH year, not a thousand. Otherwise, BibleGod would be authoring mass confusion. BibleGod (given half a brain) would be sure to use a language and time system that we understand. As Paul says in 1st Corinthians 14:9&33}

> *"In the same way, if you talk to a person in some language he doesn't understand, how will he know what you mean? You might as well be talking to an empty room"*

For example, no one could ever know what BibleGod meant by "Jesus will rise from the dead after three days" if, willy-nilly, BibleGod could mean something other than Earth days. If the "1 Day = 1,000 Years" new-math formula is NOT a bogus verse penned in by some ancient dishonest scribe, then it is entirely possible that Jesus has yet *another* thousand years to go before he's due to be resurrected, and therefore, all of you Christians are still in your "sins."

A Russian who knows how to communicate does not speak Russian to a person who only knows Spanish. Likewise, an "all-knowing" deity should be granted the benefit of the doubt, that when he said "within **one** generation" he meant one, and not a thousand.

"God Is Not a God of Confusion"

∴

1000 Year Quote = Bogus

2nd Peter 3:3-14

My Comments (con't)
The Lord is Not Slow

2Pt 3:9   The Lord is ***not slow*** about His **promise**…

2Pt 3:12   …*WAITING FOR* and hastening the coming of the day of God. (Darby [#21])

2Pt 3:13   But according to His **promise we are** *LOOKING FOR* new heavens and a new earth…

2Pt 3:14   Therefore, beloved, since **you look for these things**, be diligent…

The Lord is Not Slow
Like A Herd of Turtles

∴

Due 1st Century

The Promise:
The promise in question can be found in Matthew 16:27-28 & 24:34, where Jesus in both cases reinforces the degree of promise with a preface of "Truly I say unto you…". What was the promise? Taken together, the promise was to return within the era of the 1st Century. "Peter" states that "the Lord" is not slow about fulfilling his promise. It is therefore reasonable to conclude that "Peter" and Jesus both blew it, as 2,000 years is, by any normal human standards, slow.

Within Their Lifetime:
They are told to "**look for**" and "**wait for**" certain things, and that "the Lord" would not be slow in making these things show up. Since ***DEAD PEOPLE CAN NOT "LOOK FOR" OR "WAIT FOR" THINGS***, the things they were to look & wait for had to be **within their lifetime.**

> "***Words have no meaning*** *if a statement like this may refer to some event **still future**, and perchance distant, which cannot be 'looked for' because it is not within view, nor 'hasted unto' because it is **indefinitely** remote."*
> The Parousia p.324 [#33]

Therefore it is reasonable to conclude that the events they eagerly awaited were due to occur back in their own era.

149

2nd Peter 3:3-14

My Comments (con't)
2nd Peter = Matthew 24

The 24th chapter of Matthew has already been shown to be a listing of events that were expected within the 1st Century. If 2nd Peter is a parallel of the chapter in Matthew (and it clearly is, see table below) then it is also clear that the events of 2nd Peter were due within the 1st Century.

2nd Peter Chapter 3			St. Matthew Chapter 24
Words spoken by Jesus	3:2	24:4	Words spoken by Jesus
"The last days"	3:3	24:6	"The end"
"Promise of his coming"	3:4	24:37	"Coming of the Son of Man"
Noah's flood	3:6	24:37	Noah's flood
Astronomical disasters	3:10,12	24:29	Astronomical disasters
Heaven & Earth replaced	3:13	24:35	Heaven & Earth pass away.

2nd Peter 3:3-14

Commentaries & Quotes

New American Standard Bible, Study Edition: Intro to 2ⁿᵈ Peter [#38]	The authorship, date, and destination of the second letter of Peter are <u>**extremely uncertain**</u>. No New Testament writing had a more **difficult time** establishing itself in the Canon. Scholars, both ancient and modern, have <u>**seriously doubted**</u> its Petrine composition… the first time it is definitely mentioned is by Origen, and this is to question it… Eusebius says 'As for the current second epistle, it has <u>***not***</u> come down to us as canonical…
Harper's Bible Dictionary p.544 [#39]	Internal evidence and historical facts do <u>***not***</u> support Peter's authorship. Differences in style, language, and point of view between 1ˢᵗ and 2ⁿᵈ Peter indicate that the books were written by <u>**different authors**</u>. Perhaps neither was by Peter… The early church **doubted** that it was a genuine letter of Peter's… (the) evidence all indicates that **this Epistle was written about the middle of the 2ⁿᵈ** century by an unknown author who used Peter's name as a pseudonym.
Westminster Dictionary of the Bible p.474 [#40]	Critics are not agreed concerning the date and authorship of this epistle. The author describes himself as 'Symeon Peter…' yet many difficulties confront the acceptance of this testimony… <u>**Calvin**</u> entertained doubts as to its **genuineness**, and <u>**most**</u> modern scholars regard it as the work of an <u>**unknown**</u> author, who c. <u>**A.D. 150**</u> wrote in the name of the great Apostle Peter in order to secure a wider hearing.
Smith's Bible Dictionary p.523 [#41]	This Epistle of Peter presents questions of difficulty… <u>**doubts**</u> as to its genuineness were entertained by the early Church; in the time of <u>**Eusebius**</u> it was reckoned <u>**among the disputed books**</u>… ***<u>Many reject the Epistle altogether as SPURIOUS</u>***.
The Quest of the Historical Jesus Dr. Albert Schweitzer pp.22-23 [#36]	It appears, then, that THE HOPE OF THE PAROUSIA WAS THE <u>**FUNDAMENTAL THING**</u> IN PRIMITIVE CHRISTIANITY… Accordingly, the main problem of primitive dogmatics was the **DELAY of the Parousia.** Already in Paul's time the problem was **pressing**, and he had set to work in 2ⁿᵈ Thessalonians to discover **all possible and impossible reasons** why the second coming should be **delayed**. Reimarus mercilessly exposes the position of the apostle, who was **OBLIGED TO <u>FOB PEOPLE OFF</u> SOMEHOW OR ANOTHER.** The author of **2ⁿᵈ Peter**… undertakes to restore the confidence of Christendom once for all with the **SOPHISM** ["SOPHISM: Any false argument… for deceiving someone" (Dictionary.com)] of <u>**THE THOUSAND YEARS**</u> which are in the sight of God as one day, **ignoring the fact** that in the promise the reckoning was by <u>***man's***</u> years, <u>**not**</u> by God's. 'Nevertheless it served the turn of the Apostles so well with those **simple** early Christians, that after the first believers had been bemused with it, and the period originally fixed had **elapsed**, the Christians of later generations, including Fathers of the Church, could continue even after to feed themselves with **empty hopes**.' ***THE SAYING OF CHRIST ABOUT THE GENERATION WHICH SHOULD NOT DIE OUT BEFORE HIS RETURN CLEARLY FIXES THE EVENT AT NO VERY DISTANT DATE*** [FROM 33 CE].

2nd Peter 3:3-14 (con't)

Commentaries & Quotes (con't)

Last Days Madness Gary DeMar p.294 [#34]	In light of the time texts, how should 2nd Peter 3:8 be applied? First, there is nothing in this passage or in any other passage that tells us that any time text should be filtered through 2nd Peter 3:8. Second, if time texts are fluid in relation to 2 Peter 3:8, then **we could never know what God means relative to time**. ...Are dispensationalists willing to admit that the thousand years of Revelation 20 can be reduced to a single day? *...IS JESUS STILL IN JOSEPH OF ARIMATHEA'S TOMB, SINCE THREE DAYS REALLY MEANS THREE THOUSAND YEARS?*
The Interpreter's Bible Vol. 7 p.153 [#42]	When the New Testament writers said 'soon' they meant 'soon' *in relation to their own time*. If 'with the Lord one day is as a thousand years' then civilizations may continue through **two million years**, as well as two thousand.
Why I Became an Atheist John Loftus p.312 [#205]	**SECOND PETER IS ALSO A FORGERY.** James D.G. Dunn states the scholarly consensus: 'If **ANY** document in the New Testament is pseudonymous **it is this one**. Its language and style is so very different from that of 1st Peter. It is clearly post-Pauline and reflects an anxiety over the **DELAY OF THE PAROUSIA** which would be unlikely WERE PETER HIMSELF STILL **ALIVE**.
Who Wrote The New Testament? Dr. Burton Mack p.213 [#208]	So Peter is an **apostle**, writing to remind his readers, that they should **remember** the words of the **apostles**! The **FICTION** should be clear.
Lost Christianities Dr. Bart Ehrman p.234 [#209]	The final book of the New Testament to be written was probably 2 Peter, a book almost universally recognized by critical scholars to be **pseudonymous**, not actually written by Simon Peter but one of many Petrine **FORGERIES** from the second century.
Abingdon Bible Handbook p.332 [#216]	Most scholars today believe that Peter could **not** have been the author but that the letter was written in his name by a disciple and admirer. ...**Prominent leaders (Origen, Eusebius, and Jerome) expressed or reported serious doubts that Peter the apostle wrote this letter**. ...The letter's wordy, pompous Greek style ill fits Peter. The author of II Peter borrowed extensively from the letter of Jude. This seems **STRANGE** for the eminent Peter, but not so strange for a lesser figure. And the late date of Jude (about the end of the first century) puts the later **II Peter long after Peter's death**, which occurred between **A.D. 64 and 67**. ...Precisely who our author was is unknown. He probably was a Gentile Christian who wrote sometime between **A.D. 100 and 150**, probably nearer the later date.
Resurrection: Myth or Reality? John S. Spong p.95 [#223]	The expectation of the **near return** of the ascended Lord of heaven **had begun to fade**, and with it Christianity was **evolving** into something the earliest Christians had never anticipated.
Forged Dr. Bart D. Ehrman p.21-22 [#234]	The book of 2 Peter was **REJECTED** by a number of early church fathers, as discussed by both Jerome and Eusebius, but none more straightforwardly than the notable Christian teacher of Alexandra Didymus the Blind, who argued that "**THE LETTER IS FALSE** and so is not to be in the canon". Peter, in other words, **DID NOT ACTUALLY WRITE IT**... even though the author claimed to be Peter.

2nd Peter 3:3-14 (con't)

Commentaries & Quotes (con't)

Critical & Exegetical Handbook to The General Epistles Joh. Huther pp.351-356 [#217]	Its [2nd Peter] genuineness (has) been **called into question by many**... Previous to Clemens it is sought for in vain in the apostolic and in the older Church Fathers... How can it be explained that there are **no certain traces of the epistle in the second century?**
History & Eschatology Karl Bultmann [#224]	Obviously the fact that the expected coming of Christ **FAILED TO TAKE PLACE** gave rise to disappointment and doubt. (p.37) The problem of eschatology grew out of the fact that **THE EXPECTED END OF THE WORLD** <u>FAILED</u> **TO ARRIVE**... and that history went on. (p.380) ...the <u>FAILURE</u> of the Parousia of Christ to take place. (p.40) How did the developing Church endure and overcome its disappointment that **THE PAROUSIA OF CHRIST FAILED TO MATERIALIZE?** ...It is a fact that the Christians gradually became accustomed to waiting. ...But eschatology was never abandoned, rather the **EXPECTED END OF THE WORLD** was removed into an indefinite future.
The Moral Landscape Dr. Sam Harris p.154-155 [#229]	Many religious groups... have anchored their worldviews to **SPECIFIC** *TESTABLE PREDICTIONS* ...When the date arrives, and with it the **ABSOLUTE REFUTATION** of a cherished doctrine, many members of these groups **RATIONALIZE THE FAILURE OF PROPHECY** with remarkable agility. In fact, such crises of faith are often attended by **INCREASED** proselytizing and the manufacture of **FRESH** prophecy.
Forged Dr. Bart Ehrman p.70 [#234]	One of the reasons **VIRTUALLY ALL SCHOLARS AGREE THAT PETER DID <u>NOT</u> ACTUALLY WRITE THIS LETTER** is that the situation being presupposed appears to be of **MUCH LATER TIMES**. When Peter himself died- say, the year **64** under Nero- there was still an eager expectation that Jesus would return soon; not even a full generation had passed since the crucifixion. It was only with the passing of time that the Christian claim that all would take place "**WITHIN THIS GENERATION**" (Mark 13:30) and before the disciples had "tasted death" (Mark 9:1) **STARTED TO <u>RING HOLLOW</u>**. By the time 2 Peter was written, Christians were having to **DEFEND** themselves in the face of opponents who **MOCKED** their view that the end was supposed to be **IMMINENT**. So "Peter" has to explain that even if the end is thousands of years off, it is still right around the corner by God's calendar; everything is still on schedule. ...**2 PETER ALMOST CERTAINLY COULD NOT HAVE BEEN WRITTEN BY PETER.**

2nd Peter 3:3-14 (con't)

Commentaries & Quotes (con't)

Jesus, Interrupted Dr. Bart Ehrman [#233]	The book called 2 Peter was **WRITTEN LONG *AFTER* PETER'S DEATH**, by someone who was disturbed that some people were denying that the end was coming soon, and one can understand why there might be doubters as the years rolled by. (p.135) ------------------------- **WHAT HAPPENS WHEN THIS EXPECTED END DOESN'T HAPPEN?** What happens when the apocalyptic scenarios that Jesus expected to occur in "this generation" **NEVER COME?** When Paul's expectation that he will be alive at the second coming of Christ is **RADICALLY DISCONFIRMED BY HIS OWN DEATH?** When the resurrection of the dead is delayed interminably, making a **MOCKERY** of the widespread belief that it will happen "**SOON**"? (p.264-265) One thing that happens, of course, is that **some people begin to MOCK.** That is the problem addressed in the last book of the New Testament, 2 Peter, whose author insists that when God says that it will all happen **very soon**, he means by the **DIVINE** calendar, not the **HUMAN**. And one needs always to remember that "with the Lord, a day is as a thousand years and a thousand years as one day" (2 Peter 3:8). Following this logic, if the end is supposed to come next **TUESDAY**, it could be a Tuesday **FOUR THOUSAND YEARS FROM NOW**. (p.265)
The Case Against Christianity Dr. Michael Martin p.23 [#236]	Further, Aquinas's appeal to fulfilled biblical prophecy to justify the rationality of believing the assumptions of Christianity on faith is plagued by the problem of **UNFULFILLED PROPHECIES**. One of the most notorious of these is Jesus' **FALSE** prophecy of the **IMMINENCE** of his Second Coming.
Who Tampered With The Bible Patricia Eddy p.186 [#237]	During the late half of the first century, the early church experienced some **EMBARRASSMENT** when **THE APOSTLES WERE STARTING TO DIE** and Jesus had **NOT** returned to herald the end of the world and the last judgment.
The Life of Jesus Critically Examined David Strauss p.584 [#76]	Already in the first age of Christianity, when the return of Christ was delayed longer than had been anticipated, there arose, according to 2 Peter iii. 3f., **SCOFFERS**, asking: **WHERE IS THE PROMISE OF HIS COMING...** Peter, in his second epistle, resorts to the **PREPOSTEROUS** expedient of appealing to the divine mode of reckoning time, in which a thousand years are equal to one day. Such inferences from the discourse before us would inflict a **FATAL** wound on Christianity; hence it is natural that exegetists should endeavor by all means to **OBVIATE** [i.e. eliminate difficulties] them.

2nd Peter 3:3-14 (con't)	
Commentaries & Quotes (con't)	
Forgery in Christianity Joseph Wheless [#246]	Dubbing these reasonable but disturbing inquirers "scoffers," the **CRAFTY** Peter tried in **TYPICAL PRIESTLY FORM** to **SQUIRM OUT** of the embarrassing situation created by the positive promises of the Christ… with the **SHIFTY** rejoinder…" (p.96) Bishop Eusebius, the first Church Historian, says of II Peter that it was "controverted and **NOT ADMITTED** into the canon… **UNAPOSTOLIC** in origin. …The genuineness of I Peter **CANNOT** be maintained. Most probably it was not written before **112 A.D.** (pp.233-234)

Preterism-   Damn The Facts, Save The Savior!!!

*There is a relatively new faction in Christianity (A new faction? What a surprise!) that has taken a new tact towards trying to explain away the false prophecies in the New Testament concerning the Second Coming of Jesus. Rather than saying that these prophecies are not saying what they obviously are saying (the standard Christian cop-out), this group freely admits that, yes, Jesus promised to return within one generation of 33 CE. Their catch is that Jesus did **indeed** come back, in 70 AD, but the reason nobody saw him is because he was **invisible**. Sort of like the other night when I had Jimmy Hoffa and Elvis over for dinner, and nobody saw them, because they were invisible too.*

Of course, like all Christian groups, this group has already subdivided into several warring camps. Two of the several divisions are known as Full Preterists, and Partial Preterists. I will deal with both of these groups in this section. What I intend to show is that their explanation goes against their own Bible, as well as common sense. Obviously, I can't PROVE an invisible Jesus DIDN'T come back in 70 AD, but neither can they prove an invisible unicorn is NOT standing behind them at this very moment ready to attack!

Greatest Woe in History?

> For then shall be great tribulation, such as was not since the beginning of the world
> to this time, no, nor ever shall be. (Matthew 24:21 [#19])

Jesus predicted that at his second coming, there would be disasters such as never before seen, nor ever to be matched. This being the case, the Preterists have a hard time fitting this part of Jesus' prophecy into the era of 70 AD. As everyone (except the Preterists) seems to know, no such catastrophes affected the entire world at that time. Of course, if they were INVISIBLE catastrophes, that would explain it!

Nothing happened in 70 AD that even came close to the raw body count of Noah's Flood, where it is claimed that the loving BibleGod murdered the entire population of Earth, save eight. This being the case, how come no one but modern Preterists seem to have noticed that the entire population of our planet (save maybe one or two) got wiped out in 70 AD??? It sure would be nice if they would come up with some evidence to back up this claim. Of course, if the evidence were invisible…

Jesus also predicted that *his* tribulation would forever hold the world's record for blood & guts. This is another claim that seems hard (and distasteful!) to swallow, seeing how at most about a million Jews tragically died in 70 AD, as opposed to 6 million during World War Two, not to mention the twenty million Russians starved to death by Stalin, or the three million Cambodians murdered by Pol Pot. As gory as 70 AD was, it was by no means the greatest woe in human history.

Of Concern to Gentiles 1,000 Miles Away?

On the other hand, as some Preterists claim this "tribulation" was meant to be an event restricted to Israel concerning the Jews and their religion, centered around the environs of Jerusalem itself, why on earth would Paul trouble the poor Gentiles living a thousand miles away in Corinth about it??? Why would Paul give them many warnings to be ready, aware, awake, and avoid marriage in light of the Second Coming of Jesus??? In reality, a nuclear bomb could have obliterated the entire Middle East, and it would have had little if any impact whatsoever on the people in Rome or Greece. This is another piece of the Preterist puzzle that they fail to explain.

Invisible Signs are Not Signs!

The Preterists pull an old Jehovah's Witness trick, applying it to 70 AD, in that they claim that all sorts of signs DID take place, but that they were INVISIBLE signs!!! They claim things happened in a make-believe temple in their make-believe heaven by their make-believe gods. The real miracle in this stunt is that their followers believe them!!! But listen and study for yourself what Jesus says- it seems that signs by their very nature are visible.

> *And then shall [A] __APPEAR__ the [B]__SIGN__ of the Son of man in __heaven__: and then shall [C]__ALL__ the tribes of the earth mourn, and they shall [D]__SEE__ the Son of man __coming in the clouds of heaven__ with power and great [E]__GLORY__.* (Mt 24:30 [#19])

A) APPEAR:

(Strong's #5316)
1) to bring forth into the light, cause to shine, shed light
2) shine
  2a) to shine, be bright or resplendent
  2b) to **become evident**, to be brought forth into the light,
    come to view, appear
    2b1) of growing vegetation, to come to light
    2b2) to appear, be **seen**
    2b3) expo**sed to view**
  2c) to **meet the eyes, strike the sight**, become clear or manifest
    2c1) to be **seen**, appear
  2d) to appear to the mind, seem to one's judgment or opinion (NOTE: This is the last and therefore, the least likely definition)

It is obvious that which sheds light, shines, is resplendent, becomes evident, appears, is seen, is exposed to view, strikes the sight (all the primary meanings) is visible. An invisible rabbit pulled out of a hat is none of these things.

B) SIGN:

(Strong's #4592)
1) a sign, mark, token
  1a) that by which a person or a thing is **distinguished** from
    others and is known
  1b) a sign, prodigy, portent, i.e. an unusual occurrence,
    transcending the common course of nature
    1b1) of signs portending remarkable events soon to happen
    1b2) of miracles and wonders by which God authenticates the men
      sent by him, or by which men prove that the cause they are
      pleading is God's

A "sign" is a credential or proof. An "invisible sign" is almost a __contradiction in terms__. For a sign to have ANY value at all, it must be visible. An invisible sign that proves anything actually proves nothing.

C) ALL:

(Strong's #3956)
AV - all 748, all things 170, every 117, all men 41, whosoever 31,
    everyone 28, whole 12, all manner of 11, every man 11,
    no + 3756 9, every thing 7, any 7, whatsoever 6,
    whosoever + 3739 + 302 3, always + 1223 3, daily + 2250 2,
    any thing 2, no + 3361 2, not tr 7, misc 26; 1243
1) individually
  1a) each, **every**, any, all, **the whole, everyone, all things,
  everything**
2) collectively
  2a) some of all types

ALL of the people on Earth are promised to witness this event, not just the rabble rousers living in Israel. This did not happen in 70 AD.

D) SEE:

(Strong's #3700)
  optanomai {op-tan'-om-ahee} or optomai {op-tom-ahee}
a (middle voice) prolonged form of the primary (middle voice)
  optomai {op'-tom-ahee}, which is used for it in certain
  tenses, and both as alternate of 3708; TDNT - 5:315,706; v
AV - see 37, **appear** 17, **look** 2, **show (one's) self** 1, **being seen** 1; 58
1) to look at, **behold**
2) **to allow one's self to be seen, to appear**

*For them to "see" Jesus "appear" he must be **visible**.*

E) GLORY:

 (Strong's #1391)
from the base of 1380; TDNT - 2:233,178; n f
AV - glory 145, glorious 10, honour 6, praise 4, dignity 2,
    worship 1; 168
1) opinion, judgment, view
2) opinion, estimate, whether good or bad concerning someone
  2a) in the NT always a good opinion concerning one, resulting
    in praise, honour, and glory
3) **splendour, brightness**
  3a) of the moon, sun, stars
  3b) **magnificence**, excellence, preeminence, dignity, grace
  3c) majesty
    3c1) a thing belonging to God
      3c1) the kingly majesty which belongs to Him as supreme
        ruler, majesty in the sense of the absolute
        perfection of the deity
    3c2) a thing belonging to Christ
      3c2a) the kingly majesty of the Messiah
      3c2b) the absolutely perfect inward or personal
        excellency of Christ; the majesty
    3c3) of the angels
      3c3a) as **apparent** in their **exterior brightness**

4) a most glorious condition, most exalted state
  4a) of that condition with God the Father in heaven to which
      Christ was raised after He had achieved his work on earth
  4b) the glorious condition of blessedness into which is
      appointed and promised that true Christians shall enter
      after their Saviour's return from heaven

*For "glory" to be __SEEN__ by all the tribes of the earth, it should be very **bright**, thus obviously __visible__. Note the references to things astronomically bright and readily apparent. This does **not** fit in at all with Preterist theory.*

The SIGN of Jesus, whatever it was, would appear visibly in the sky, to been SEEN by ALL men on earth, resulting in their becoming depressed. Then, ALL the men of planet earth, just as they had visibly SEEN the "sign" will now visibly SEE an EXTREMELY bright and visible and well-advertised Jesus descending down from among the clouds. Something this bright and visible couldn't hide if it wanted to. Note all the various words that even in their definitions, use terms of absolute visibility:

apparent, splendour, brightness sun, stars, see, appear, show, be seen, exterior brightness, light, shine, shed light, resplendent, come to view, to meet the eyes, strike the sight, become clear.

There is no way something that is described thusly could have been done in secret in front of the entire world. The return of Jesus herein described was not some invisible, Jehovah-Witness type pie-in-the-sky. It was predicted to be **the most visible world-wide event in history**. This ties in very well with other terminology used by Jesus, such as the lightning analogy (Mt 24:27) that is VERY visible from one end of the sky to the other, to which he compares his coming. With lightning-like visibility, trumpets blaring, apparitions floating around visibly in the sky-- this does NOT seem to be describing the Preterist theory of an invisible, secret ceremony taking place in a galaxy, far far away.

Every N.T. Usage of the Word "SIGN" Indicates
Eyeball Visibility (KJV [#19] Except as Noted)

Mt 12:38 Then certain of the scribes and of the Pharisees answered, saying, Master, we would see a *SIGN* from thee.

Mt 12:39 But he answered and said unto them, An evil and adulterous generation seeketh after a *SIGN*; and there shall no *SIGN* be given to it, but the *SIGN* of the prophet Jonas.

Mt 16:1 The Pharisees also with the Sadducees came, and tempting desired him that he would **shew** them a *SIGN* from heaven.

Mt 16:4 A wicked and adulterous generation seeketh after a *SIGN* and there shall no *SIGN* be given unto it, but the *SIGN* of the prophet Jonas. And he left them, and departed.

Mt 24:3 And as he sat upon the mount of Olives, the disciples came unto him privately, saying, Tell us, when shall these things be? and what [shall be] the *SIGN* of thy coming, and of the end of the world?

Mt 24:30 And then shall **appear** the *SIGN* of the Son of man in heaven ((where the clouds are, i.e. the **sky**)): and then shall all the tribes of the earth mourn, and they shall **see** the Son of man coming in the **clouds of heaven** with power and great glory.

Mt 26:48 Now he that betrayed him gave them a *SIGN*, saying, Whomsoever I shall kiss, that same is he: hold him fast.

Mr 8:11 And the Pharisees came forth, and began to question with him, seeking of him a **SIGN** from heaven, tempting him.

Mr 8:12 And he sighed deeply in his spirit, and saith, Why doth this generation seek after a **SIGN**? verily I say unto you, There shall no **SIGN** be given unto this generation.

Mr 13:4 Tell us, when shall these things be? and what [shall be] the **SIGN** when all these things shall be fulfilled?

Mr 14:44 Now the one who was betraying him had given them a **SIGN** saying, "The one whom I kiss—he is the one. Arrest him and lead him away under guard! [Lexham #169]

Lu 2:12 And this [shall be] a **SIGN** unto you; Ye shall find the babe wrapped in swaddling clothes, lying in a manger.

Lu 2:34 And Simeon blessed them, and said unto Mary his mother, Behold, this [child] is set for the fall and rising again of many in Israel; and for a **SIGN** which shall be spoken against;

Lu 11:16 And others, tempting [him], sought of him a **SIGN** from heaven.

Lu 11:29 And when the people were gathered thick together, he began to say, This is an evil generation: they seek a **SIGN**, and there shall no **SIGN** be given it, but the **SIGN** of Jonas the prophet.

Lu 11:30 For as Jonas was a **SIGN** unto the Ninevites, so shall also the Son of man be to this generation.

Lu 21:7 And they asked him, saying, Master, but when shall these things be? and what **SIGN** [will there be] when these things shall come to pass?

Lu 23:8 Now Herod was very glad when he saw Jesus; for he had wanted to see Him for a long time, because he had been hearing about Him and was hoping to see some sign performed by Him. (NASB [#1])

Joh 2:18 Then answered the Jews and said unto him, **What SIGN shewest thou unto us**, seeing that thou doest these things?

Joh 4:54 This is again a second **SIGN** that Jesus performed when He had come out of Judea into Galilee. (NASB [#1])

Joh 6:14 Therefore when the people saw the **SIGN** which He had performed, they said, "This is truly the Prophet who is to come into the world." (NASB [#1])

Joh 6:30 They said therefore unto him, **What SIGN shewest thou then, that we may see**, and believe thee? What dost thou work?

Joh 10:41 Many came to Him and were saying, "While John performed no **SIGN**, yet everything John said about this man was true." (NASB [#1])

Joh 12:18 For this reason also the people went and met Him, because they heard that He had performed this **SIGN.** (NASB [#1])

Ac 4:16 Saying, "What should we do with these men? For that a remarkable **SIGN** has taken place through them is evident to all those who live in Jerusalem, and we are not able to deny it! (Lexham [169])

Ac 4:22 For the man on whom this **SIGN** of healing had been performed was more than forty years old. (Lexham [#169])

Ac 12:17 Peter made a **SIGN** with his hand to tell them to be quiet. He explained how the Lord led him out of the jail, and he said, "Tell James and the other believers what happened." Then he left to go to another place. (New Century [#97])

Ac 13:16 And Paul, rising up and making a **SIGN** with the hand, said, Israelites, and ye that fear God, hearken. (Darby [#21])

Ac 28:11 And after three months we departed in a ship of Alexandria, which had wintered in the isle, whose **SIGN** was Castor and Pollux.

Ro 4:11 And he received the **SIGN** of circumcision, a seal of the righteousness of the faith which…

1Co 1:22 For the Jews require a **SIGN** and the Greeks seek after wisdom:

1Co 11:10   For this reason a woman ought to have a **SIGN** of authority on her head. (Mounce [#161])

1Co 14:22   Wherefore tongues are for a **SIGN**, not to them that believe, but to them that believe not.

2Th 3:17   The greeting is by my hand, Paul's, which is a **SIGN** of genuineness in every letter: this is how I write. (Lexham [#169])

Re 12:1   And a great **SIGN** appeared in heaven: a woman clothed with the sun and with the moon under her feet, and on her head a crown of twelve stars. (Lexham [#169])

Re 12:3   And another **SIGN** appeared in heaven, and behold, a great fiery red dragon, having seven heads and ten horns, and on his heads were seven royal headbands. (Lexham [#169])

Re 15:1   And I saw another **SIGN** in heaven, great and marvelous, seven angels having the seven last plagues; for in them is filled up the wrath of God.

Retreat into Figurative Language!

For the last few thousand years, reality has been slowly but surely beating more and more of Christianity into the corner of "Figurative Language". This pretzeling of scripture, the figurization of difficult passages into harmless fluff, started way back at the beginning. The early church father known as Origen excused Biblical malarky thusly:

A spiritual truth often exists embodied in a corporeal falsehood   [P. 42 #76]

And to demonstrate that, it is described how he neutralized one such problem verse, the one in Matthew 4:8, where the evil Satan brings Jesus to a very tall mountain, and from the top of this mountain, all the kingdoms of the world are visible. This might work on a flat earth with clean air, but is physically impossible on a round earth with dirty air. We read Origen trying to explain away the problem:

It is not to be understood *__literally__* that Satan showed to Jesus all the kingdoms of the earth from a mountain, because this is impossible to the bodily eye...(it was merely) a *__vision__*. [p. 43 #76]

The general Christian practice is when a verse turns out to be total bullshit, do not admit the obvious-- that the verse is in **_ERROR_** (the Christian brain starts to short circuit at the very thought!), rather, merely **MAKE UP YOUR OWN WORD DEFINITIONS** and thus redirect the interpretation of said verse. It is nothing more than playing word games. It is very similar to the general who, when ordered never to retreat, rather ordered a full charge-- to the rear!!! This Christian double-speak, shades of Orwell's *1984*, and President Clinton's "is-is" fiasco, might go something like this...

"Oh, you thought I said I was going to <u>hit</u> you? I wasn't going to <u>physically</u> hit you,
I was merely going to take my <u>spiritual</u> boot and shove it up your <u>spiritual</u>..."

ass you might guess, this wouldn't work in THE **_REAL_** WORLD. Real people would end up punching you out, because real people don't put up with such BS. But many Christians do. They've lived an imaginary life in an imaginary universe for so long they've grown numb to being lied to by themselves & others.

This "spiritualization" of embarrassing verses is exemplified by the <u>Flat Earth</u> "debate". Several verses in the Bible clearly teach a flat earth, so based upon that, the medieval church also taught a flat earth. But each time in history that the Bible has gone up against science, science has eventually won out, and another chunk of the Bible evolves from literal to "spiritual" interpretation.

Another example of doctrinal evolution can be found in the Mormon religion. Any student of Mormonism can see, in a compressed time frame, this evolutionary process going on-- the same process that Christianity has been drifting through for 2,000 years. As more evidence comes to light that Mormonism doesn't *have* any evidence...

"well, golly gee, it's not that all those things were FALSE (Kaibob forbid!),
but that we were wrong for taking them literally!!! Why, they were meant to be
taken SPIRITUALLY!"

And thus Mormons have defused the ticking bomb of reality which had threatened the church, they have built this "deflector shield" against any future "bombs" that may yet be discovered. "Joe Smith a liar? So what! Joe Smith a false prophet? So what! Those things were never meant to be taken literally."

The Preterist View seems to be ***more of the same***. Christianity has tired of having "egg on it's face" the past 2,000 years, due to the no-show second act of it's star, so now it's time to realize that, golly gee, all those second-coming verses that most people had thought were LITERAL actually turn out to be "spiritual", and must not be taken at face value. It's not that Jesus screwed up in his "prophecies", but the READERS of those prophecies, the "victim", it is **he** that screwed up. Blame it on the victim, in order to leave the offending false prophet off the hook. The Preterist View is traveling down the exact same road that has been so often traveled by Christians. IF Jesus' prophecies were actually true to start with, as history has marched on, more and more of the prophecies would have been fulfilled in an obvious way, and by now the world should have been saying, "Of course Jesus was a true prophet! Any idiot knows that!" Instead, people like the Preterists are out there with magnifying glasses, looking under rocks in the hopes of finding something to salvage from the false Second Coming prophecies of Jesus. Good luck.

Saving The Savior

The Preterist theory is nothing more than a SALVAGE OPERATION, attempting to save Jesus from the consequences of his own false prophecies. They are off hunting in the land of "spiritual fulfillments" for an invisible Jesus visible only to the "spiritual" eye- whatever the hell that is. It does not have the ring of truth, only the ring of trying to cover up blown prophecies. It is ***exactly*** the same thing the Jehovah Witnesses did after their 1914 debacle. "Yes, Jesus came- just as we predicted! But he came in a SPIRITUAL way, that's why you can't see him." Of course, the return of Jesus became invisible only AFTER, never BEFORE, the time limits are blown. How convenient.

Real truth, as time marches on, gets confirmed more and more. New evidences come to light, more loose pieces of the puzzle fit in. For example, look at the theory that the earth orbits the sun. There has now accumulated so much additional evidence to back up this theory, that those that doubt it are now considered crack pots. Contrast this to the Second Coming prophecies of Jesus. As time has marched on, Jesus looks worse and worse. Preterism is merely the last-ditch effort, a spiritual equivalent to the Ptolemaic geo-centric system, getting ever more complicated, ever more complex, in a failed attempt to explain away and/or obfuscate bogus Biblical prophecies. "Oh what a tangled web we weave, when at first we practice to deceive."

Temple's Been Destroyed Several Times Already!

The temple that Solomon built, the first temple, was said to be the finest building on earth at the time, it being destroyed in 586 BC by the Babylonians. The second temple, built by the returning exiles did not survive in whole either. The temple in which Jesus taught (temple #3) was the result of a complete remodeling and enlarging by Herod the Great between 20 and 4 BC. The fact is, temples come and temples go. In fact, temples don't even count, if you believe what Jesus said to the woman at the well in John 4:19-24

> *The woman saith unto him, Sir, I perceive that thou art a prophet. Our fathers worshipped in this mountain; and ye say, that in Jerusalem is the place where men ought to worship. Jesus saith unto her, Woman, believe me, the hour cometh, when ye shall neither in this mountain, nor yet at Jerusalem, worship the Father. Ye worship ye know not what: we know what we worship: for salvation is of the Jews. But the hour cometh, and now is, when the true worshippers shall worship the Father in spirit and in truth: for the Father seeketh such to worship him. God [is] a Spirit: and they that worship him must worship [him] in spirit and in truth.*

The Preterist view is that the end of the temple was an event of worldwide proportions, fulfilling all sorts of prophecies in the New Testament. But these prophecies of the destruction of the temple also foretell of universal doom, cosmic catastrophes, i.e. world-wide events. Nothing like that happened in 70 AD when the temple was destroyed. The sun still shone on the children playing in Athens, and 99% of mankind was totally unaware of what was happening in Jerusalem that day. The end of the temple was by no means the earthshaking catastrophe the Preterists claim. The temple was obsolete anyway, according to Jesus himself, so what's the big deal? The Preterist view of the temple's destruction doesn't fit the reality.

Partial Preteristism = Bunk

The Partial Preterists believe that end-time predictions of Matthew 24 were fulfilled during the first century, but those of 2nd Thessalonians were meant for later. The problem this runs into is revealed by simple algebra, you know, that stuff you thought you'd never have a use for! As you'll (maybe) recall,

$$\textbf{IF} \quad A=B \quad \textbf{AND} \quad B=C \quad \textbf{THEN} \quad A=C$$

I believe it was called the *Distributive Law*. Well, as close as mere words allow, when it comes to prophecies,

$$\textbf{IF}$$
$$\text{Matthew 24} \quad = \quad \text{1}^{st}\text{ Thessalonians}$$
$$\textbf{AND}$$
$$\text{1}^{st}\text{ Thessalonians} \quad = \quad \text{2}^{nd}\text{ Thessalonians}$$
$$\textbf{THEN}$$
$$\text{Matthew 24} \quad = \quad \text{2}^{nd}\text{ Thessalonians}$$

I intend to show that this is the case. The Prophecy of Matthew 24 = The Prophecy of 2 Thessalonians. What is the big deal about that, you may ask. Thanks for asking. The "big deal" is that it totally disproves the Partial Preterist position. You see, the prophecies in the letters to Thessalonica require fulfillment within the first century, before 71 AD to be precise, as the **temple** is assumed to be still standing within the era that these prophecies are due to take place, as well as the more obtuse fact that Paul expected fulfillment within the lifetimes of the Thessalonians. And what is the problem with that? The problem is that the general Resurrection, and Judgment Day are *__also__* due to take place within this *__same__* time frame, the era of the temple. ***This would place the general Resurrection and Judgment Day within the first century*** - things that we know for sure did NOT happen. The end result? The Partial Preterist position, though giving it a good try, nevertheless fails to rescue Jesus from his false prophecies. Jesus still remains a false prophet to those that honestly consider the evidence, as he clearly predicted things which did not happen within the time frame he himself laid down.

What follows is a chart that compares these three sections of prophecy. Paul usually doesn't parallel any of the gospel stories, so to see how closely his two letters follow the script here is quite surprising. I wonder if I am the first to have noticed this? It is also another bit of evidence that this was the common teaching of the early church. I believe that, when laid side-by-side, it will become obvious to the casual observer that these three sections of prophecy are all referring to the **same** event: the Second Coming.

The Partial Preterists are wrong for dividing these up, some events for the 1st Century, other events for who knows what century in the future. And what are these events?
- ♦ Destruction of Jerusalem and the temple.
- ♦ The visible return of Jesus to earth.
- ♦ The so-called "rapture" of the saints.
- ♦ The Judgment of all evil men before the throne of God.
- ♦ The general resurrection from the dead of all mankind.

Needless to say, the FACT that you the reader are sitting around reading this sentence right now proves that the end did *NOT* come when it was predicted to come. And please don't bother criticizing me if I forgot to dot an "i" or cross a "t" in this brief but broad synopsis of Christian end-time myths. Christians *themselves* can't straighten out their *own* mess regarding the final scenario-- so don't expect anyone else to do any better.

A Trilogy of Prophecy: Matthew & 1st and 2nd Thessalonians

A Trilogy of Prophecy		
Showing That These Three Books Are All Prophesying The Same Event		
Matthew	**1st Thessalonians**	**2nd Thessalonians**
24:3) The sign of your coming.	4:15) When the Lord comes.	2:1) The coming of our Lord.
24:9) (persecutions)		1:4) (persecutions)
		2:8) The "man of lawlessness" is killed by the 2nd coming of Jesus. This was a FIRST CENTURY individual, and thus the 2nd coming is locked into the first century
24:15 The abomination, standing in THE holy place, i.e. the temple.		2:3-4) The man of lawlessness, sitting in the temple.
24:21) Great tribulation	1:10) Retribution	1:8) Dealing out retribution.
24:21) Tribulation unparalleled in history.	2:16) Wrath to the utmost.	
24:22) Days of wrath cut short to preserve Christians.	1:10) Jesus delivers Christians from the wrath to come.	
25:30) "Sinners" get cast into outer darkness.		1:9) "Sinners" get eternal destruction away from Jesus.
24:24) False wonders and signs.		2:9) False wonders and signs.
24:4,5,24) False prophets and deceivers.		2:2) False teachers and deceivers.
24:27) Jesus as visible as a lightning flash in the sky. (i.e. extremely bright)		1:7-8) Jesus revealed (i.e. made visible) from heaven (i.e. in the sky), in BLAZING FIRE (i.e. extremely bright).
	4:16-17) The dead in Christ shall be resurrected.	
25:31) With angels.		1:7-8) With angels.
24:30; 25:31) Great glory.		1:10) Will reveal his glory.
24:31) Trumpet blast.	4:16) Trumpet blast.	
24:30) Jesus "coming on the clouds"(i.e. in the sky, the "heavens").	4:16) Jesus descending from heaven.	
24:30) Jesus in the clouds.	4:17 Jesus in the clouds.	
24:30) ALL the tribes of planet earth will SEE with their eyes the 2nd coming. Not a local, or hidden, event.		
25:31+) All nations will stand before Jesus at his coming.	2:19; 3:13) We will stand before Jesus at his coming.	
24:10) An apostasy precedes Jesus' return.		2:3) An apostasy precedes Jesus' return.
24:42) Keep awake!	5:6) Keep awake!	
25:5) Some are sleeping.	5:6) Some are sleeping.	
24:43) Will come like a thief in the night.	5:2,4) Like a thief in the night.	
24:4) Let no one deceive you.		2:3) Let no one deceive you.
24:42) Which day your Lord is coming.	5:2) The day of the Lord.	2:2) The day of the Lord.
24:37-39, 48-51) Sense of complacency, all is normal, precedes Jesus' return.	5:3) Sense of complacency, peace & safety, precedes Jesus' return.	
24:40-42, 31) Christians gathered from earth up to Jesus / angels gather up Christians.	4:17) Christians gathered from earth up to Jesus.	2:1) Christians gathered from earth up to Jesus.
24:39) Their destruction comes unexpectedly.	5:3) Their destruction comes unexpectedly.	
25:5) Some Christians drowsy, asleep while waiting for Jesus.	5:5-6) Don't sleep! Be alert.	
25:31-46) Judgment Day.	3:13) Judgment Day.	1:8-9) Judgment Day.

A Cloudy Theory: The Invisible Jesus

Another feature of Preterism is that the **invisible** Jesus returning to earth in 70 AD returned in invisible clouds. Easy to say, harder to prove. Also hard to back up from the Bible, as I will show that the Bible promises a **visible** Jesus returning amongst **visible** clouds.

The Preterists have a difficult time with the clouds mentioned in connection with the return of Jesus, because it is obvious that if Jesus were to return amongst the visible clouds of the sky, he could not be the *invisible* Jesus of the Preterist camp. Therefore the Preterists strive to rationalize this problem away by doing what a lot of dishonest Christians do when confronted with words they don't like: they redefine. Clouds are visible by definition. Preterists need *invisible* clouds. Presto chango! Claim these are invisible, figurative, spiritual or whatever clouds, and the problem is solved.

But the problem remains, as they can not cite even **one** Biblical reference to back up their goof-ball contention. **_All_** clouds in the Bible are real clouds. There are **_no_** invisible clouds, such as are required by the Preterist position. They take plain verses, twist the hell out of them, speculate on "war clouds" and "ancient battles" and hope no one looks at their position too closely. They go through all sorts of mental gymnastics in an attempt to make those real clouds of Jesus' return go away. However, they have no more luck in that than do our weathermen on TV. Those pesky visible clouds just won't go away!

You want to know what's *really* invisible? The verses in the Bible promising an **invisible** Preterist Jesus returning to the Earth amongst **invisible** clouds. As for the whole thing being visible, there are plenty of verses promising that}

And then shall *appear*
((Only something that is <u>visible</u> may "appear"))
the sign
((A sign that is invisible is no sign))
of the Son of man in _heaven_:
((This means the sky, obviously <u>visible</u>))
and then shall all the tribes of the earth mourn, and they shall
see
((They shall WHAT???? THEY SHALL <u>SEE</u>! With this, their invisible Jesus just "disappeared"))
the Son of man *coming in the clouds*
*((Are clouds visible? Of course! Clouds are some of the **<u>MOST</u>** visible items of planet Earth, even visible from outer space))*
of heaven with power and *great glory*
((Glory resulting from everyone <u>seeing</u> the wondrous event)).
(Matthew 24:30 also Mk 13:26) (KJV [#19])

Then we which are alive [and] remain shall be caught *up*
((Why "up"? Because that's where the real clouds of the real sky are when you're on the ground!))
together with them in the *clouds*, to meet the Lord in the *air*.

((Clouds are found in the air- this is obvious to all, and I feel stupid for having to point out the obvious to people, but here goes: dear Preterists, these are REAL clouds UP floating around in a REAL sky))

and so shall we ever be with the Lord.

(1ˢᵗ Thessalonians 4:17 KJV [#19])

Behold, he cometh *with (the) clouds*

((Sounds like everyday, normal clouds to me! If he meant something different, how would he then describe REAL clouds, if not in these same terms?????))

and *every*

(the word "every" would include every "spiritual" eye as well as every fleshly eye, thus giving the boot to the old "spiritual eye" excuse. The word "every" means "without exception" per Webster's Dictionary. The Preterists, pro-dictionary when it supports their position, end up hypocritically arguing with the dictionary over this verse.)

eye shall <u>see</u> him

((Gee! Just as clouds are very visible due to their being way up in the sky, so will Jesus also be visible, as he will be SEEN, by EYES, amongst the CLOUDS. It can't get much more specific than that! <u>SEEN</u>, by <u>EYES</u>, among <u>CLOUDS</u>- no invisible Jesus' here!))

and they [also] which pierced him: and all kindreds of the earth shall wail because of him. Even so, Amen.

(Rev. 1:7 KJV [#19])

And when he ((Jesus)) had spoken these things, while they *beheld*

((i.e. while they were <u>looking</u> with their physical, fleshly non-spiritual <u>eyeballs</u>))

he was taken up; and a *cloud*

((A WHAT? did he say a CLOUD???? I guess it was a <u>VISIBLE</u> cloud, as they wrote about it, and thus could see it.))

received him *out of their sight*.

((Only a REAL cloud could have <u>blocked their vision</u>. This was therefore no figurative cloud, nor a spiritual cloud. Notice also that most of the ascent of Jesus was <u>visible</u>. Not until Jesus reached orbital velocity was their vision blocked. Likewise, the return of Jesus is to be visible as well.))

And while they *looked*

((Looked with what? With their <u>eyes</u>!!! What kind of eyes? Eyes of "perception"? Eyes of "spiritual insight"? "Spiritual" eyes? No! They used their good old, fleshly, human eyes.))

steadfastly toward heaven

((Heaven, per the Bible, is where clouds are- i.e. the sky.))

as he went up, behold, two men stood by them in white apparel; Which also said, Ye men of Galilee,

why stand ye *gazing*

(Once again, the fact of being visible is emphasized. One can not "gaze" at an invisible Jesus.)

up into heaven? This same
Jesus, which is taken up from you into heaven,
shall so come in like manner
as ye have seen *him go into*
heaven.
(Acts 1: 9-11 KJV [#19])

It can't get much plainer than this. As Jesus physically and very **VISIBLY** blasted off thru **visible** clouds into outer space,

"IN LIKE MANNER"

shall he **visibly** return thru **visible** clouds to Earth. For the Preterists to read this verse, and totally (deliberately?) miss what it's saying, is strong testimony to their own self-delusion. In spite of this verse, they continue to teach that an **invisible** Jesus returned to the Earth in **figurative** "clouds of war" in 70 AD. In light of the above verse, the only appropriate response I can think of to the theological hair-splitting of the Preterists is

HORSE MANURE ! ! !

(We are) looking
*(How in the hell could they be out "looking" for something for which it is **impossible** to look for, i.e. an invisible Jesus returning to Earth? It is painfully obvious that a **visible** Jesus is what was promised.)*
for the... appearing
*(Let's see... they are **looking** for the **appearing**... hmmm, sure sounds like something that would be visible. If I can "see" this, why can't our Preterists???)*
of the great God and our Savior, Jesus Christ.
*(This nails it down as a Second Coming passage. They are looking for a **visible** Jesus to return.)*
(Titus 2:13 KJV [#19])

<u>WATCH</u> therefore; for ye know not what hour your Lord doth come. (Mt 24:42 KJV [#19])

<u>WATCH</u> therefore, for you know neither the day nor the hour wherein the
Son of Man cometh. (Mt 25:13 KJV [#19])

Take ye heed, <u>WATCH</u> and pray; for ye know not when the time is. (Mk 13:33 KJV [#19])

<u>WATCH</u> ye therefore; for ye know not when the master of the house cometh. (Mk 13:35 KJV)

And what I say unto you I say unto all, <u>WATCH</u>! (Mk 13:37 KJV [#19])

It is physically impossible to watch for something that can't be watched. If the invisible Jesus of the Preterist theory is correct, Jesus is asking the impossible from his followers. Jesus may just as well have ordered them to say prayers in the corners of round rooms as to expect them to view an unviewable Second Coming. You can only <u>WATCH</u> for that which is <u>WATCHABLE</u>.

Primitive Theories of Clouds

We tend to take for granted the knowledge of what clouds really are. Our problem is, we live in an era of routinely flying thru clouds in 747's at 600 miles per hour, and not thinking twice about it. However, thousands of years ago, people had no good reasons to believe that clouds weren't solid objects that could support weight. Hell, even most of us as kids day dreamed as much. Therefore, it's not surprising to find statements in ancient documents that, when written, were written as *literal*, but since then have evolved into *figurative* due to advances in science. For example, in Psalms we find a reference to the Hebrew god using clouds as chariots:

> Who layeth the beams of his chambers in the waters: **who maketh the clouds his chariot**: who walketh upon the wings of the wind. (Psalms 104:3 KJV [#19])

It seems to us to be figurative language, but remember: the concept of riding on clouds was not beyond the realm of possibility for the ancient Hebrews. Did they think of clouds as transportation for their god? Yes they did. Here is a verse that seems to be saying as much:

> Behold, **the LORD rideth upon a swift cloud**, and shall come into Egypt: and the idols of Egypt shall be moved at his presence... (Isaiah 19:1 KJV [#19])

Please note that all of the clouds we've encountered so far have been real, actual clouds. We have yet to run into the invisible variety as required by the Preterist position. Let's look at some more clouds. You will see that these also were real, and very visible. In fact, if the children of Israel had the Preterist type of cloud leading them thru the wilderness (i.e. an invisible cloud), they all would have gotten lost and died in the desert the first month!

> And the LORD went before them by day in a pillar of a (visible) **cloud**, to lead them the way; and by night in a pillar of fire (visible fire) to give them light; to go by day and night: He took not away the pillar of the **cloud** by day, nor the pillar of fire by night, [from] before the people. (Exodus 13:21-22 KJV [#19])

This cloud was as visible and real as the clouds that Jesus spoke of. The Preterists need invisible clouds to support their theory, but I'm afraid we'll not see any invisible clouds anywhere in the Bible!

Another verse adds to the evidence that these clouds were real and visible:

> And the angel of God, which went before the camp of Israel, removed and went behind them; and the pillar of the **cloud** went from before their face, and stood behind them: And it came between the camp of the Egyptians and the camp of Israel; and it was a **cloud** and darkness [to them], but it gave light ((LIGHT! Visible LIGHT! Not invisible, but real)) by night [to these]: so that the one came not near the other all the night. (Exodus 14:19-20 KJV [#19])

The Old Testament apocrypha was accepted by the early church as authoritative writings. Even the New Testament quotes from them as an authoritative source, in Jude 14. The people that wrote the New Testament did not limit their study of scriptures to what we have labeled THE OLD TESTAMENT. That means that their usage of the word "cloud" would have also been influenced by how it was used in the apocrypha. Let's look at some examples from the apocrypha:

> And they (angels) took me up onto their wings, and carried me up to the first heaven, and **PLACED ME ON THE CLOUDS**. And, behold, they were moving. And there I perceived the air higher up, and higher still I saw the ether. And they placed me on the first heaven. And they showed me a vast ocean, much bigger than the earthly ocean. (2 Enoch 3)

> How many chariots has the Holy One? He has chariots of the cherubim...He has chariots of wind...**He also has the chariots of swift cloud**, as it is written, "See! the Lord comes, riding a swift cloud." He has the **chariots of clouds**, as it is written, "I am coming to you in a dense cloud." (3 Enoch 24)

> And as I said these things **a cloud came and seized me and took me up again to the heavens**. And I saw many judgments and I wept bitterly... (Greek Apocalypse of Ezra, 5:7-8)

Along the same line as these, we find in Harper's Bible Dictionary that:

...clouds were experienced and perceived as an awesome manifestation of divine power by the Canaanites and ancient Israelites. The Ugaritic texts call the storm god Baal "Cloud Rider." Israel applied *the same title* to God. [#160]

So BibleGod & Baal share the same nickname, "Cloud Rider". If the worshippers of Baal believed their god zoomed around on clouds that were literal, why would their neighbors USING THE EXACT SAME VERBIAGE, think those clouds figurative??? It is only the prejudice of the modern Christian for their BibleGod that excuses all such UN-scientific thinking found in the Christian scriptures, but condemns the exact same verbiage when found in non-Christian scriptures.

I think the problem is that we tend to look at this ancient book through the eyes of modern man. We airplane savvy jet-setters know by heart that clouds are very nebulous, and of no harm whatsoever to an airplane that flies straight into/through one. But why should we assume that ancient people, who had never touched a cloud, would know this? It is unreasonable to assume that out of all the ancient people who used terms like "riding on a cloud", only the Israelis understood it to be figurative. HOW, if they knew this to the exclusion of their neighbors, did they know this? Did they have airplanes? The same can be said for stars. They wrote of stars falling to the earth. Should they have known better??? Is there any way on earth they could have known about stars being billions of miles away, fired by nuclear fusion and propelled at enormous velocities through empty space? Of course not! But we, with our almost unconscious feeling for science, seeing all through the spectacles of modern man, automatically translate all such Biblical passages into "Figurative Language." This is WRONG! We have to take these passages as THEY wrote them, not as we, thousands of years later, interpret them. We are merely reading back into the text that which doesn't exist. It is cultural bias, and most people aren't even aware of it.

Every Listing of the word CLOUD

Cloud

Being a Listing of Every Occurrence of the Word "Cloud"
from the Old & New Testament, American Standard Version [#10],
and not even ONE supports what the Preterists claim about "Clouds".

Old Testament: Clouds

Genesis 9:13 I do set my bow in the **CLOUD**, and it shall be for a token of a covenant between me and the earth.

Genesis 9:14 And it shall come to pass, when I bring a **CLOUD** over the earth, that the bow shall be seen in the **CLOUD**,

Genesis 9:16 And the bow shall be in the **CLOUD**; and I will look upon it, that I may remember the everlasting covenant between God and every living creature of all flesh that is upon the earth.

Exodus 13:21 And Jehovah went before them by day in a pillar of **CLOUD**, to lead them the way, and by night in a pillar of fire, to give them light; that they might go by day and by night:

Exodus 13:22 the pillar of **CLOUD** by day, and the pillar of fire by night, departed not from before the people.

Exodus 14:19 And the angel of God, who went before the camp of Israel, removed and went behind them; and the pillar of **CLOUD** removed from before them, and stood behind them:

Exodus 14:20 and it came between the camp of Egypt and the camp of Israel; and there was the **CLOUD** and the darkness, yet gave it light by night: and the one came not near the other all the night.

Exodus 14:24 And it came to pass in the morning watch, that Jehovah looked forth upon the host of the Egyptians through the pillar of fire and of **CLOUD**, and discomfited the host of the Egyptians.

Exodus 16:10 And it came to pass, as Aaron spake unto the whole congregation of the children of Israel, that they looked toward the wilderness, and, behold, the glory of Jehovah appeared in the **CLOUD**.

Exodus 19:9 And Jehovah said unto Moses, Lo, I come unto thee in a thick **CLOUD**, that the people may hear when I speak with thee, and may also believe thee for ever. And Moses told the words of the people unto Jehovah.

Exodus 19:16 And it came to pass on the third day, when it was morning, that there were thunders and lightnings, and a thick **CLOUD** upon the mount, and the voice of a trumpet exceeding loud; and all the people that were in the camp trembled.

Exodus 24:15 And Moses went up into the mount, and the **CLOUD** covered the mount.

Exodus 24:16 And the glory of Jehovah abode upon mount Sinai, and the **CLOUD** covered it six days: and the seventh day he called unto Moses out of the midst of the **CLOUD**.

Exodus 24:18 And Moses entered into the midst of the **CLOUD**, and went up into the mount: and Moses was in the mount forty days and forty nights.

Exodus 33:9 And it came to pass, when Moses entered into the Tent, the pillar of **CLOUD** descended, and stood at the door of the Tent: and *Jehovah* spake with Moses.

Exodus 33:10 And all the people **saw** the pillar of **CLOUD** stand at the door of the Tent: and all the people rose up and worshipped, every man at his tent door.

Exodus 34:5 And Jehovah descended in the CLOUD, and stood with him there, and proclaimed the name of Jehovah.

Exodus 40:34 Then the **CLOUD** covered the tent of meeting, and the glory of Jehovah filled the tabernacle.

Exodus 40:35 And Moses was not able to enter into the tent of meeting, because the **CLOUD** abode thereon, and the glory of Jehovah filled the tabernacle.

Exodus 40:36 And when the **CLOUD** was taken up from over the tabernacle, the children of Israel went onward, throughout all their journeys:

Exodus 40:37 but if the **CLOUD** was not taken up, then they journeyed not till the day that it was taken up.

Exodus 40:38 For the **CLOUD** of Jehovah was upon the tabernacle by day, and there was fire therein by night, in the sight of all the house of Israel, throughout all their journeys.

Leviticus 16:2 and Jehovah said unto Moses, Speak unto Aaron thy brother, that he come not at all times into the holy place within the veil, before the mercy-seat which is upon the ark; that he die not: for I will appear in the **CLOUD** upon the mercy-seat.

Leviticus 16:13 and he shall put the incense upon the fire before Jehovah, that the **CLOUD** of the incense may cover the mercy-seat that is upon the testimony, that he die not:

Numbers 9:15 And on the day that the tabernacle was reared up the **CLOUD** covered the tabernacle, even the tent of the testimony: and at even it was upon the tabernacle as it were the appearance of fire, until morning.

Numbers 9:16 So it was alway: the **CLOUD** covered it, and the appearance of fire by night.

Numbers 9:17 And whenever the **CLOUD** was taken up from over the Tent, then after that the children of Israel journeyed: and in the place where the **CLOUD** abode, there the children of Israel encamped.

Numbers 9:18 At the commandment of Jehovah the children of Israel journeyed, and at the commandment of Jehovah they encamped: as long as the **CLOUD** abode upon the tabernacle they remained encamped.

Numbers 9:19 And when the **CLOUD** tarried upon the tabernacle many days, then the children of Israel kept the charge of Jehovah, and journeyed not.

Numbers 9:20 And sometimes the **CLOUD** was a few days upon the tabernacle; then according to the commandment of Jehovah they remained encamped, and according to the commandment of Jehovah they journeyed.

Numbers 9:21 And sometimes the **CLOUD** was from evening until morning; and when the **CLOUD** was taken up in the morning, they journeyed: or *if it continued* by day and by night, when the **CLOUD** was taken up, they journeyed.

Numbers 9:22 Whether it were two days, or a month, or a year, that the **CLOUD** tarried upon the tabernacle, abiding thereon, the children of Israel remained encamped, and journeyed not; but when it was taken up, they journeyed.

Numbers 10:11 And it came to pass in the second year, in the second month, on the twentieth day of the month, that the **CLOUD** was taken up from over the tabernacle of the testimony.

Numbers 10:12 And the children of Israel set forward according to their journeys out of the wilderness of Sinai; and the **CLOUD** abode in the wilderness of Paran.

Numbers 10:34 And the **CLOUD** of Jehovah was over them by day, when they set forward from the camp.

Numbers 11:25 And **Jehovah came down in the CLOUD**, and spake unto him, and took of the Spirit that was upon him, and put it upon the seventy elders: and it came to pass, that, when the Spirit rested upon them, they prophesied, but they did so no more.

Numbers 12:5 And **Jehovah came down in a pillar of CLOUD**, and stood at the door of the Tent, and called Aaron and Miriam; and they both came forth.

Numbers 12:10 And the **CLOUD** removed from over the Tent; and, behold, Miriam was leprous, as *white as* snow: and Aaron looked upon Miriam, and, behold, she was leprous.

Numbers 14:14 and they will tell it to the inhabitants of this land. They have heard that thou Jehovah art in the midst of this people; for thou Jehovah art seen face to face, and thy **CLOUD** standeth over them, and thou goest before them, in a pillar of **CLOUD** by day, and in a pillar of fire by night.

Numbers 16:42 And it came to pass, when the congregation was assembled against Moses and against Aaron, that they looked toward the tent of meeting: and, behold, the **CLOUD** covered it, and the glory of Jehovah appeared.

Deuteronomy 1:33 who went before you in the way, to seek you out a place to pitch your tents in, in fire by night, to show you by what way ye should go, and in the **CLOUD** by day.

Deuteronomy 4:11 And ye came near and stood under the mountain; and the mountain burned with fire unto the heart of heaven, with darkness, **CLOUD**, and thick darkness.

Deuteronomy 5:22 These words Jehovah spake unto all your assembly in the mount out of the midst of the fire, of the **CLOUD**, and of the thick darkness, with a great voice: and he added no more. And he wrote them upon two tables of stone, and gave them unto me.

Deuteronomy 31:15 And Jehovah appeared in the Tent in a pillar of **CLOUD**: and the pillar of **CLOUD** stood over the door of the Tent.

Judges 20:38 Now the appointed sign between the men of Israel and the liers-in-wait was, that they should make a great **CLOUD** of smoke rise up out of the city.

Judges 20:40 But when the **CLOUD** began to arise up out of the city in a pillar of smoke, the Benjamites looked behind them; and, behold, the whole of the city went up *in smoke* to heaven.

1 Kings 8:10 And it came to pass, when the priests were come out of the holy place, that the **CLOUD** filled the house of Jehovah,

1 Kings 8:11 so that the priests could not stand to minister by reason of the **CLOUD**; for the glory of Jehovah filled the house of Jehovah.

1 Kings 18:44 And it came to pass at the seventh time, that he said, Behold, there ariseth a **CLOUD** out of the sea, as small as a man's hand. And he said, Go up, say unto Ahab, Make ready *thy chariot*, and get thee down, that the rain stop thee not.

2 Chronicles 5:13 it came to pass, when the trumpeters and singers were as one, to make one sound to be heard in praising and thanking Jehovah; and when they lifted up their voice with the trumpets and cymbals and instruments of music, and praised Jehovah, *saying*, For he is good; for his lovingkindness *endureth* for ever; that then the house was filled with a **CLOUD**, even the house of Jehovah,

2 Chronicles 5:14 so that the priests could not stand to minister by reason of the **CLOUD**: for the glory of Jehovah filled the house of God.

Nehemiah 9:12 Moreover in a pillar of **CLOUD** thou leddest them by day; and in a pillar of fire by night, to give them light in the way wherein they should go.

Nehemiah 9:19 yet thou in thy manifold mercies forsookest them not in the wilderness: the pillar of **CLOUD** departed not from over them by day, to lead them in the way; neither the pillar of fire by night, to show them light, and the way wherein they should go.

Job 3:5 Let darkness and the shadow of death claim it for their own; Let a **CLOUD** dwell upon it; Let all that maketh black the day terrify it.

Job 7:9 As the **CLOUD** is consumed and vanisheth away, So he that goeth down to Sheol shall come up no more.

Job 26:8 He bindeth up the waters in his thick clouds; And the **CLOUD** is not rent under them.

Job 26:9 He incloseth the face of his throne, And spreadeth his **CLOUD** upon it.

Job 30:15 Terrors are turned upon me; They chase mine honor as the wind; And my welfare is passed away as a **CLOUD**.

Job 37:11 Yea, he ladeth the thick **CLOUD** with moisture; He spreadeth abroad the **CLOUD** of his lightning:

Job 37:15 Dost thou know how God layeth *his charge* upon them, And causeth the lightning of his **CLOUD** to shine?

Psalms 78:14 In the day-time also he led them with a **CLOUD**, And all the night with a light of fire.

Psalms 99:7 He spake unto them in the pillar of **CLOUD**: They kept his testimonies, And the statute that he gave them.

Psalms 105:39 He spread a **CLOUD** for a covering, And fire to give light in the night.

Proverbs 16:15 In the light of the king's countenance is life; And his favor is as a **CLOUD** of the latter rain.

Isaiah 4:5 And Jehovah will create over the whole habitation of mount Zion, and over her assemblies, a **CLOUD** and smoke by day, and the shining of a flaming fire by night; for over all the glory *shall be spread* a covering.

Isaiah 18:4 For thus hath Jehovah said unto me, I will be still, and I will behold in my dwelling-place, like clear heat in sunshine, like a **CLOUD** of dew in the heat of harvest.

Isaiah 19:1 The burden of Egypt. Behold, **Jehovah rideth upon a swift CLOUD**, and cometh unto Egypt: and the idols of Egypt shall tremble at his presence; and the heart of Egypt shall melt in the midst of it.

Isaiah 25:5 As the heat in a dry place wilt thou bring down the noise of strangers; as the heat by the shade of a **CLOUD**, the song of the terrible ones shall be brought low.

Isaiah 44:22 I have blotted out, as a thick **CLOUD**, thy transgressions, and, as a **CLOUD**, thy sins: return unto me; for I have redeemed thee.

Isaiah 60:8 Who are these that fly as a **CLOUD**, and as the doves to their windows?

Lamentations 2:1 How hath the Lord covered the daughter of Zion with a **CLOUD** in his anger! He hath cast down from heaven unto the earth the beauty of Israel, And hath not remembered his footstool in the day of his anger.

Lamentations 3:44 Thou hast covered thyself with a **CLOUD**, so that no prayer can pass through.

Lamentations 2:1 How hath the Lord covered the daughter of Zion with a **CLOUD** in his anger! He hath cast down from heaven unto the earth the beauty of Israel, And hath not remembered his footstool in the day of his anger.

Lamentations 3:44 Thou hast covered thyself with a **CLOUD**, so that no prayer can pass through.

Ezekiel 1:4 And I looked, and, behold, a stormy wind came out of the north, a great **CLOUD**, with a fire infolding itself, and a brightness round about it, and out of the midst thereof as it were glowing metal, out of the midst of the fire.

Ezekiel 1:28 As the appearance of the bow that is in the **CLOUD** in the day of rain, so was the appearance of the brightness round about. This was the appearance of the likeness of the glory of Jehovah. And when I saw it, I fell upon my face, and I heard a voice of one that spake.

Ezekiel 8:11 And there stood before them seventy men of the elders of the house of Israel; and in the midst of them stood Jaazaniah the son of Shaphan, every man with his censer in his hand; and the odor of the **CLOUD** of incense went up.

Ezekiel 10:3 Now the cherubim stood on the right side of the house, when the man went in; and the **CLOUD** filled the inner court.

Ezekiel 10:4 And the glory of Jehovah mounted up from the cherub, *and stood* over the threshold of the house; and the house was filled with the **CLOUD**, and the court was full of the brightness of Jehovah's glory.

Ezekiel 30:18 At Tehaphnehes also the day shall withdraw itself, when I shall break there the yokes of Egypt, and the pride of her power shall cease in her: as for her, a **CLOUD** shall cover her, and her daughters shall go into captivity.

Ezekiel 32:7 And when I shall extinguish thee, I will cover the heavens, and make the stars thereof dark; I will cover the sun with a **CLOUD**, and the moon shall not give its light.

Ezekiel 38:9 And thou shalt ascend, thou shalt come like a storm, thou shalt be like a **CLOUD** to cover the land, thou, and all thy hordes, and many peoples with thee.

Ezekiel 38:16 and thou shalt come up against my people Israel, as a **CLOUD** to cover the land: it shall come to pass in the latter days, that I will bring thee against my land, that the nations may know me, when I shall be sanctified in thee, O Gog, before their eyes.

Hosea 6:4 O Ephraim, what shall I do unto thee? O Judah, what shall I do unto thee? for your goodness is as a morning **CLOUD**, and as the dew that goeth early away.

Hosea 13:3 Therefore they shall be as the morning **CLOUD**, and as the dew that passeth early away, as the chaff that is driven with the whirlwind out of the threshing-floor, and as the smoke out of the chimney.

New Testament: Clouds

Matthew 17:5 While he was yet speaking, behold, a bright **CLOUD** overshadowed them: and behold, a voice out of the **CLOUD**, saying, This is my beloved Son, in whom I am well pleased; hear ye him.

Mark 9:7 And there came a **CLOUD** overshadowing them: and there came a voice out of the **CLOUD**, This is my beloved Son: hear ye him.

Luke 9:34 And while he said these things, there came a **CLOUD**, and overshadowed them: and they feared as they entered into the **CLOUD**.

Luke 9:35 And a voice came out of the **CLOUD**, saying, This is my Son, my chosen: hear ye him.

Luke 12:54 And he said to the multitudes also, When ye **see** a **CLOUD** rising in the west, straightway ye say, There cometh a shower; and so it cometh to pass.

Luke 21:27 And then shall they **see** the Son of man coming in a **CLOUD** with power and great glory.

Acts 1:9 And when he had said these things, as they were looking, he was taken up; and a **CLOUD** received him out of their sight.

1 Corinthians 10:1 For I would not, brethren, have you ignorant, that our fathers were all under the **CLOUD**, and all passed through the sea;

1 Corinthians 10:2 and were all baptized unto Moses in the **CLOUD** and in the sea;

Hebrews 12:1 Therefore let us also, seeing we are compassed about with so great a **CLOUD** of witnesses, lay aside every weight, and the sin which doth so easily beset us, and let us run with patience the race that is set before us,

Revelation 10:1 And I saw another strong angel coming down out of heaven, arrayed with a **CLOUD**; and the rainbow was upon his head, and his face was as the sun, and his feet as pillars of fire;

Revelation 11:12 And they heard a great voice from heaven saying unto them, Come up hither. And they went up into heaven

Revelation 14:14 And I saw, and behold, a white **CLOUD**; and **on** the **CLOUD** *I saw* one **sitting** like unto a son of man, having on his head a golden crown, and in his hand sharp sickle.

Revelation 14:15 And another angel came out from the temple, crying with a great voice to him that **sat** on the **CLOUD**, Send forth thy sickle, and reap: for the hour to reap is come; for the harvest of the earth is ripe.

Revelation 14:16 And he that **sat** on the **CLOUD** cast his sickle upon the earth; and the earth was reaped.

2nd Peter 3:3-14

Preterism Impossible

<u>2nd Peter 3:7</u> … the present **HEAVENS AND EARTH** by His word are being reserved for **FIRE**, kept for the day of judgment and destruction of ungodly men.

<u>2nd Peter 3:10</u> …the day of the Lord will come like a thief, in which **the HEAVENS will pass away with a roar and the ELEMENTS will be DESTROYED with intense heat, and the EARTH and its works will be BURNED UP.**

<u>2nd Peter 3:12</u> (You should be) looking for and hastening the coming of the day of God, on account of which **the HEAVENS will be DESTROYED by burning, and the ELEMENTS will melt with intense heat!**

2nd Coming = Destruction of the Earth & Universe ∴ **Preterist Position Impossible** 	If Jesus returned in 70 CE, then everything mentioned above also must have happened. And for those Preterists who want to ignore dictionaries, below are definitions of the three items that are slated for total & complete destruction down to the atomic level. For Preterism to be correct, billions of galaxies and trillions of stars and planets- including our own- were all annihilated in 70 CE.

"The Heavens"
> Strong's #3772 ouranos {oo-ran-os'}
> 1) the vaulted expanse of the sky with all things visible in it
> 1a) <u>the universe, the world</u>

"The Elements"
> Strong's #4747 stoicheion {stoy-khi'-on}
> 1b) **the elements from which all things have come**, the material causes of the universe
> 1c) **the heavenly bodies**, either as parts of the heavens or (as others think) because in them the elements of man, life and destiny were supposed to reside.

"The Earth"
> Strong's #1093 ge {ghay}
> 1) arable land
> 2) the **ground**, the earth as a standing place
> 3) the main land as opposed to the sea or water
> 4) the **earth as a whole**
> 4a) the earth as opposed to the heavens
> 4b) **the inhabited earth**, the abode of men and animals
> 5) a country, land enclosed within fixed boundaries, a tract of land, territory, region

OK now, let me check… Yup, the Earth is still here. That's a fact, a fact that totally disproves Preterism. And I'll take facts over theological hot air any day!

Gary Demar's Book   LAST DAYS MADNESS   is Mad

Christian author and Preterist proponent Gary DeMar wrote one of the best selling books on Preterism, entitled "Last Days Madness". In it he exemplifies one of the biggest flaws in Preterist reasoning, that of an assumptions built upon another assumption which has been built upon even more assumptions etc, until the reader himself, a bit dizzy by now, upon reaching the end of the section, forgets that the

DRAMATIC CONCLUSION

*presented as hard **fact**, never really got past the mere **assumption** stage. This is a common tactic of cult writings, and Gary appears quite skilled in the art. So below is but a brief review of Gary DeMar's book, pointing out a small sampling of the many assumptions found within the book. Were I to make it an exhaustive listing, who knows, but in the words of the Apostle John, "the world itself could not contain the books".*

Last Days Madness [#34]
Gary DeMar, American Vision Inc.
Atlanta, GA 1994

ASSUMPTION: THE SUPPOSITION THAT SOMETHING IS TRUE. A FACT OR STATEMENT TAKEN FOR GRANTED.

Page 98, bottom two sentences, Gary quotes from Kirk, saying that Jesus was describing a local event in Matt. 24, Luke 19, and not the second coming. Up to this point, he has offered nothing to support this claim, and introduces the claim as if out of thin air. The claim needs support, as it claims Matt. 24 "makes it clear that Jesus was describing a **LOCAL** event..." What Mt. 24 makes "clear" is that "...immediately AFTER the tribulation of those days" stars will fall, ALL the tribes of the earth will mourn and THEY (**ALL** the tribes) will SEE Jesus (where?) in the clouds, and then the elect will be gathered from all over the entire earth. THIS is what is clear to the reader, and even though Gary offers hair brained "explanations" of these much later in the book, his statement, placed here without any support, is at this point only an assumption.

Page 117, middle of second paragraph, he starts to use a phrase that becomes commonplace later in the book. Gary is getting the reader used to substituting his own pet phrase "coming in judgment" for the more common phrase, "Second Coming." Until this concept has had some evidence to back it up, at this point in the book, it remains merely an assumption.

Page 120, last paragraph, Gary calls Titus, the Roman general, "God's representative." Once again, merely an assumption at this point.

Page 27, last paragraph, Gary writes of 1 Peter 4:7, that the "end of all things" meant the Old Covenant passing away. A reader of 1 Peter would conclude, from verse 1:4-5, that it rather refers to heaven. A reader would be left hanging with an unanswered question.

Page 56, about the 4th sentence, Gary writes that the Old Covenant came to an end in 70 AD. Why 70 AD? Why not 33 AD when Jesus died and the temple curtain was torn from top to bottom? No direct evidence is offered to support ANY exact date. To assume a date without evidence is to assume.

Page 57, he quotes Milton Terry as saying that the temple being destroyed is what was in mind in Heb. 12:26, "shaking of heaven and earth." This weird interpretation is presented without any explanation, thus, another mere assumption.

Page 58, middle paragraph, he says, "we must conclude that the idea of 'coming' in this context is different from the way many contemporary Christians understand the concept of 'coming.'" Gary ASSUMES we MUST conclude that. Well, I conclude something totally different! I conclude that Jesus was in error in his so-called prophecies of returning!!!

Page 73, middle paragraph, Gary says the Greek word means the **INHABITED** earth. Then he goes on to ASSUME that it is limited to the **ROMAN EMPIRE**, and then ASSUMES that JC would return after the gospel had been preached to the Roman Empire, and ASSUMES that return would be a "return in judgment upon Jerusalem," and not the BIG second coming. I say, a stack of cards, no matter how high, is still a stack of cards. Just because the "Holy Spirit" was ignorant of North & South America and Australia doesn't excuse OUR ignorance. WE KNOW BETTER. Or should.

Even More Assumptions...

For him who has ears to hear (and a goodly supply of patience) on the following pages are more assumptions you can check out on your own}

74, 91, 92, 132, 138, 154, 157, 159, 160, 161,
162, 163, 164, 165, 182, 204, 227, 291, 292,
306, 314, 315, 317, 318, 328, 329, 349

A Final Word Regarding Preterism

The Preterist theory is that Jesus' Second Coming occurred in 70 AD, but no one saw it, because "it was all invisible." The Preterist theory can not exist without one turning a blind eye towards many clear and plain verses in the Bible and leaving many questions unanswered.

As for Full Preterists, if they claim the Second Coming to be only a local event concerning Israel, then they must believe that the destruction of Jerusalem (a local event) killed more people than a world-wide flood. If they claim the Second Coming to be a **world-wide event** which took place in 70 CE, why did nobody in the entire world, not a single solitary individual, notice? And they can't explain why, if the Second Coming was just a **local event** only of concern to those in Jerusalem, then why was Paul writing to Gentile Corinthians 800 miles away to run for cover, duck & hide, and prepare for it??? They can't explain away all the Second Coming verses in the New Testament that clearly state a very visible and public return, so therefore they instead twist the definitions around until the words cease to mock and undercut their theory. They make figurative the literal, and literalize the figurative bing bang boom, using only their imagination and the support of their theory as the criteria. Ignoring the fact that the ONLY signs in the New Testament are VISIBLE signs, they create a new species of sign: the _**INVISIBLE**_ sign, created solely, once again, to support their theory, their theory existing solely to save their savior from being a False Prophet.

Partial Preterists ignore or try to explain away that fact that Judgment Day and The Resurrection are promised in the New Testament to take place concurrent with the return of Jesus. Neither of these happened in 70 AD. And their mutilation of the word "cloud" should earn all of them a hot spot in their mythical hell. The mental and verbal contortions they resort to, to save their savior from being a False Prophet, are truly hard to explain; one must experience it first hand (but please, try not to laugh in their face- it's rude).

Frankly, I think the reason that Preterism is still around, is that big-name mainline scholars can't stop laughing long enough to take it seriously. Sorry, but if Gary DeMar's book is a fair representation of the "mighty" Preterist view, I'm very disappointed.

Another reason mainline scholars can't really attack Preterism is that the next best viable alternative to it is what I've presented in this book: Jesus was a **FALSE PROPHET**, as he failed to return within the time limit laid down by himself & his Apostles, in The New Testament. To save their savior, **any** excuse will do- any card they can keep up their sleeve might come in handy to save their savior from his false prophecies- even Preterism. For Christians who want to remain willfully ignorant, Preterism beats the alternative of Jesus & Company having been documented prodigious liars and false prophets.

Conclusion

To the best of my knowledge, I have covered the verses in the New Testament that deal with the Second Coming. All data points have ended up in the same column of "Second Coming Due First Century." Not one legitimate verse ever places the Second Coming hundreds or thousands or millions of years in their future. Jesus & Company of the 1st Century clearly expected & prophesied & promised the Second Coming to occur within the lifetime of the folks they spoke & wrote to. But the Second Coming never happened within the time limits they themselves laid down, thus showing themselves to be false prophets.

As I stated in the introduction to this book, when I started this study of the Second Coming, I was a Christian. I had no foresight that such a study would lead me to conclude that Jesus had been a false prophet. I, an adult, was merely trying to answer a question that the teenage me had asked years previous.

So thus having weighed the evidence and "kicked against the goads" eventually every single data point eventually leads to only one conclusion:

Jesus, even if he were the son of god, even if he walked on water and had been resurrected from the dead, Jesus had also been a FALSE PROPHET. This conclusion is iron clad and inescapable. My conclusion was my conclusion; your conclusion is obviously up to you. Take your time, think it over, let it percolate. When you finally get to deciding, it will be one of, if not the biggest, decision in your life.

As for my journey thru life, regardless of the years and efforts I had put into the Christian faith, I drew the line at worshipping a false prophet. They had stoned such in Old Testament times; how could I then in good conscience worship such a man? So at that point I walked away from Christ & Christianity, and have had no regrets since. My final recommendation to you, reader, if you are truly a seeker of truth, is found in the words of Jesus, Luke 10:37, and that is to

Go &
do likewise

Bibliography

Bibliography

1	**New American Standard Bible**, The Lockman Foundation, La Habra CA, 1963
2	**The New Testament in Modern Speech**, Richard F. Weymouth, The Pilgrim Press, Boston, 1930, 1912
3	**Young's Literal Translation of the Holy Bible**, Robert Young (1898), Baker Book House, Grand Rapids, Mich.
4	**Concordant Literal New Testament**, Concordant Publishing Concern, Canyon Country, CA 1976
5	**The Emphasized New Testament**, J.B. Rotherham, Kregel Publications, Grand Rapids, MI 1967
6	**The New International Version Interlinear Greek-English New Testament**, with The Nestle Greek Text with a Literal English Translation by Rev. Alfred Marshall, Zondervan Publishing House, Grand Rapids, MI 1976
7	**Westcott & Hort Greek Text**, 1881, Public Domain
8	**The American Heritage Dictionary of the English Language**, Third Edition, Houghton Mifflin Co, 1992
9	**The Amplified New Testament**, Lockman Foundation, La Habra CA, 1958
10	**American Standard Version**, (1901), Star Bible Pub. Inc., Fort Worth, TX
11	**The Scholars Version**, found within **The Five Gospels**, Robert Funk, Macmillan Pub. Co, New York, 1993
12	**The Complete Bible: An American Translation**, J.M. Powis Smith & Edgar J. Goodspeed, The University of Chicago Press, Chicago, Illinois, 1963
13	**The Modern Language New Testament: The New Berkeley Version**, Dr. Gerrit Verkuyl, Zondervan Pub. House, Grand Rapids, MI, 1971
14	**Today's English Version**, aka **Good News Bible**, Thomas Nelson Publishers, Nashville, TN 1976
15	**The New Testament in Modern English**, J.B. Phillips, Macmillan Company, New York, 1966
16	**The New International Version**, Zondervan Publishing House, Grand Rapids, MI, 1976
17	**New Revised Standard Version**, National Council of Churches, Oxford Univ. Press, NY 1989
18	**Revised Standard Version**, Thomas Nelson Inc., NY 1971
19	**Authorized Version (King James Version)**, 1611
20	**Bible in Basic English**, Cambridge University Press, NY 1965
21	**Darby Bible**, J.N. Darby, 1881
22	**21st Century King James Version**, Deuel Enterprises 1994
23	**A Literal Translation of The Bible**, Jay P. Green, Hendrickson Pub., Peabody, Mass 1987
24	**Green's Modern King James Version**, Sovereign Grace Trust Fund, J.P. Green, 1993
25	**The New English Bible**, Oxford University Press, 1970
26	**The New Jerusalem Bible**, Henry Wansbrough, Publisher: Darton, Longman & Todd, 1985
27	**The Bible: A New Translation**, James Moffatt, Harper & Bro's, 1935
28	**The Holy Bible in Modern English**, Ferrar Fenton, Destiny Publishers, 1966
29	**The New American Bible**, Catholic Book Pub. Co., New York, 1970
30	**An American Translation**, William Beck, Holman Bible Pub., Nashville, TN 1976
31	**The Living Bible**, Tyndale House Publishers, Wheaton, Il, 1971
32	**Webster's Seventh New Collegiate Dictionary**, Merriam Co.,Publishers, Springfield, Mass. 1965
33	**The Parousia**, J. Stuart Russell, T. Fisher Unwin Pub., London, 1887
34	**Last Days Madness**, Gary DeMar, American Vision Inc., Atlanta, GA 1994
35	**Luke and the Last Things**, A.J. Matill, Western N.C. Press, Dillsboro, NC, 1979
36	**The Quest of the Historical Jesus**, Dr. Albert Schweitzer, Macmillian, NY, 1968
37	**The Search for the Twelve Apostles**, W. S. McBirnie, Tyndale House, Wheaton, IL, 1973
38	**The New American Standard Bible, Study Edition**, Holman Company, New York, 1975
39	**Harper's Bible Dictionary**, Madeleine & J. Lane Miller, Harper & Bro's, NY 1952
40-A	**The Westminster Dictionary of the Bible**, John Davis, Westminster Press, Philadelphia, 1944
40-B	**The *New* Westminster Dictionary of the Bible**, Henry Gehman, Westminster Press, Philadelphia, 1970

41	**Smith's Bible Dictionary,** Barbour Books, Westwood, NJ 1987
42	**The Interpreter's Bible,** misc. volumes, Abingdon Press, New York, 1953 etc
43	**An Expository Dictionary of New Testament Words,** W.E. Vine, Revell Co., Old Tappan, NJ 1966
44	**Future Survival,** Pastor Chuck Smith, The Word for Today, Costa Mesa, CA 1978
45	**The Harper Collins Bible Dictionary,** Paul J. Achtemeier, Gen. Editor, Harper, S.F. 1996
46	**The International Standard Bible Encyclopedia,** Vol. 2, Geoffrey W. Bromiley, Gen. Editor, Eerdman's Pub. Co., Grand Rapids, Mich 1982
47	**The Interpreter's Dictionary of the Bible,** Abingdon Press, NY 1962
48	**Mercer Dictionary of the Bible,** Watson Mills, Gen. Ed., Mercer Univ. Press, Macon, GA 1990
49	**Nelson's Illustrated Bible Dictionary,** Herbert Lockyer, Gen. Ed., Thomas Nelson Pub., NY 1986
50	**The Oxford English Dictionary,** 2nd Edition, (20 vol. set), Clarendon Press, Oxford 1989
51	**The Popular and Critical Bible Encyclopaedia,** Samuel Fallows, Howard-Severance Co., 1906
52	**Peloubet's BibleDictionary,** Universal Book & Bible House, Philadelphia, 1925
53	**Wycliffe Bible Encyclodedia,** Moody Press, Chicago, 1975
54	**Concise Dictionary of The Bible,** Lutterworth Press, London, 1967
55	**The Expositor's Bible Commentary,** D.A. Carson, Zondervan, Grand Rapids MI, 1985, Vol. 8, p. 507, as quoted by DeMar [#34] on page 44
56	**Commentary on the Gospel of Mark,** William Lane, Eerdmans, Grand Rapids, MI, 1974
57	**The Eerdmans Bible Dictionary,** Eerdmans Pub. Co., Grand Rapids, MI 1987
58	**Cyclopaedia of Biblical, Theological, and Ecclesiastical Literature,** Rev. John M'Clintock, James Strong, Baker Book House, Grand Rapids, MI 1969
59	**The New International Dictionary of New Testament Theology,** Zondervan, Grand Rapids, 1986
60	**Exegetical Dictionary of the New Testament,** edited by Horst Balz & Gerhard Schneider, Eerdmans Pub. Co., Grand Rapids, 1978
61	**The Imperial Bible-Dictionary,** Vol. II, Rev. Patrick Fairbairn, Blackie & Son, London, 1885
62	**Greek and English Lexicon of the New Testament,** Edward Robinson, Harper & Bro's, NY 1882
63	**The New Analytical Greek Lexicon,** Wesley J. Perschbacher, Hendrickson, Peabody, Mass 1992
64	**The Analytical Lexicon to the Greek New Testament,** William Mounce, Zondervan, Grand Rapids, MI 1993
65	**Thayer's Greek-English Lexicon of the New Testament,** Joseph H. Thayer, AP&A, Grand Rapids, MI (reprint of 1889 original)
66	**A Greek-English Lexicon of the New Testament,** Arndt and Gingrich, Univ. of Chicago Press, Chicago, 1958
67	**Theological Dictionary of the New Testament,** Gerhard Kittel, Eerdmans, Grand Rapids, MI 1964
68	**New Bible Dictionary,** Douglas, Hillyer, and Wood, Inter-Varsity Press, Downers Grove, IL 1996
69	**Easton's Bible Dictionary,** M. G. Easton, Pantianos Classics, 1893 1st Published
70	**Bible Commentary,** Vol. 1, Charles Scribner's Sons, NY 1901
71	**Peake's Commentary on the Bible,** Nelson, 1980
72	**The NIV Matthew Henry Commentary,** Zondervan, Grand Rapids, MI 1992
73	**The Decline and Fall of the Roman Empire,** Edward Gibbon, Penguin Books, NY 1985
74	**World's Last Night,** C.S. Lewis, Harcourt & Brace, NY 1988
75	**A Greek And English Lexicon of the New Testament,** Edward Robinson, Harper & Brothers Pub., New York, 1882
76	**The Life of Jesus Critically Examined,** David F. Strauss, Sigler Press, Ramsey, NJ 1846, 1892, 1994
77	**Commentary on the New Testament,** Thomas Scott, Vol. 1
78	**A Critical and Exegetical Commentary on the Gospel According to St. Mark,** Ezra P. Gould, Charles Scribner's Sons, NY 1896, as quoted in "This Generation Shall Not Pass" by John Bray, Box 90129, Lakeland, FL 33804 Feb. 1995, p. 7
79	**He Shall Have Dominion,** Kenneth L. Gentry, Institute for Christian Economics, PO Box 8000, Tyler, TX 75711, p. 162, as quoted in "This Generation Shall Not Pass" by John Bray, Box 90129, Lakeland, FL 33804 Feb. 1995, p.8
80	**The Word of Truth,** Dale Moody, Eerdmans, Grand Rapids, MI 1981, as quoted in "This Generation Shall Not Pass" by John Bray, Box 90129, Lakeland, FL 33804 Feb. 1995, p.10

81	**Jesus and the Kingdom of God,** G.R. Beasley-Murray, Eerdmans, Grand Rapids, MI 1986, as quoted in "This Generation Shall Not Pass" by John Bray, Box 90129, Lakeland, FL 33804 Feb. 1995, p. 20
82	**Meyer's Commentary on the New Testament,** Heinrich Mayer, Hendrickson Pub, Peabody, Mass, 1983 edition of 1852 original, as quoted in <u>"This Generation Shall Not Pass"</u> by John Bray, Box 90129, Lakeland, FL 33804 Feb. 1995, p. 20
83	**The Four Gospels: With a Commentary,** Abiel A. Livermore, (((Pub? City?))) p. 288, as quoted in "This Generation Shall Not Pass" by John Bray, Box 90129, Lakeland, FL 33804 Feb. 1995, p. 25
84	**The Expositor's Greek Testament,** Vol. 1, Bruce and Dods, reprinted by Eerdman's, Grand Rapids, 1983
85	**The Broadman Bible Commentary,** Vol. 8, Clifton Allen, ed., Broadman Press, Nashville, TN 1969
86	**The Gospel According to St. Matthew,** Alan Hugh M'Neile, Macmillan & Co., London 1949
87	**The Gospel According to Matthew,** R.T. France, Eerdmans, Grand Rapids, MI, 1985
88	**The Gospel of Matthew,** Theodore H. Robinson, Harper & Bro's, NY, 1927
89	**A Commentary on The Gospel According to St. Matthew,** Floyd Filson, Adam & Charles Black Pub., London, 1960
90	**Word Pictures In The New Testament,** Vol. 1, Archibald T. Robertson, Harper & Bro's, NY 1930
91	**Primitive Christian Eschatology,** E.C. Dewick, Cambridge University Press, Cambridge, 1912
92	**The Eschatology of Jesus,** Lewis Muirhead, Andrew Melrose Pub., London, 1904
93	**The Wycliffe Bible Commentary,** Charles Pfeiffer (OT) & Everett Harrison (New Testament), Moody Press, Chicago, 1962
94	**The Jerome Biblical Commentary,** Vol. II, Pretice Hall, Pub., Englewood Cliffs, NJ 1962
95	**The Holy Bible,** Ronald Knox, Sheed & Ward Inc., NY 1950
96	**The Modern Reader's Bible,** Richard Moulton, Macmillan Co., London, 1920
97	**The Everyday Bible, New Version,** Word Pub., Dallas TX 1988
98	**The New World Translation of the Holy Scriptures,** Watch Tower…, Brooklyn, NY 1984
99	**The Bible in Living English,** Steven Byington, Watch Tower…, Brooklyn, NY 1972
100	**Holy Bible- Contemporary English Version,** American Bible Society, NY 1995
101	**The New Testament,** E.E. Cunnington; Marshall, Morgan & Scott Ltd., London 1930
102	**Centenary Translation of the New Testament,** Henry B. Montgomery, The American Baptist Publication Society, Philadelphia, 1924
103	**The Twentieth Century New Testament,** Fleming Revell Co., NY 1904
104	**The New King James Bible,** Thomas Nelson Pub., Nashville, TN 1979
105	**The New Life Testament,** Gleason Ledyard, Christian Lit. Foundation, Canby, OR, USA 1969
106	**The New Testament,** H.T. Anderson, Standard Pub. Co, Cincinnati, 1918
107	**The New Testament,** (Revision of the Challoner-Rheims Version), St. Anthony Guild Press, Paterson, NJ 1941
108	**The Riverside New Testament,** William G. Ballantine, Houghton Mifflin Co., NY 1923
109	**The New Testament,** John Wesley (1790), John Winston Co., Philadelphia, 1938
110	**The Good News According To Matthew,** Henry Einspruch, Lederer Foundation, Baltimore, 1964
111	**The New Testament in Basic English,** S.H. Hooke, Dutton & Co., NY 1941
112	**The Authentic New Testament,** Hugh Schonfield, Dennis Dobson Ltd., Great Britain, 1955
113	**The Corrected English New Testament,** Samual Lloyd, Putnam's Sons, NY 1905
114	**The Four Gospels: A New Translation,** Charles C. Torrey, Harper & Bro's Pub., 1933
115	**The New Testament- According To The Eastern Text,** George M. Lamsa, A.J. Holman Co., Philadelphia, 1940
116	**God's New Covenant- A New Testament Translation,** Heinz W. Cassirer, Eerdmans Pub. Co., Grand Rapids, MI 1989
117	**Tyndale's New Testament,** William Tyndale (1534), Yale Univ. Press, New Haven, 1989
118	**Bible Review,** Hershel Shanks, editor. Marcus Borg, Washington DC, August 1994, p. 16
119	**The Historical Jesus and the Kingdom of God,** Richard Hiers, Univ. of Florida Press, Gainesville, FL 1973
120	**Apocalypse of The Gospels,** Milton Terry (1819), chapter 18 reprinted and its pages renumbered in 1992 by John Bray, PO Box 90129, Lakeland, FL 33804

121	**A Critical and Exegetical Commentary on the Gospel according to St. Matthew,** The Int'l Critical Commentary, W.C. Allen, Charles Scribner's Sons, NY 1907
122	**The Holy Bible with an Explanatory and Critical Commentary,** F.C. Cook, Scribner's, NY, Vol. 1, 1903
123	**Bertrand Russell on God and Religion,** Al Seckel, editor. Prometheus Books, Buffalo, NY 1986
124	**St. Paul verses St. Peter: A Tale of Two Missions,** Michael Goulder, Westminster John Knox Press, Louisville, Kentucky, 1994
125	**Encyclopedia of Bible Difficulties,** Gleason Archer, Zondervan, Grand Rapids, MI, 1982
126	**The Great Tribulation,** David Chilton, Dominion Press, Ft. Worth, TX 1987
127	**Commentary on the Gospel of Luke,** Norval Geldenhuys, Eerdmans, Grand Rapids, MI, 1951, pp. 538, 539, as quoted in *Last Days Madness*, Gary DeMar, [#134] p.168
128	**Saint Matthew,** J.C. Fenton, Westminster Press, Philadelphia, 1963 as quoted in *This Generation Shall Not Pass,* 1995, John Bray, PO Box 90129, Lakeland, FL 33804, p.13
129	**Josephus, The Jewish War,** English Translation by H. St. J. Thackeray, vol. III, Harvard Univ. Press, London, 1961
130	**Reasonable Faith,** William Lane Craig, Crossway Books, Wheaton, Ill, 1994
131	**Davis Dictionary of the Bible,** John D. Davis, Baker Book House, Grand Rapids, MI 1924
132	**Today's Dictionary of the Bible,** T.A. Bryant, Bethany House Pub., Minneapolis, MN 1982
133	**Cruden's Dictionary of Bible Terms,** Alexander Cruden, Baker Book House, Grand Rapids, MI 1958
134	**The Cyclopaedia of Biblical Literature,** Vol. 1, John Kitto, Ivison & Phinney Pub., New York, 1857
135	**A Dictionary of the Bible and Christian Doctrine in Everyday English,** Albert Truesdale, Beacon Hill Press, Kansas City, MO 1986
136	**Dictionary of The Bible,** John McKenzie, Bruce Pub. Co, Milwaukee, WI 1965
137	**The Comprehensive Critical and Explanatory Bible Encyclopaedia,** Edward Robinson, O.A. Browning & Co. Pub., Toledo, Ohio, 1881
138	**Dictionary of The Bible,** William Smith, Houghton, Mifflin & Co., Boston, 1881
139	**A Biblical and Theological Dictionary,** Richard Watson, B. Waugh and T. Mason Pub., New York, 1832
140	**Matthew,** Douglas Hare, John Knox Press, Louisville, Kentucky, 1993
141	**Critical and Exegetical Hand-Book To The Gospel of Matthew,** Heinrich Meyer (1883), Alpha Pub., Winona Lake, IN 1980
142	**The Wesleyan Bible Commentary,** Vol. 4, Ralph Earle, Baker Book House, Grand Rapids, 1966
143	**The New Unger's Bible Dictionary,** Merrill Unger, Moody Press, Chicago, 1988
144	**Hard Sayings of The Bible,** W. Kaiser, P. Davids, F.F. Bruce, M. Brauch, InterVarsity Press, Downers Grove, Ill, 1996
145	**A Dictionary of the Bible,** James Hastings, Hendrickson Pub., Peabody, Mass., 1988
146	**New Century Bible: The Gospel of Matthew,** Oliphants Pub., London, 1972
147	**Jesus and 'This Generation',** Evald Lovestam, Wallin & Dalholm Pub., Lund, Stockholm, 1995
148	**A Comprehensive Lexicon of the Greek Language,** John Pickering, Sanborn & Company, Boston, 1857
149	**Keyword Concordance,** Concordant Pub. Concern, Saugus, CA 1970
150	**A Manual Greek Lexicon of the New Testament,** G. Abbott Smith, T.&T. Clark, Edingurgh, 1921
151	**A Greek-English Lexicon,** Henry Liddell & Robert Scott, Clarendon Press, Oxford 1948
152	**Webster's New World Dictionary for Young Readers,** Prentice Hall, New York, 1989s
153	**Jesus And The Last Days,** George R. Beasley-Murray, Hendrickson Pub., Peabody, Mass. 1993
154	**A Commentary on the Revelation of John,** George Eldon Ladd, Eerdmans, Grand Rapids, 1972
155	**New Handy Webster Dictionary,** World Pub. Co., NY 1959
156	(Pre-published translation of the NT from Aramaic → English) Victor Alexander, web page: http://www.v-a.com/bible/aramaic.html
157	**The Prophecy of the Destruction of Jerusalem,** N. Nisbett, Simmons & Kirkby, Pub., London, 1787; Reprinted 1992 by John Bray, PO Box 90129, Lakeland, FL 33804
158	**Matthew 24 Fulfilled,** John L. Bray, John L. Bray Ministry Pub., Lakeland, FL, 1996
159	**International Standard Version,** ISBN #1891833049 Davidson Press, June 2003
160	**Harper's Bible Dictionary,** Harper & Row, San Francisco, 1985

161	**Mounce Reverse Interlinear New Testament,** Robert H. Mounce & William D. Mounce, 2011
162	**Disciples' Literal New Testament,** Michael J. Magill, 2011 Reyma Publishing
163	**Easy to Read Version,** Bible League Int'l, 2006
164	**English Standard Version,** Crossway- Good News Pub, 2016
165	**1599 Geneva Bible,** Tolle Lege Press
166	**God's Word Translation,** God's Word Mission Society, 1995
167	**International Children's Bible,** Tommy Nelson, Harper Collins Christian Publishing, 2015
168	**Jubilee Bible 2000,** Russell M. Stendal, Ransom Press, 2020
169	**Lexham English Bible,** Logos Bible Software, 2012
170	**Names of God Bible,** Baker Publishing Group, 2011
171	**New American Bible Revised Edition,** Confraternity of Christian Doctrine, 2010
172	**New English Translation,** Biblical Studies Press, 2017
173	**New International Reader's Version,** Biblica, 2014
174	**New Life Version,** Barbour Publishing, 2003
175	**New Living Translation,** Tyndale House Foundation, 2015
176	**Orthodox Jewish Bible,** Artists for Israel Int'l, 2011
177	**Tree of Life Translation of The Bible,** The Messianic Jewish Family Bible Society, 2015
178	**The Voice,** Ecclesia Bible Society, Thomas Nelson, 2012
179	**World English Bible,** Public Domain
180	**Wycliffe Bible,** Terence P. Noble, 2001
181	**The Original New Testament,** Dr. Hugh Schonfield, The Hugh & Helene Schonfield World Service Trust, 1985
182	**BRG Bible,** BRG Bible Ministries, El Dorado, AK 2012
183	**Christian Standard Bible,** Holman Bible Publishers, 2017
183	**Common English Bible,** Publisher: Common English Bible
184	**Complete Jewish Bible,** David H. Stern, Messianic Jewish Publishers, 1998
185	**Douay-Rheims 1899 American Edition,** John Murphy Company, Balitimore Maryland, 1899
186	**Evangelical Heritage Version,** Wartburg Project, 2019
187	**English Standard Version Anglicised,** Good News Publishers, Harper Collins,
188	**Good News Translation,** American Bible Society, 1992
189	**Holman Christian Standard Bible,** Holman Bible Publishers, Nashville TN, 2009
190	**Modern English Version,** Charisma House, Military Bible Association, 2014
191	**New International Version UK,** Biblica Inc., 2011
192	**New King James Version,** Thomas Nelson, 1982
193	**New Matthew Bible,** Ruth Magnusson, Baruch House Publishing, 2016
194	**New Revised Standard Version, Anglicised,** National Council of the Churches of Christ, 1989
195	**New Revised Standard Version, Anglicised Catholic Edition,** National Council of the Churches of Christ, 1995
196	**New Revised Standard Version Catholic Edition,** National Council of the Churches of Christ, 1989
197	**New Testament for Everyone,** Nicholas Thomas Wright, Society for Promoting Christian Knowledge, 2011
198	**The Passion Translation,** Broadstreet Publishing Group, 2017
199	**Revised Geneva Translation,** Five Talents Audio, 2019
200	**Expositor's Bible Commentary (Abridged): New Testament,** Kenneth L. Barker, Zondervan Publishers, 2004
201	**Bible Review,** Editor: Hershel Shanks, August 1994
202	**The Jesus Party,** Dr. Hugh Schonfield, Macmillian Pub, NY NY 1974
203	**Blaming Jesus for Jehovah,** Dr. Robert M. Price, Tellectual Press, Valley WA, 2015
204	**Why I Believed,** Kenneth W. Daniels, K.W. Daniels Pub, 2009
205	**Why I Became an Atheist,** John W. Loftus, Prometheus Books, Amherst NY, 2012
206	**Leaving The Fold,** Edward Babinski, Prometheus Books, Amherst NY, 1995
207	**The Book Your Church Doesn't Want You to Read,** Tim Leedom, Editor, Kendall/Hunt Pub, 1993
208	**Who Wrote The New Testament?** Dr. Burton L. Mack, Harper Collins, San Francisco, 1995
209	**Lost Christianities,** Dr. Bart D. Ehrman, Oxford Univ. Press, 2003
210	**The Incredible Shrinking Son of Man,** Dr. Robert M. Price, Prometheus, Amherst NY, 2003
211	**Mounce Concise Greek-English Dictionary of The New Testament,** William Mounce, 2011
212	**Word Biblical Commentary Vol. 36: John,** George R. Beasley-Murray, Word Books Pub, Waco 1987

213	**The New Testament,** Samuel Davidson, Henry & King Co. Pub, London, 1875
214	**The New Testament in Modern Speech,** Ernest Hampden Cook, editor, Pilgrim Press, Boston, 1909
215	**Texts Explained or Helps to Understand the New Testament,** F.W. Farrar, F.M. Barton, 1899
216	**Abingdon Bible Handbook,** Edward P. Blair, Abingdon Press, New York, 1975
217	**Critical and Exegetical Handbook to The General Epistles,** Joh. Ed. Huther, 1883
218	**How To Defend The Christian Faith,** John R. Loftus, Pitchstone Pub, Durham NC, 2015
219	**The Greek Testament: Vol. 1,** Henry Alford, Moody Press, Chicago 1968
220	**Critical & Exegetical Hand-Book to the Gospel of Matthew,** Heinrich A. W. Meyer, Alpha Pub, 1980
221	**The Historical Jesus,** John Dominic Crossan, Harper Pub, San Francisco, 1992
222	**Mythology's Last Gods,** William R. Harwood, Prometheus Books, Buffalo, 1992
223	**Resurrection: Myth or Reality?** Bishop John Shelby Spong, Harper Collins, San Francisco, 1994
224	**History and Eschatology,** Dr. Rudolf Karl Bultmann, Edinburgh Univ. Press, 1957
225	**Jesus' Proclamation of The Kingdom of God,** Johannes Weiss, Fortress Press, Philadelphia, 1892
226	**The Message from Patmos,** David Clark, Baker Pub, Grand Rapids, 1989
227	**God is Not Great,** Christopher Hitchens, Twelve Pub, New York, 2007
228	**Is Christianity Good for The World?** Christopher Hitchens vs Douglas Wilson, Cannon Press, 2008
229	**The Moral Landscape,** Dr. Sam Harris, Free Press Pub, New York, 2010
230	**The God Delusion,** Dr. Richard Dawkins, Houghton Mifflin, New York, 2006
231	**Atheism Explained,** David Ramsay Steele, Open Court Pub, Chicago, 2008
232	**God's Problem,** Dr. Bart D. Ehrman, Harper One, New York, 2008
233	**Jesus, Interrupted** Dr. Bart D. Ehrman, Harper One, New York, 2009
234	**Forged,** Dr. Bart D. Ehrman, Harper One, New York, 2011
235	**James the Brother of Jesus,** Dr. Robert Eisenman, Viking Penguin Pub, New York, 1997
236	**The Case Against Christianity,** Dr. Michael Martin, Temple Univ. Press, Philadelpha, 1991
237	**Who Tampered With The Bible,** Patricia Eddy, Winston-Derek Pub, Nashville, 1993
238	**The Bible Handbook,** Ball, Foote, Bowden, Smith, American Atheist Press, Austin TX, 1986
239	**Treatise on The Gods,** H.L. Mencken, John Hopkins Univ. Press, Baltimore, 1930, 1946, 1997
240	**Jesus: Apocalyptic Prophet of The New Millennium,** Dr. Bart D. Ehrman, Oxford Univ. Press, 1999
241	**Porphyry's Against The Christians,** R. Joseph Hoffmann, Prometheus, Amherst NY, 1994 (300-350 CE)
242	**The True Believer,** Eric Hoffer, Harper & Row, New York, 1951
243	**Evolving Out of Eden,** Dr. Robert M. Price, Edwin A. Suominen, Tellectual Press, Valley WA, 2013
244	**Twilight of The Idols / The Anti-Christ,** Dr. Friedrich Nietzsche, Penguin Group Pub, 1990
245	**Misquoting Jesus,** Dr. Bart D. Ehrman, Harper Pub, San Francisco, 2005
246	**Forgery in Christianity,** Joseph Wheless (1930), ISBN 1-56459-225-1, Kessinger Pub, Kila MT,
247	**Four Views on the Book of Revelation,** Kenneth L. Gentry's chapter, Pate- Editor, Zondervan, Grand Rapids, 1998
248	**God Without Dogma,** Hugo Fruehauf, Xlibris Pub, 2010
249	**The Kingdom of The Cults,** Walter Martin, Bethany House Pub, Minneapolis, 1997
250	**End Times,** Pastor Chuck Smith, Calvary Chapel, Maranatha House Pub, Costa Mesa CA, 1978
251	**The Prophecy of Matthew 24,** Bishop Thomas Newton, 1754, pub. John Bray Min, Lakeland FL 1991
252	**What Happened in A.D. 70?** Edward E. Stevens, Kingdom Pub, Bradford PA, 1997
253	**Beyond The End Times,** John Noe, Preterist Resources Pub, Bradford PA, 1999
254	**NIV Study Bible Notes,** Zondervan, 2011
255	**The Time Is At Hand,** Charles T. Russell, pp.98-99 (1889 edition) / p.101 (1908 edition)
256	**Testing The Prophecies of Joseph Smith,** Ed Decker, "Saints Alive" website, web ref as of Oct 2020} http://saintsalive.com/testing-the-prophecies-of-joseph-smith/

Room For Notes...

Room For Notes...

Room For Notes...

Room For Notes...

Printed in Great Britain
by Amazon